Tainted by Suspicion

The Secret Deals and Electoral Chaos of Disputed Presidential Elections

Fred Lucas

Tainted by Suspicion: The Secret Deals and Electoral Chaos of Disputed Presidential Elections

© 2016 Fred Lucas All Rights Reserved
Print ISBN 978-1-941071-40-3
ebook ISBN 978-1-941071-41-0

This book is sold subject to the condition that it shall not, by way of trade or otherwise, be lent, resold, hired out or otherwise circulated without the publisher's prior consent in any form of binding or cover other than that in which it is published and without a similar condition including this condition being imposed on the subsequent purchaser.

STAIRWAY PRESS—SEATTLE

Cover Design by Guy Corp
www.GrafixCorp.com

STAIRWAY PRESS

www.StairwayPress.com
1500A East College Way #554
Mount Vernon, WA 98273 USA

Richard:
Hope you enjoy.
Fred Lucas

Dedication

For my wife Basia, who always has my undisputed vote.

Acknowledgements

There are many folks to thank for this book.

Certainly my wife Basia, my mom and my sisters were all very supportive. In particular, my sister Angela always contributed worthwhile advice for the project.

Stairway Press is a great company to work with—I thank Ken Coffman for his great advice and editing, as well as Chris Benson for his ideas on getting word out about the book.

I am also very grateful to the various academics who lent their insights to this book. My goal was to make it as much journalism as history, drawing on real experts to provide context about how things were and how things might have been. In evaluating what America might have been like under a President Aaron Burr or a President Al Gore, I sought to offer a diversity of informed opinion rather than another "what if" book.

My former editor at TheBlaze, Scott Baker, also expressed his enthusiasm for this book and I want to say I was very blessed to be covering the White House and the current presidential contest for a first class news operation that never forgot about serving the public.

Also, a special thanks to all of the truly great presidential historians whose work I drew upon for the details of past elections, who made things clear how our nation's political history was not so different from the polarizing political climate today.

On that note, I should probably thank the colorful cast of presidential candidates in 2016—who have made things very entertaining, and with any luck, might also prompt interest in how the most controversial presidential elections from the past shaped the country we live in today.

Contents

Introduction 7
What is it with Florida Anyway? 7
   And Other Observations 7

PART I 11
John Adams vs. Thomas Jefferson 11
CHAPTER ONE 12
The President vs. The Vice President 12
   Round One 13
   Scandal and Near War 13
   The Presidential Candidates 15
   The Vice Presidential Candidates 18
   Safe Place for a Bible 22
   The Grand Adams-Royals Conspiracy Theory 24
   Conservatives and Liberals 26
   How Burr Delivers the Election 29
   Let it be One Whom We Can Oppose 32

CHAPTER TWO 35
73-73 35
   Not be so Mad 38
   Stretch of the Constitution 40
   Burr's 'Critical Moment' 41
   Civil War was Expected 42
   Adams and Jefferson Walk and Talk 43
   Another Revolution 46
   'What a Lesson to America and the World' 48

CHAPTER THREE 54
President Burr 54
   Federalist Loyalty? 56
   Impeachment? 58

Burr and Slavery 59
　　Burr and the Louisiana Purchase 62
　　Burr's Real-Life Presidency 64
　　Burr Re-Election 72

PART II 75

John Quincy Adams vs. Andrew Jackson 75

CHAPTER FOUR 76

Democracy Arrives 76
　　'Good Feelings' Fade 77
　　Voting Boom, Caucus Collapse 81
　　The Proud Democrat 84
　　Caucusing for Crawford 87
　　A President's Son 89
　　The Great Compromiser 90
　　Second Thoughts 94
　　Conservatives and Liberals 94

CHAPTER FIVE 97

'The People Have Been Cheated' 97
　　'Political Weathercocks' 99
　　Alleged Deal 101
　　Days of Trial 104

CHAPTER SIX 109

President Jackson—Four Years Early 109
　　No Democratic Party 112
　　Trail of Tears Earlier 115
　　Paving the Way for President Calhoun? 117
　　Killing the Bank 122

PART III 126

Rutherford B. Hayes vs. Samuel Tilden 126

CHAPTER SEVEN 127

Reform Campaign 127

Democrats and the Klan 129
Democratic Tide 130
Reform Candidates.. 132
Conservatives and Liberals... 137
Bloody Shirt and Accusations 138
Suppressing the Black Vote 140

CHAPTER EIGHT 144

Compromise of 1877 144
Shenanigans and Rulings 148
Election Moves to D.C... 150
Electoral Commission 153
Wormley House 160
Nation Reacts 164

CHAPTER NINE 170

President Tilden 170
'Negro Supremacy' Alarmism 172
Civil Service Reform 181
Tildenomics... 183
Political Consequences 185

PART IV 190

Non-Disputed Controversies 190

CHAPTER TEN 191

Cleveland Uninterrupted... 191
Cleveland's Challenging First Term 192
Trouble with Trade 193
Harrison's Road to the Nomination............................ 195
Conservatives and Liberals... 198
The Campaign 199
Scandals and Scurrilous Charges 201
Election Results.. 203
Cleveland's Earlier Second Term 205

CHAPTER ELEVEN 208

Kennedy, Nixon and the Minimal Challenge.......................208
    Caution on Race 209
    Road to the Nomination..210
    Conservatives and Liberals...212
    Religion and Debates 213
    Jackie Robinson and Harry Bellefonte 214
    Alabama 'Absurdity' 215
    'Down to the Wire'...220
    'Gross and Palpable Fraud'...222
    President Nixon, Eight Years Early 228

PART V 233

George W. Bush vs. Al Gore 233

CHAPTER TWELVE..234

Clash of Dynasties 234
    Politics of Personality 236
    Primary Problems..239
    Clinton Fatigue..241
    Third Party Spoilers 243
    Rats and Chains and 30-Second Spots...........................245
    Electoral College Expectations 246

CHAPTER THIRTEEN...248

36 Days...248
    The War for Florida..250
    Rage over Butterflies 252
    Disenfranchising Soldiers 255
    State Courts 256
    'Trying to Kidnap Electors'..257
    'Stick with the Appeal'...258
    Supreme Court Decides 262
    Victory and Defeat 265
    Bush Wins Another Recount 270

CHAPTER FOURTEEN...274

President Gore..274

Gore's Green Agenda 276
Gore the War President... 279
The Iraq Question 280
Gore, Patriot Act and Gitmo 286
Difference on the Home Front....................................... 288
Four More for Gore? 289

CONCLUSION.. 292

Did Anyone Really Steal Anything? 292

END NOTES... 295

Tainted by Suspicion

Introduction

What is it with Florida Anyway?

And Other Observations

DURING THE HEAT of the 1876 election dispute, President Ulysses S. Grant wrote one of his generals to say:

> No man worthy of the office of President should be willing to hold it if counted in or placed there by fraud. Either party can afford to be disappointed in the result, but the country cannot afford to have the result tainted by suspicion of illegal or false returns.

As it turned out, the 1876 election was still tainted in the eyes of many Americans—just as the elections of 1824 and 2000 were, with large segments of the population believing their president was selected instead of elected. The means to settle these disputes were not satisfying to the public, but America's tradition of orderly and peaceful transfer of power was maintained.

The question above is based on the oddity that one state

would play such a big role in controversial presidential elections. First, in 1876, Florida was the most closely contested of the four states in question during the Hayes-Tilden election. In 2000, it was the only state in question for the Bush-Gore dispute. There were of course two other elections that dragged out—in 1800 and 1824—that had nothing to do with Florida.

Above all, the elections described in this book demonstrate the resolve of Americans to rise above politics and keep America together even in fragile circumstances. Even today, that's not a guarantee in many countries. The election outcome in the Ivory Coast election in 2010 led to a civil war. The 2014 presidential election in Ukraine prompted Russia to intervene with hostile actions against the new government.

At least twice in American history, an election could have led to war. The country was particularly vulnerable in 1800. America was still in its infancy when the presidential election that was supposed to be Adams vs. Jefferson and ended up being Jefferson vs. Burr was thrown to the House of Representatives. Some Federalist lawmakers plotted to maintain power by disregarding the Constitution, while some Jefferson supporters were planning to take up arms. The other example, when the nation was on the brink occurred in 1876—just more than a decade after the Civil War. Democratic supporters were chanting "Tilden or blood," while some Democrats in Congress feared President Grant, the renowned general, would use the military to ensure Hayes was his successor. In each year, both sides of the dispute managed to keep their heads to avoid self destruction.

As angry as much of the public became over the outcomes of those contests, an actual war was unlikely as a result of the controversial 1824 and 2000 elections.

The imperfections of democracy (to use the term quite loosely, since the Electoral College is perhaps the biggest star of this story) that occurred ever so often never brought the system down. The story of these four elections, plus two honorable mentions—in 1888 and 1960—also underscore two points about political polarization today.

The first point is that it's not new. For all the wailing about how divided the country is along partisan and ideological lines today, we should ask: compared to when? Compared to the 1960s? Compared to the 1860s? Compared to when a sitting vice president would gun down a former treasury secretary in a duel? The story of the campaigns that went down to the wire also tells us that America is more than able to survive internal political tensions and unite.

Most, if not all of history, should face the questions of how, why and what if?

For this book, disputed presidential elections are defined by presidential campaigns decided by another branch of government after an extended period. In 1800 and 1824, the House of Representatives chose the president. In 1876, an electoral commission made up of members of the House, Senate and Supreme Court picked the winner. In 2000, the Supreme Court essentially decided after the dispute worked its way through the Florida courts.

It should be noted that of the four presidents to emerge from these odd situations—Thomas Jefferson, John Quincy Adams, Rutherford B. Hayes and George W. Bush—there were no claims that Jefferson was selected rather than elected. That election was of a different nature because the constitution allowed for an Electoral College tie between Jefferson and running mate Aaron Burr. It was well understood in the lead up to the election that Jefferson was running for president and Burr for vice president.

Two elections that I referred to as honorable mentions get less attention, but nonetheless warrant mention. Neither the 1888 election, where Benjamin Harrison won the electoral vote but lost the popular vote, nor the 1960 election filled with irregularities, were formally disputed. But these elections—particularly 1960—

prompted questions for decades. There have been numerous other very close elections—1968, 1976 and others—that don't approach being called disputed.

It's notable that of the four elections chronicled in these pages, only the 2000 election was truly open for all Americans. The 1800 election allowed the popular vote in six of the 16 states, and of those six states only property-owning white males could cast ballots. Though much was made of the popular vote in 1824, just 18 of the 24 states allowed voters to choose electors, although the property restrictions had been significantly relaxed. Key to the 1876 election was the black vote guaranteed under the Fifteenth Amendment. But, intimidation of black voters was central to that election. Also, women were not allowed to vote in those days.

Two of these disputed elections involved the sons of former one-term presidents running for president against a Tennessee politician. Also, Harrison was the grandson of a former president. Four elections—1824, 1876, 1888 and 2000—involved the Democratic Party (or at least what became known as the Democratic Party) coming up short when the Electoral College was inconsistent with the popular vote. At no point did the modern Republican Party end up on the short end of a disputed election or an electoral-popular vote split.

The story of the presidency is about how men shaped history and how they were shaped by history. So, how many outcomes were inevitable regardless of who held the office? For example, as you'll read later, there is significant dispute about whether Al Gore, had he won the Florida recount, would have invaded Iraq the same as George W. Bush did. Also, would an earlier Andrew Jackson term have allowed the creation of the modern Democratic Party? Would Reconstruction in the South have ended the same way under Samuel Tilden as under President Hayes? And just imagine if Aaron Burr had been the third president of the United States.

PART I

John Adams vs. Thomas Jefferson

CHAPTER ONE

The President vs. The Vice President

HE WASN'T A candidate, but Alexander Hamilton was possibly the leading political player in the election of 1800. As the nation's first Treasury Secretary wielding immense power in the first presidential administration, he set out to be a kingmaker in crowning the third president of the United States. He perhaps crowned the king he and most American political observers least expected.

King is a term that must be used judiciously, considering the American Revolution was about casting off the shackles of the British crown. Ultimately, for all his brilliance, Hamilton was a man who carried deep vendettas, and made the political personal.

As revered as George Washington was, few seemed moved by his warning against factions during his farewell address. The first president was twice elected by acclamation, but for all practical purposes governed as a Federalist. He was far removed from the fierce electioneering that had devolved into factionalism by the time the first contested presidential election came.

Round One

In 1796, Vice President John Adams, carrying Washington's view of federalism, and former Secretary of State Thomas Jefferson, leader of the anti-federalist Democratic-Republicans, tangled in the first contested presidential campaign. The two factions were fairly unorganized that year, but each side would demonstrate the strategy of regional balance early. Adams, a New Englander, had Thomas Pinckney, a distinguished diplomat from South Carolina, as his running mate. Jefferson, the Virginian, had New Yorker Aaron Burr at his side. Four years later, the names were the same and the only thing that would change is that the Federalists picked the younger brother of Pinckney, Charles, to run with Adams in 1800.

It ended in the election of Adams—the ideological successor to Washington, winning the presidency with 71 electoral votes to Jefferson's 68. Jefferson, as the second runner up, became vice president. The fact that two opponents would govern together was, to some, evidence of a constitutional flaw.

Without disputing the matter, Jefferson accepted the vice presidency, believing it a good idea to work with a moderate Federalist against the Hamiltonians. Jefferson wrote to Madison:

> It is to be considered whether it would not be on the whole for the public good to come to a good understanding with him. [1]

Scandal and Near War

The United States had begun trading with Britain, with which France was at war. The French insisted that anyone trading with Britain was an act of war. French navy officials began boarding American trade ships and seizing cargo.

The Directory, the pre-Napoleon ruling regime in France,

refused to accept an American envoy to the country and decided to cut commercial relations with the young country seeking to establish an economic foothold. French Foreign Minister Charles Maurice de Talleyrand asserted in 1798 that France refused to negotiate with America unless the government would first pay a substantial bribe.

Adams reported the apparent act of extortion to Congress, and the Senate printed the correspondence, in which the Frenchmen were referred to only as "X, Y, and Z." One of the first American political scandals to have a name was the XYZ Affair. The bribery scandal pumped up the popularity of the Adams administration and led to a Federalist landslide in the 1798 midterm elections. Congress approved money for the naval conflict with France and passed the Alien and Sedition Acts, the latter which led to the demise of Adams. It was an attempt to curb criticism of the administration, but resulted in making him more unpopular.

Adams and his Federalist administration led the nation into a quasi-naval war with France, in what might have marked an early divide about hawkish foreign policy vs. more restraint. His vice president, Jefferson, strongly opposed the military involvement against the French, whom he had sympathies for. But Jefferson also had troubles with militarization—which he feared would empower the federal government to oppress the public. [2]

As vice president, Jefferson was still one of the authors of the Virginia and Kentucky Resolutions that declared the Alien and Sedition Act to be unconstitutional, and there was broad belief that states could nullify federal laws. [3]

Under the Alien and Sedition Act—later found unconstitutional by the Supreme Court after it had already expired—the president was allowed to expel or imprison any immigrant who was considered to be dangerous and or treasonous. It further authorized prison terms or fines for anyone who distributed "any false, scandalous, and malicious writings" that could promote the overthrow of the government. This gave the government very broad interpretation, which is difficult to imagine today. The Adams administration had 15 opposition newspaper editors jailed. But framed in the context of the fears of the revolutionary bloodletting in France, to some, it might seem comparable to the USA Patriot Act in post-9/11 America, or surveillance by the National Security Agency.

However, Adams proved to be a moderate on the defense front. The quasi-war with France never turned into anything more, as Adams negotiated a peace with France. That enraged Hamilton, who had a distinguished record on the battlefield in the Revolutionary War, rising to the rank of Major General, and serving on the staff of General Washington.

The Presidential Candidates

A great founder, Adams had a tumultuous four years in office and always watched his back for Vice President Jefferson. The 1796 campaign certainly had its moments of mudslinging between the two men who would both die on the Fourth of July, but the political discourse of an 1800 rematch devolved to political warfare. It would be the last time the vice president challenged a president, primarily because of the constitutional change prompted by these controversial elections.

There was no set national Election Day at the time for all states to select their electors. In the absence of popular voting, states were left to decide themselves. The only real Election Day would be on Wednesday Dec. 3, when electors would meet in their respective state capitals and cast their votes.

Adams was the only candidate to have never owned slaves. At that time, one in six Americans living in the country were enslaved. There was of course Jefferson's complex approach of being personally opposed to slavery but still owning slaves. Pinckney of South Carolina was also a slave owner. Even Burr, the

New Yorker, had previously owned slaves. Every state had at least limited slavery except for Adams' own Massachusetts and nearby Vermont.[4]

Born in the Massachusetts Bay Colony in 1735, Adams was a Harvard-educated attorney who served in the Continental Congress. He served as a diplomat in France and Holland during the Revolutionary War, a cause he strongly supported. He returned to the United States to be elected as the first vice president of the United States, under George Washington.

The most influential member of the Washington administration was most definitely Hamilton, and Adams was aware of this. The vice president told his wife Abigail Adams:

> My country has in its wisdom contrived for me the most insignificant office that ever the invention of man contrived or his imagination conceived.[5]

Though Jefferson was obviously not his choice to be part of his administration, it might have given Adams some relief that his foe was cast into insignificancy.

Born in 1743 in Albemarle County, Virginia, Jefferson inherited about 5,000 acres from his mother. He studied at the College of William and Mary. In 1772 he married a widow, Martha Wayles Skelton, and the two lived in his famous Monticello home in Charlottesville, Virginia.

Jefferson served the Virginia House of Burgesses, later the Continental Congress, and authored the Declaration of Independence at the age of 33. In 1786 he authored the Virginia Statute of Religious Freedom. But it was a year prior to that—1785—that he succeeded Benjamin Franklin as the minister to France, where he became sympathetic with the French Revolution, or at least the thinking behind it. That sympathy prompted the conflict with Hamilton and abbreviated his time as Washington's Secretary of State, which lasted only from 1790 to

1793. In 1796, he stepped up to run for president.

There is much complaint about how long presidential campaigns last today. The 1800 campaign, before there were actual voters to persuade and big money to raise, began about a year before the voting, almost as long as today's elections, and a departure from 1796, when the campaign began about three months before the Electoral College convened.

Though a fierce campaign to be sure, it wasn't fiercely fought by the candidates themselves, who both stayed above of the fray, allowing political operatives, journalists of the partisan press and other surrogates do their dirty work. For his part, President Adams was toothless and barely able to speak publicly. So when it got nasty, the candidates themselves didn't sling the mud. Both parties had massive barbecues and booze-fests across the 16 states to get the public charged up.

That year, 10 of the 16 existing states actually had the state legislatures choose the electors. The other six states chose their electors by popular vote. However, state legislators—who were directly elected—were considered a proxy vote for president that year, as it would be these state governments that would pick the electors for that state.

A few states sought to change the way electors are picked, such as in the Democratic-Republican leaning Georgia. The Federalist-leaning New England states also altered how things were done. Because both houses of each state legislature essentially had to agree on the set of electors, Pennsylvania and South Carolina had trouble arriving at a position until just days before the election.

Meanwhile, the states of Kentucky, Virginia, Maryland, Rhode Island, North Carolina and Tennessee wrestled with whether the winners in their states would get all of their state's electoral votes—as is the case in most states today whether a candidate carries the state by 1 percent or 20 percent—or would there be proportionality, allowing the individual electors to cast their individual votes. This was significant, because it would allow parties—depending on the state—to have a significant advantage, or disadvantage. Winning all of the state's electoral votes could be a big boon.

Virginia—which seemed to like being the first at everything at the time—was the first state to choose its electors in January. Though heavily Democratic-Republican, there were some Federalist elected officials. So, the majority was sure to change the rules to "general ticket" voting—or a winner take all system. The change was spearheaded by James Madison. [6]

The Vice Presidential Candidates

Incredibly important to this contest were the two vice presidential candidates, chiefly Aaron Burr, who was running with Jefferson (though not as a ticket as we know today) but also Charles Pinckney of South Carolina (who was running with Adams). Both Burr and Pinckney were presidential candidates.

Under the structure, each party picked two presidential candidates, with an understanding—but no formal designation—of who would become president and who would be vice president. The idea was that electors would place each first and second, since the second runner up in an election became the vice president. The lack of the presidential-vice presidential tickets we know today is why we had an Adams-Jefferson administration for four years.

Burr, born in 1756 in Newark, New Jersey, was the son of a minister. He first considered following in his father's footsteps, before deciding it wasn't the life for him. Like his rival Hamilton, he became an aide to General Washington. Washington had more than a few problems with the pompous young Colonel Burr, but admired his ability enough to entrust him with monitoring British troop movements in New York.

Burr married Theodosia Bartow Prevost, the widow of a

British army officer, in 1782. In just 12 years, Burr was a widower when his wife died, but they had one child named Theodosia, after her mother.

He started his political career serving one term in the New York Assembly beginning in 1784. He actually joined forces with Alexander Hamilton to support Richard Yates in the 1789 New York Governor's race. Yates lost to George Clinton, but Clinton appointed Burr as the state attorney general and orchestrated his appointment to the U.S. Senate in 1791. Clinton and Burr would go on to have a complex relationship.

Burr's move to the U.S. Senate came at the expense of ousting Sen. Philip Schuyler, who happened to be Hamilton's father-in-law. This was one of the first points of animosity between Burr and Hamilton.

Burr, though legendary for his lack of any ideology or principles, was a staunch partisan Democratic-Republican in the Senate and opposed the foreign policy of his old boss—President George Washington—while also voting against most of Washington's nominees, including a failed attempt to block John Jay from serving in the Supreme Court.

He had the endorsement of the Democratic-Republicans to be vice president under Jefferson in 1796. However, after that vote that year, he came in fourth place, since half of the Democratic-Republicans didn't cast their second ballot for Burr— a far cry from what would happen four years later.

Burr retired from the U.S. Senate in 1797 and returned to the New York state Assembly in 1798, where he was more bipartisan, and supported defensive measures to protect New York harbors from the French after the "XYZ Affair." Some in his party had their misgivings about him, and also worried about questions involving his finances. Burr was out of office the next year—but he still had plenty of political clout.

Burr continued to be a vocal opponent of the Alien and Sedition Acts, and made up for some lost ground among fellow partisans. Nevertheless, the popular choice among most Democratic-Republicans for vice president in 1800 was George Clinton. Luckily for Burr, Clinton didn't want the job, at least not then.

Jefferson also had misgivings about his running mate, but nevertheless used his influence to be sure all 21 Virginia electors would cast their second vote for Burr. He may have worked too hard to ensure those votes, as it turns out.

Burr actively campaigned for Jefferson in several states. At stops in New England, he asserted, "The Matter of V.P—is of very little comparative consequence." He speculated on a Jefferson-Adams administration, and simply insisted he was doing everything possible to ensure a Jefferson presidency.[7]

On the other side, Pinckney, born in 1746, came from an aristocratic family that had close ties to the British. His father was the colonial chief justice and a member of the Royal Council. His father even moved to London in 1753 and the young Charles enrolled in Westminster preparatory school, and grew up to practice law being admitted into London's bar in 1769.

After coming to the states, he had a close association with the planter class of South Carolina, which would seem to make him fit well among Jeffersonians. But he also supported a strong national government—which prompted him to eventually side with the Hamilton faction.

In a time when plenty of elite gentlemen were eager to join the military as a means of boosting their prestige, Pinckney joined the socially elite 1st Regiment of South Carolina militia, which made him lieutenant. He entered elected office in 1770 as part of the South Carolina legislature and was a regional attorney general three years later. He married Sarah Middleton, who was the daughter and sister of South Carolina political leaders, further affirming his gentleman status.

Despite those family and social ties with England, he rejected the British loyalist argument, and happily supported the revolution. He stepped aside as a politician to be a fulltime soldier leading the 1st Regiment as a senior company commander, and was part of the successful defense of Charleston in June 1776 against British forces led by General Sir Henry Clinton and moved up to the rank of colonel. Since hostilities had cooled in the south, Pinckney sought to serve under General Washington near Philadelphia in 1777. Joining Washington's staff also allowed him to build a political network, such as Hamilton and James McHenry.

When South Carolina was under threat from the British again, Pinckney returned in 1778. His defense of Charleston was less successful in 1780, as this time the British invasion was successful, and Pinckney was among those in the state who became a prisoner of war. His British captors sought to persuade him to turn away from the American cause, he famously said:

> *If I had a vein that did not beat with the love of my country, I myself would open it. If I had a drop of blood that could flow dishonorable, I myself would let it out.*
> [8]

As the fighting had ended, Pinckney was freed in 1782 under a prisoner exchange and promoted to brigadier general. His wife died in 1784 and in 1785, a man named Daniel Huger wounded him in a dual, but he survived. Hamilton might have been wise to learn from Pinckney's misfortune.

Like Hamilton, Pinckney believed the goals of the American Revolution couldn't be achieved unless the states were bound politically, economically, and militarily, putting him solidly in what would become the Federalist camp.

He represented South Carolina at the Constitutional Convention in Philadelphia in 1787 and helped establish a South Carolina state Constitution in 1790. He seemed to have retired from politics after that, declining political office from President

Washington, but by 1796 he accepted the position of ambassador to France. This put him in the middle of the XYZ Affair. When the French officials pushed the bribe, he famously responded, "not a six pence." [9]

Pinckney considered the French demand for a bribe as an affront to America's honor. He returned home and President Adams appointed him as leader of the Provisional Army the Federalists pushed to raise in response to the troubles with France.

Safe Place for a Bible

The forces behind Adams attacked Jefferson for deism and alleged his lack of religiosity, or a godless Jacobin, as they called him. Jacobin was a term for French radical, stressing Jefferson's backing of the French Revolution. The Connecticut Courant (today the Hartford Courant) even said, a Jefferson presidency would mean:

> ...*murder robbery, rape, adultery and incest will all be openly taught and practiced, the air will be rent with the cries of the distressed, the soil will be soaked with blood, and the nation black with crime.*

That's supercharged political hyperbole to be sure, but it was an apt description of what happened after the French Revolution. That's not likely what Jefferson and other American supporters of the uprising envisioned would be the outcome, but it's very easy to see how being pro-French was cause for alarm during that era.

Those who engage in handwringing every time religion enters the political arena should take a look at 1800.

Timothy Dwight, the Congregationalist clergyman president of Yale University, painted a grim picture of a Jefferson win, predicting the "Bibles will be cast into a bonfire," with children "chanting mockeries against God," and "our wives and daughters the victims of legal prostitution, soberly dishonored, speciously polluted, the outcast of delicacy and virtue; and the loathing of God and man ... our sons the disciples of Voltaire and the dragoons of Marat."

New York pastor John Mason authored the *Voice of Warning to Christians in the Ensuing Election* and declared that Jefferson:

> ...*writes against the truths of God's word; who makes not even a profession of Christianity.* [10]

Many other prominent ministers joined in dire warnings against a Jefferson presidency. It might well seem like they were piling on, but again, the French Revolution was very fresh on the minds of the American public. The French Revolution began with high-minded rhetoric before descending mass murderous cleansing of the Christian church in the country. So, while such an urgent warning seemed over the top—particularly when in the context of describing so revered a figure as Jefferson, a staunch supporter of religious liberty by the way—French-phobia wasn't unfounded.

In one of the more humorous anecdotes to come out of Paul F. Boller's book *Presidential Elections*, a Connecticut woman fearing a Jefferson victory brought her Bible to the only Jefferson supporter she knew. She told him she feared a Jefferson regime would destroy all Bibles, and wanted her friend to hold on to hers so it would be safe. The man disputed the premise, but said, "...if all Bibles are to be destroyed, what is the use of bringing yours to me? That will not save it when it is found." The woman responded, "It will be perfectly safe with you. They'll never think of looking in the house of a Democrat for a Bible."

It was perhaps to combat the constant godless attack and the French comparisons that Jefferson asserted that year, "I have sworn upon the altar of God eternal hostility against every form of tyranny over the mind of man."

Federalists didn't confine their attacks to religion, but hurled several charges at Jefferson to make him untenable. They claimed he was a coward as wartime governor of Virginia; they claimed he cheated British creditors and they claimed he cheated a widow out of an estate valued at tens of thousands of dollars. They even hit him on his alleged affairs with his slaves.

In order to reassure the country, he was not a wild-eyed radical, Jefferson wrote a long "profession of my political faith," and referred it to Elbridge Gerry, a Democratic-Republican standing for governor of Massachusetts and future vice president. The profession, which Gerry was only supposed to circulate among friends, asserted that Jefferson had a strong belief in republicanism, or representative government, as opposed to mob rule. Secondly, that he had a commitment to the U.S. Constitution, with which many in the Democratic-Republican camp were never fully on board. [11]

The Grand Adams-Royals Conspiracy Theory

The Democratic-Republicans didn't treat President Adams any better. Prominent journalist Benjamin Franklin Bache, publisher of the *Philadelphia Aurora* wrote the president, "...old, querulous, bald, blind, crippled, toothless Adams." He also accused Adams of trying to "...gasconade like a bully and to swagger as if he were emperor of all Russians." Pushing the monarch narrative, Bache referred to Adams as his "serene highness" and said Adams was "a man divested of reason and wholly under the domination of his passions." [12]

Jefferson is widely believed to have put another editor, James Callender, a deeply unethical journalist, on his payroll. Callender wrote the president was "...a repulsive pedant," and "...hideous, hermaphroditical character which has neither the force and firmness of a man, nor the gentleness and sensibility of a woman."[13]

Callender was among those jailed under the Alien and Sedition Act. Though he served as a martyr for the Democratic-Republicans, Jefferson didn't bail him out when asked because he did not want to be publicly associated with Callender.

Federalists weren't the only party that could stir hysteria about another country. The Democratic-Republicans concocted a conspiracy theory that Adams wanted to reunite with Britain. Something that likewise would seem outlandish today, but certainly believable in that age given the close time proximity to independence. If nothing else, it fed the narrative of aristocratic Federalists.

Long before the Truthers and Birthers came the theory that went like this: President Adams was conspiring with the Royal Family to reunite the United States of America as a colony of Britain by having one of his sons marry the daughter of King George III. The original story included George Washington, but since Washington could do no wrong in the eyes of most, he was portrayed as a good guy. After making two prior pleas that Adams rejected, Washington came to his successor wearing a Revolutionary uniform and threatened to stab him with his sword if Adams went forward with the diabolical plan.

Apparently unable to stop with a good conspiracy theory, the story elaborates by swiping the running mate, saying Pinckney went to England as part of the deal to procure four mistresses, two for each. Adams simply found this comical.

He joked:

> I do declare on my honor, if this be true, General Pinckney has kept them all for himself and cheated me out of my two.

Abigail Adams said that there was enough "abuse and scandal" during the election year "to ruin and corrupt the minds and morals of the best people in the world." [14]

The bizarre tale has some underpinnings in the realm of policy debate. As many were concerned about Jefferson's love for France, there was similar concern about Adam's continued respect for Britain. There was no doubt about his commitment to the American Revolution, but he continued to see merit in a constitutional monarch for other countries, while he believed direct democracy was dangerous—a slippery slope to French anarchy.

Conservatives and Liberals

It's always tough to impose today's philosophical views on that of the past, but on balance, Adams, Hamilton and the Federalists were probably conservatives while Jefferson and the Democratic Republicans were liberals. That said, the modern Democratic Party's lineage to Jefferson is very questionable. The term 'conservative' was not widely used in those days, whereas liberal typically meant freedom as in John Locke, who had a libertarian philosophy. Jefferson captured a libertarian spirit well, thus is quite admired by most modern conservatives.

It would be puzzling to many in the modern era to understand how the Federalists—who favored strong central government—would be conservative, while the Democratic-Republicans—who preferred decentralization and States rights—could be liberal. But there were broader issues at stake.

The Federalists favored an industrial modernized economy as supported by most Republicans, from Abraham Lincoln, Dwight Eisenhower, Ronald Reagan and the modern conservative movement. The Jeffersonians preferred a more limited agriculture-based economy. But this view led to a perspective of using rhetoric to champion the common man and assail the comfortable.

Perhaps most of all, assessing any right-left divide for that

Tainted by Suspicion

time revolved around France.

The French Revolution created an intense fear that something akin to it would come to the young republic of the United States of America. Conservatives felt their task was to defend society from upheaval while the Democratic-Republicans had significant French sympathies. By contrast, the Federalists were conservatives because they sought to defend tradition and civilization for which the French Revolution seemed to pose the biggest risk.

Jefferson was swept up with French civilization and philosophy. Long before the American Revolution. Jefferson heralded reason above traditional institutions. [15]

As historian Bernard A. Weisberger, author of *America Afire: Jefferson, Adams and the First Contested Election*, explained in a 2000 C-Span interview:

> Adams was a conservative who didn't have a very high opinion of popular judgment. He did believe in self-government, but he also believed that, in the end, people were easily seduced by rank and riches and glamour, and he believed that society was in a constant state of class war; not quite class warfare, but the poor and the rich would always be trying to get the advantage of each other. And so you needed a stable, steady government, particularly a strong executive to hold them in check. While not particularly religious, he respected tradition and authority.
>
> Jefferson, on the other hand, was a philosophical radical, much more of a philosophical than a governmental radical, as it turned out. But Jefferson believed in the triumph of reason; he was a child of the Enlightenment. And he was sure that if humanity got rid of all the superstitions and idolatry, i.e. revealed religion and reverence for monarchy and aristocracy,

> *the world would get better and better. And he thought that in the mass of ordinary people, by whom he meant usually small-land holders, there was a natural elite of intelligence, which could be brought out by a universal system of public education. And if such a system were in place, democracy could prosper without a great deal of authority, without a great deal of government.*
>
> *So there's an optimistic vs. hard-boiled view of human nature that separated them.* [16]

Just as today, the modern Democratic party engages in fiery class-warfare rhetoric. In those days, Jefferson's party took jabs at the class of people they called "stockjobbers," who today would be called fat cats or one-percenters. Democratic-Republicans believed "stockjobbers," or the investor class, gained unearned wealth and held stock in the National Bank, hence the name.

James Madison shared this view that the investor class—or those who weren't farmers—were unproductive and less deserving of wealth. The same class resentment wasn't felt toward wealthy plantation owners or anyone rich from agriculture, who the Democratic-Republicans believed visibly produced something for society. Stockjobbers, Jeffersonians believed, were simply loathsome people that didn't grow things, but rather shuffled papers and drove up prices for the working man. [17]

The Federalists of course had a different point of view, believing the National Bank was important to the wealth of the nation—similar to the Bank of England.

Pulitzer Prize winning author Edward J. Larson, who wrote *A Magnificent Catastrophe: The Tumultuous Election of 1800, America's First Presidential Campaign*, contends that it isn't such a difficult distinction when looking at Federalists and the Jeffersonians. Larson said:

> *Government has little to do with it. Liberals believed in*

> *increasing individual freedom, or classic liberalism. Conservatives, or classic conservatives, believed in social order and tradition.*

Adam Carrington, a professor of politics at Hillsdale College, sees a good bit of nuance in making the comparison of liberalism and conservatism then and now. He said:

> *The modern Republican Party transcends a little bit into both Hamiltonian and Jeffersonian elements. The Republican party certainly believes in giving more power to the states. It's doubtful anyone knew how massive the federal government would grow at the time and questionable as to whether Hamilton would have approved. Hamiltonians were the party of free markets and building up business and free labor. Economically, that would make them more conservative. The modern Democratic party has some crossover as well.*

How Burr Delivers the Election

The North was strong for Federalists. New England was easily going to Adams, but Jefferson had a chance of winning if he could carry New York. Without New York, he would have to win New Jersey and Pennsylvania, which the Democratic-Republicans thought nearly impossible. Burr knew the political climate and electorate in the state, and realized the key to controlling the legislature would be winning 13 assembly seats in New York City. He recruited the best candidates for the seats and helped organize and strategize their campaigns. Jefferson repeated Burr's message to Madison that, "if the city election of New York is in favor of the republican ticket, the issue will be republican."

Though it was George Clinton who named Burr to the U.S. Senate, the two would be rivals. Burr talked Jefferson's first choice for a running mate out of political retirement to run for governor of New York. Burr's thinking was that Clinton, a popular six-term former governor, could have enough coattails to sweep Democratic-Republicans into office.

Burr also recognized a gem in a social club known as the Society of St. Tammany, which he helped turn into the first political machine in getting out the vote for Democratic-Republican legislative candidates by holding out the promises of government goodies and jobs on the other side as payback for delivering the vote. After demonstrating the power of New York politicos, it stopped being a social club and became the powerful political force known as Tammany Hall, which defined the New York state Democratic party well into the 20th Century, with immense clout in the national Democratic party. [18]

On Election Day in May, Burr spent 10 hours campaigning at one New York polling place, and an understudy spent 15 hours at another, all to get the vote out for their party. For his part, Hamilton worked hard to keep the Federalists in charge of New York, but was outflanked by Burr. The Democratic-Republican candidates carried the New York City assembly districts, marking a huge victory for Burr and his party and a severe blow to Hamilton's pride. [19]

It was a far more devastating blow to the Federalists, as the new legislative majority was nearly certain to ensure the Democratic-Republicans carried New York's 12 electoral votes.

The fate of Adams and the Federalists was all but decided by the New York elections. Adams won all 12 of New York's electoral votes in 1796, critical since he won the election by just three electoral votes nationally. The president was devastated by the news.

Burr's clever maneuvering wasn't all that carried the day. There was a significant shift in New York City, the heart of Hamilton's vision for industry and manufacturing. It would seem surprising that such an area would back the party of a farm-based economy, but the Democratic-Republican arguments—what might broadly be called populism or even class warfare—found its appeal in Manhattan.

Hamilton begrudgingly acknowledged that for New York City voters it was "a question between the Rich & the Poor." Many workers, and even newly wealthy business entrepreneurs that didn't come from aristocracy, viewed Federalists as the party of social monarchy. [20]

An absolutely giddy Virginia Congressman John Dawson declared, "The [Federalist] party are in a rage & despair." Meanwhile, Abigail Adams sadly wrote it "is generally supposed that N York would be the balance" for the election. [21]

In today's context, imagine the news anchors calling the definitive swing state on a presidential election night, all but sealing the deal. In this case, the ultimate swing state was called months before Election Day, with the New York state legislative races serving as a proxy vote to select electors.

Still, Hamilton wouldn't give up. He wrote New York Governor John Jay asking him to call the lame duck Federalist legislature into session to pass a bill taking elector selection away from the newly elected Democratic-Republican legislatures and giving it directly to voters. This, keep in mind, was coming from the party that feared too much democracy.

Hamilton told Jay:

> *In times like these in which we live, it will not do to be over scrupulous.*

He added that it was important to…

> *…prevent an atheist in religion, and a fanatic in politics, from getting possession of the helm of State.*

Jay, however, moved closer to the scrupulous side, never

responded to Hamilton, but filed his letter away with the notation, "Proposing a measure for party purposes, which I think would not become me to adopt." [22]

Burr's triumph in New York was in fact a clear demonstration of what we have seen throughout modern presidential elections—the best organization wins. Understanding how to use the media helps even more. There were plenty of Federalist newspapers, but the Democratic-Republicans set up a formal Committee of Correspondence, a national network of sorts for newspapers to promote Jefferson and denounce Adams.[23]

Let it be One Whom We Can Oppose

While the Democratic-Republicans had strong organization throughout the country, the Hamilton-Adams rift left the Federalists fractured.

It was perhaps Hamilton's propensity to truly loathe political rivals, or even allow his emotions to create heated rivalries, that helped determine this election. He was extremely angry with Adams for being overly moderate and not going to full-scale war with France in 1798, a conflict in which he hoped to be a glorious general.

The break between the moderate Adams Federalists and Hamilton's High Federalists helped make the president's party dysfunctional against the Democratic-Republican well-organized apparatus. America's first and still best Treasury secretary hated Jefferson for being a dangerous radical. As for Burr, it was probably based on more personal and practical reasons. Burr was an old rival in New York politics, whom Hamilton found loathsome and void of any moral compass.

As today, it's easy to imagine elements of either party being so annoyed by sellout candidates they would just as soon lose the election, believing a defeat could even be better for their party's future and ideological strength as opposed to a squishy moderate who will give away the store to the other side. This was essentially how Hamilton felt about the choice of Adams and Jefferson.

Hamilton said:

> *If we must have an enemy as the head of government, let it be one whom we can oppose, and for whom we are not responsible, who will not involve our party in the disgrace of his foolishness and bad measures...* [24]

So why was he eager to shift the New York election to the Federalists? He had a plan.

As would have been the case with anyone involved, there seemed to Hamilton barely a reason to think Burr would be president. The enemies to focus on would be Jefferson and Adams, and he hatched a plot to ensure neither enemy would head the government.

High Federalists wanted Hamilton to lead the party into battle with Jefferson instead as the presidential candidate. Hamilton knew this was not practical, so he orchestrated a way to get Pinckney elected president instead of Adams. He hit several New England states to push the idea in the heart of Federalism. It is ironic that by happenstance, it was the opposing party that nearly saw the vice presidential designate take the top prize.

During the George Washington administration, Hamilton had the first president's ear while Jefferson was simply tolerated. As president, Adams wouldn't bend to Hamilton's whims. Though the sedition law seemed overly sweeping by most measures, Hamilton and his supporters believed Adams wasn't stern enough. Hamilton was also certain he would have more influence over Pinckney than the more independent Adams.

Hamilton's 50-page letter excoriating Adams leaked into the Democratic-Republican newspapers. The surrounding publicity closed off any future hopes of Hamilton ascending to the presidency—and it didn't do a lot of good for Adams re-election campaign. In a message targeted at Federalists in South Carolina, Hamilton wrote:

> *Few go as far in their objections as I do. Not denying to Mr. Adams patriotism and integrity and even talents of a certain kind, I should be deficient in candor, were I to conceal the conviction, that he does possess the talents adapted to the administration of government, and that there are great intrinsic defects in his character, which unfit him for the office of chief magistrate.*

Burr got a copy and leaked it to Democratic-Republican newspapers around the country. The letter titled *The Public Conduct and Character of John Adams* ran to the great humiliation of the president and Hamilton.

Educator Noah Webster and other political writers jumped to the president's defense. And, just as Hamilton might prefer Jefferson run the country, Adams preferred to serve under Jefferson than to owe any victory to Hamilton.

Adams expressed his own frustration of Hamilton, even blaming him for the loss of New York:

> *Hamilton is an intriguant, the greatest intriguant in the world—a man devoid of every moral principal—a bastard... Mr. Jefferson is an infinitely better man, a wiser one, I am sure, and if President, will act wisely. I know and would rather be vice president under him or even minister resident at Hague than indebted to such a being as Hamilton for the presidency.* [25]

As it would turn out, Adams wouldn't have to owe anything to Hamilton, but another candidate would.

CHAPTER TWO

73-73

ELECTION DAY IN 1800 was held on Dec. 3 when electors met in state capitals to make their selections. While the ballots wouldn't be opened until February 1801, the Jeffersonians were rejoicing—quite preemptively as it turned out considering the long slog ahead. The *Baltimore American* declared, "The Jig's Up ... Be glad America."

Jefferson wrote Burr on Dec. 15 to congratulate his presumed vice president:

> *Although we have not official information of the votes for President & Vice President, and cannot have until the first week in Feb, yet the state of the votes is given on such evidence, as satisfies both parties that the two republican candidates stand highest...*

Almost as an afterthought, the letter continues:

> *I understand several of the high-flying federalists have expressed their hope that the two republican tickets may be equal, & their determination in that case to prevent*

> *a choice by the H of R, (which they are strong enough to do,) and let the government devolve on a President of the Senate. Decency required that I should be so entirely passive during the late contest that I never once asked whether arrangements had been made to prevent so many from dropping votes intentionally, as might frustrate half the republican wish; nor did I doubt, till lately, that such had been made.* [26]

Burr wrote back saying that even if the election did go to the House of Representative, he was certain there would be enough Jefferson voters to carry nine states—enough to win. [27]

The Federalists were soundly defeated.

Pinckney, Hamilton's choice for president, came in last place with 64 electoral votes. President Adams got 65 electoral votes. He came in behind Jefferson's 73 electoral votes. The problem is that Burr also got 73 votes.

Jefferson and Burr were both running as Democratic-Republicans for president. Again, these factions were not fully-functioning political parties that nominated candidates as we see today. But the plan was simple enough. The Jeffersonians were supremely confident based on the unpopularity of Adams and from the New York victory of getting the first and second spot. The idea of candidates was based on trying to get a president and vice president of the same party.

Under the Constitution, each Elector cast two votes and the ultimate runner up would be the vice president. Federalists wanted one Elector to vote for John Jay rather than vice presidential candidate Pinckney to ensure Pinckney would be the vice president. One of the Democratic-Republican electors was supposed to abstain from voting for Burr. This would assure that Jefferson becomes president and Burr his vice president.

The Democratic-Republicans though couldn't pull off that superior organization when it counted, and each of those electors voted for both Jefferson and Burr for an electoral tie, 73 votes each. The theories vary. It could have been a simple accident. It could have been the Jeffersonians were afraid the party couldn't win without casting all their votes. Or, it could have been mismanagement. The problem was apparently that not a single elector was specifically asked to withhold his vote from Burr. Jefferson's longtime friend James Madison alleged that the party members were pulled into...

> ...*false assurances dispatched at the critical moment to the electors of one state, that the votes of another would be different from what they proved to be.* [28]

Virginia Gov. James Monroe asserted that because of the lack of foresight, "We remain in the hands of our enemies." [29]

Unfathomable today, not only having an actual tie, but a tie between running mates. Imagine a tie between Barack Obama and Joe Biden, who despite running as a team during the campaign, were contesting for the presidency. Of course, that could never happen, because the election of 1800 exposed a flaw in the Constitution, and it was amended for the better.

Without a definitive electoral majority, the House of Representatives decides the next president. The nation's first watershed presidential election also saw the Democratic-Republicans turnout the Federalist majority with 68-38 House majority. The new majority would have easily dispatched of the problem by simply voting for the intent of their party: Jefferson for president, Burr for vice president. However, it wasn't the new majority deciding. The new Congress wouldn't be sworn in until March 4. It was the lame duck Federalist majority of 60-46, with many members eager to create mischief for the opposition. In the House of Representatives, each state would get one vote.

Federalists did not want to install whom they viewed as that godless Jacobin, better known as Jefferson, as president. There was reason to back Burr, a northerner who opposed slavery. With Adams out of the running, Burr became a de facto Federalist candidate in the battle for the House.

Not be so Mad

While it's common today to view Burr only as the scoundrel among the founders, prominent Federalist leaders then felt they could at least live with Burr, even though he didn't support a Federalist agenda.

Federalist House Speaker Theodore Sedgwick of Massachusetts believed that Burr would not be able to govern without the help of the opposition party, thus would be bendable. The speaker even wrote in his diary that the:

> ...disposition to prefer Mr. Burr to Mr. Jefferson has been increasing until it has become increasingly unanimous.

In his diary, New York Senator Gouverneur Morris wrote:

> It seems to be the general opinion that Colonel Burr will be chosen president by the House of Representatives. [30]

Adams' Secretary of State Timothy Pickering believed that Burr could be a useful ally for Federalists, in part because he considered the man to be unprincipled. Pickering said of Burr:

> He holds no pernicious theories, but is a mere matter-of-facts man. His very selfishness prevents his entertaining any mischievous predilections for foreign nations... So that although Burr's promises were but as cobwebs to bind a giant, both the great parties in the nation would have concurred in imposing necessary

> restraints. ... He would not, because he could not have projected and procured of adoption of measures productive of so much mischief... no possible mischief was to be apprehended from him as executive chief of the union. [31]

Such acceptance of Burr didn't sit well with Alexander Hamilton, who told the House speaker that Burr:

> ...would disgrace our country abroad... His ambition aims at nothing short of permanent power and wealth in his own person. For heaven's sake, let not the Federal party be responsible for the elevation of this man. [32]

Hamilton asserted Burr's "public principles have no other spring or aim than his own aggrandizement." In other words, Jefferson may have the wrong principles, but at least he had them.

In a letter to Senator Morris, Hamilton took a scolding tone:

> I trust the Federalists will finally not be so mad as to vote for Burr. I speak with an intimate and accurate knowledge of character. His elevation can only promote the purposes of the desperate and profligate. If there be a man in the world I ought to hate it is Jefferson. With Burr I have always been personally well. But the public good must be paramount to every private consideration.

In a Dec. 27 letter to Federalist Rep. James Bayard of Delaware, who would go on to become a major player in brokering a winner, Hamilton wrote of Burr that:

> ...rest assured my dear sir this man has no principle public or private.

Hamilton further said:

> *There is no doubt but that upon every virtuous and prudent calculation Jefferson is to be preferred. He is by far not so dangerous a man and he has pretensions to character.* [33]

Stretch of the Constitution

But there was at least a hope among many Federalists of using this predicament to deny either Jefferson or Burr the prize and maintaining Federalist control over the executive branch. Federalists in the House felt they could keep voting for Burr to block Jefferson from attaining the majority he needed to become president until Inauguration day, March 4, 1801. By this time, they would assert the vacancy in the presidency wasn't foreseen by the Constitution, so it's up to Congress to pass emergency legislation to name a new president, likely the Senate President Pro Tempore or the Chief Justice, both Federalists. Had this happened, the young republic might well have imploded or gone the way of France Revolution-like tyranny—which would have ironically been spurred by political actions of the Federalists that made France their paramount fear.

In a letter to Madison, Jefferson wrote:

> *The Federalists ... openly declare they will prevent an election and will name a president of the Senate pro tem by what they say would only be a stretch of the Constitution.* [34]

Democratic-Republican Party leaders let it be known that wouldn't happen on their watch. Governors of Jefferson's party vowed not to recognize such a new Federalist government, to jail federal officers in their states and block enforcement of federal law within the states should Federalist override an election.[35]

Burr's 'Critical Moment'

Burr didn't speak publicly about his desires. He didn't publicly seek Federalist votes, nor did he publicly bow out, thus he seemed willing to have the presidency thrust upon him. He shunned the notion that he was seeking Federalist support. But prominent Federalist Robert Goodloe Harper of South Carolina urged Burr not to withdraw, saying:

> *I advise you to take no step whatsoever, by which the choice of the House of Representatives can be impeded or embarrassed. Keep the game perfectly in your own hands but do not answer this letter or any other that may be written to you by Federal men nor write to any other third party.* [36]

A diary entry from a Burr associate later claimed that Burr ally Albert Gallatin, a former Pennsylvania senator who would go on to serve as Treasury Secretary, sent him a letter warning that the Federalists were plotting to seize control, prompting a protracted deadlock. But, Gallatin said, Democratic-Republican House members from Maryland, New Jersey and New York said they were willing to vote for Burr to head off a disaster. Burr apparently told his other friends he needed to be on hand in Washington to secure the votes from the House members. Burr ally Peter Townsend said that Burr had packed and was prepared to go to Washington, but "at a critical moment, his heart failed him and he decided to remain in Albany." Townsend told the story to a business associate who recorded it in his diary. [37]

So, it's essentially hearsay. If true though, it demonstrates even the opportunistic Burr was far less impulsive than the older Burr. Perhaps regret over his inability to seize the opportunity prompted the later bizarre actions that defined his legacy.

There were other reports that Burr informed Democratic-Republican operative Samuel Smith during a meeting in Philadelphia that if the House elected him president, he would serve, asserting, "We must have a president and a constitutional one." This began to appear in newspapers, but Burr himself never spoke up publicly.

Civil War was Expected

On Feb. 11, 1801, eight of the sixteen states—one less than the simple majority required to elect the president—voted for Jefferson, while six states voted for Burr. Two states were divided and not voting. By the time it reached the fifth vote that same day, some members had switched their vote, but it was not enough to switch any states.

Thousands poured into Washington, prepared for partisan violence if there was what the Jeffersonians called "usurpation." President Adams would assert years later, "…a civil war was expected."

Monroe, in Richmond, worried about reports that Jefferson supporters were arming for revolt, and said, "Anything [like] a commotion would be fatal to us." [38]

Jefferson, during the vote count, wrote Monroe:

> We thought it best to declare openly and firmly that, once for all, that the day such an act passed, the Middle States would arm, and that no such usurpation, even for a single day, submitted to. [39]

Jefferson much preferred a constitutional convention to amend the Constitution if the Federalists continued down this road.

Though it would be Hamilton who would play a massive role in the outcome, there was a great flurry of activity that led up to the final result. Moderates in both camps didn't want to see the country torn apart should the diehard Federalists push it to the deadlock and try to appoint a president. Adams and Jefferson wanted to avoid this above all.

On the second day of balloting, the House took just one vote.

Bayard, perhaps influenced by Hamilton, felt the House had to move toward Jefferson, but he wanted to get some reassurances to make it an easier pill to swallow. He contacted Jefferson ally Samuel Smith about communicating to the vice president. Moderate Federalists were willing to bend if they could get some assurance that Jefferson would not expunge the national debt and that he would not throw out all of the Federalist officials working in government. Jefferson never gave such an assurance.

Adams and Jefferson Walk and Talk

The president and vice president met during the raging dispute and took a walk along Pennsylvania Avenue. Jefferson told Adams he was aware that Federalists wanted to install the Senate president pro tem as the chief executive. He suggested that Adams announce that he would veto such a measure because it could cause "resistance by force and incalculable consequences."

Adams told Jefferson he could simply declare that he "would not turnout Federalist officers, nor put down the Navy, nor expunge the national debt."

Of the meeting, Jefferson said he agreed to nothing in so many words, but said, "...the world must judge as to myself of the future by the past." [40]

Given that Federalists sought to portray Jefferson as a radical extremist, citing a past record might seem less than reassuring. But the Federalists were hoping for some rationale to avert a mob war but still save face.

It was perhaps a wise move for Jefferson not to commit to

anything, considering he was at an advantage, feeling that Adams probably wouldn't have bothered talking to him if he believed the Federalists could really emerge victorious.

Smith and Bayard met again, and this time, Smith brought good news. Jefferson had agreed that "...he did not think that such officers should be removed on political grounds only." That meant some of the Federalist civil servants would remain on the job. Not every Federalist was convinced by the message Bayard relayed, but Bayard insisted it's far more than they've gotten from Burr—who made no commitments. Further, the Democratic-Republicans seemed united.

After this meeting came another ballot that Bayard knew was headed for an 8-6 split. He voted for Burr again because he didn't want to cause angst among his fellow party members that he was trying to persuade.

Another controversy emerged over court appointments. For anyone who thought the politics of judicial appointments is new need only look at this era. Fearing a Democratic-Republican Congress and president would unravel what the nation had built since President Washington, the lame duck Federalist Congress passed and lame duck President Adams signed the Judiciary Act on Feb. 13, 1801. The law created about 60 new federal judgeships across all levels, the federal circuit judges and federal district judges.

The courts were now stacked with Federalist judges holding lifetime appointments, many would be around longer than their party. Many of these appointments, Adams made late into the night, earning the nickname "midnight appointments" by the Democratic-Republicans. Aside from partisanship, it was mostly sensible. Previously, Supreme Court Justices were required to travel the circuit to hear cases, which created a backlog.

Adams also nominated in late January—and the lame duck Senate confirmed—John Marshall to be the Chief Justice of the United States on Feb. 4, which the outgoing president asserted was, "...a gift to the people of the United States ... the proudest of my life."[41]

The Judiciary Act didn't ease tension for the Democratic-Republicans, but the law—establishing Federal power on the bench—could have at least contributed to talking Federalists away from the edge.

Finally, on Feb. 17, 1801, the House was about to cast the 36th ballot.

Bayard, an Adams loyalist and Delaware's lone member of the House of Representatives at the young age of 33, played a monumental role in helping to shift the race. Bayard told fellow Federalists that he could not "exclude Jefferson at the expense of the Constitution."

Bayard changed his vote from Burr to a blank ballot, and other representatives from Vermont and Maryland joined him. This shifted Maryland and Vermont from no choice into Jefferson's column, giving him 10 states he needed. South Carolina also did not cast a vote. The four Federalist members from South Carolina changed their votes from Burr to blank. Burr ended up with just four states.

These various political moves meant Jefferson was elected as the third president of the United States in the House of Representatives, owing much of his victory to his longtime ideological and political nemesis Hamilton.

In *America Afire* about the 1796 and 1800 elections, author Barnard Weisberger raises questions whether labeling Hamilton a kingmaker is a bit of lore, writing:

> *How much influence Hamilton's letter had with Bayard, or with any other recipients, is hard to guess. Certainly his divisive behavior during the campaign itself could not have increased his weight in party councils. Only inflation of the evidence allows for the conclusion that he 'swung' the final choice. But there is*

less mystery about his motive. Admiring biographers are inclined to give credit to his interest in the "public good" and praise him for burying old feuds and recognizing that Jefferson's claim to lead young America was far superior to Burr's. 'Hamilton Puts Nation Above Personal Feelings' makes a good story. But considering the violence of his language against Burr, it is also possible that in December 1800, he simply hated the man who had recently beaten him in New York State more than any other of his enemies, more than Jefferson in 1792, more than John Adams whom he was out to destroy a few months earlier.

Another Revolution

Long after he left the White House, at age 76, Jefferson reflected on his first term victory in a rather grandiose way, calling it the "Revolution of 1800." It might have seemed presumptuous for a man who campaigned as the candidate of the people to declare his ascension to the presidency as tantamount to the American Revolution of 1776.

It was, Jefferson said:

> ...as real a revolution in the principles of our government as that of 1776 was in its form; not effected indeed by the sword, as that, but by rational and peaceful instruments of reform, the suffrage of the people.

Federalist newspapers scoffed at the assertion as did Adams, the vanquished opponent. Jefferson would seek to explain to Adams that he meant the American Revolution established the supremacy of the people over the elite. [42]

Although he came in third place, Adams might well have

been re-elected if not for the most dubious words to make it into the Constitution; the notorious three-fifths clause. One of the great ironies was that the slave states that afforded slaves no human rights wanted slaves counted as a full person when it came to counting them for the Census and gaining apportionment in the House of Representatives and electoral votes. By contrast, opponents of slavery that believed humans owning another human was an abomination didn't want slaves counted at all in the Census, because they didn't want the slave states having disproportionate influence.

Not surprisingly, opponents of slavery were mostly Federalists, while supporters were generally Democratic-Republicans. That was far from consistent. The Constitution was settled on with the three-fifths compromise. This provided a dozen electoral votes for the Democratic-Republicans in 1800, as Gary Wills explained in his book *Negro President: Jefferson and the Slave Power*. It would have taken just a change in five Electoral votes to give Adams another term. If slaves had never been counted in the Census at all, Adams would have won the 1800 election.

As slavery goes, it is well known that Jefferson was more than a bit complicated on the matter as a slave owner, who may well have fathered a child with one and didn't set his slaves free in his will as George Washington did, nevertheless declared the institution an "abominable crime," believing it to be moral and economic evil that destroyed individual "industry" and undermined the owner perhaps more than the slave. His *Notes on the State of Virginia* (1781) denounced slavery. He told James Madison he was hesitant to publish it because:

> ...the terms in which I speak of slavery and of our Constitution [in Virginia] may produce an irritation which will revolt the minds of our countrymen against the reform of these two articles, and thus do more harm

than good. [43]

It is important to note Jefferson lived nearly three decades after Washington died, when Virginia laws on owner emancipation were far more restrictive, even when it came to setting slaves free in a last will and testament. In 1806, the state legislature imposed greater restriction on owners who wanted to voluntarily free their slaves. Jefferson observed in an August 1814 letter to Illinois statesman Edward Coles:

> *The laws do not permit us to turn them loose, if that were for their good: and to commute them for other property is to commit them to those whose usage of them we cannot control.*

Still, at the time, Federalist politicians and the Federalist press pointed out this contradiction. Outgoing Secretary of State Timothy Pickering, an Adams loyalist, resented that the country would be run by a "negro president," or someone elected because of the power of slave states. The Jan. 20, 1801 issue of the Boston newspaper *The New England Palladium* asserted that Jefferson would make his "ride into the temple of liberty on the shoulders of slaves." [44]

'What a Lesson to America and the World'

Ultimately though, it was not the prolonged result and intrigue that made 1800 so monumental. While not a revolution, the transition from one party to another was profound.

University of Dayton history professor Larry Schweikart, author of more than 20 books, including *What Would the Founders Say?*, said:

Tainted by Suspicion

> *The election of 1800 was probably the most important election in the nation's history, going from one ideology to another, and there was confidence that the country could survive.*

He added:

> *A peaceful transfer of power was practically unheard of in the world at that time and nobody had to die. Partisan rancor didn't stop, but people didn't come out with bayonets.*

On the morning of March 4, 1801, President Adams woke up at 4 A.M. to take a stage coach from Washington to Boston, where he would live out his life as a private citizen.

The peaceful transfer of power marked a pivotal moment, not just for America's survival during its infancy, but in setting an example for the world. Madison thought it likely Federalists would use force to maintain power and heralded the result as in a letter to Jefferson:

> *What a lesson to America and the world is given to the public will when there is no army to be turned against it.*[45]

Peacefully giving up power wasn't something that generally occurred in that time and it very easily might not have happened in this instance had Adams, Jefferson and Hamilton not had foresight to put aside their own ambitions and animosity.

This also marked America's first realignment election. While Adams was the last Federalist president, the Democratic-Republicans would control the office for another generation as the Federalist never mounted another competitive presidential campaign and withered away shortly after.

Jefferson took office at 11 A.M. wearing a simple suit, without powdered hair or wearing a sword strapped to his side—he didn't even ride the inaugural carriage to the Capitol as both his predecessors had. The simple ceremony, in Jefferson's view, was to mark a departure from pomp of the elite Federalists. He was accompanied only by the Alexandria militia. [46]

In his inaugural address, Jefferson sought to unite the country, famously saying, "We are all Republicans, we are all Federalists."

It was a mystery in those days, but a correspondence three decades later fueled speculation that a deal was struck. Former Federalist, George Baer, in an April 19, 1830 letter to Congressman Bayard's son, Richard Bayard, made the claim:

> *Having also received assurances from a source on which we place reliance, that our wishes with respect to certain points of federal policy in which we felt a deep interest, would be observed in case Mr. Jefferson was elected.* [47]

However, Jefferson always denied that he ever struck of any kind of deal with the Federalists. With regards to his vague assurance to Adams, Jefferson did not wipe out the national debt, though he paid it down by a third, and he did not get rid of all Federalist officials.

Jefferson was bitter at his vice president Burr for not simply conceding the election early on, and acted to stop his patronage appointments. He referred to the New England votes for Burr as a "declaration of perpetual war" against his administration. [48] It would of course mark just one part of yet another incredibly tough relationship between a president and vice president.

Jefferson rolled back some of the heavy national taxes, including the highly unpopular whiskey tax and did not renew the Alien and Sedition Act—again, policies that in many ways would be politically conservative by today's standards. But, in what is arguably a more dovish foreign policy, he backed down on aggression with the French and slashed the military budget. In fact, he balanced the books largely by doing away with so much of the military. Still, he wasn't just a dove, as he demonstrated after sending a naval squadron to fight the Barbary pirates.

President Jefferson was aggressive on other fronts. He moved forward with the Louisiana Purchase without Congress, accepting the implied powers of the presidency he had campaigned against. For the most part, he embraced many of the Hamilton economic policies he campaigned against. He almost invented triangulation before anyone used the phrase and was a very pragmatic and flexible leader—particularly when compared to the image the Federalist touted of a dangerous French-loving radical. He co-opted enough Federalist policies that made the opposition party unnecessary and proving himself not to be an extremist.

Before Jefferson's re-election, with a new running mate—George Clinton—the Twelfth Amendment was ratified in 1804 stating presidential electors would make separate choices for president and vice president. The amendment essentially codified the notion of political parties into the Constitution. The effect was to require factions to be far more organized in selecting candidates for office.

Benjamin Franklin's cautionary words, "A Republic, if you can keep it," were put to the test. As it turned out, Americans could keep it.

Flaws and all, these were men with enough character and intellect to realize the folly of clinging to power or risking bloodshed to obtain it. The nation truly could have been on the brink of collapse while still in its infancy, but was saved, perhaps by providence.

If the Federalists had insisted on maintaining a deadlock in the House—in what would have amounted to a coup against the

Constitution to install another Federalist in the White House—it seems certain that forces backing Jefferson, with or without his endorsement, would have not recognized this government. This could have eventually led to the Federalist government using force to uphold their government, and jeopardizing the chances for another election.

The country, at least as it was meant to be, would not have survived a civil war at this stage. One side would have won, and so convinced of the other side's evil, would have become despotic.

Had the Federalists won, stamping down an armed rebellion, America might have become something akin to a monarchy. Democracy would seem too dangerous. Lesson learned. Perhaps try again when the people are ready, but now the masses must be protected from themselves, an aristocratic class would reason.

Had the Jeffersonians prevailed through armed conflict, it might well have resulted in something similar to the French Revolution—though probably not as violent. The godlessness of the French Revolution made it doomed to fail. Americans were virtuous people, but might have been able to easily rationalize a guillotine for the tyrannical aristocrats that attempted to steal the election from the working men.

America was able to survive its Civil War six decades later only because it had become a strong nation by that time, able to endure. There would have been no endurance from an internal conflict in 1801.

The third possibility from election fallout turned bloody is that either Britain or France would seize on the opportunity to conquer the chaotic mess.

Under any of these scenarios, America would never be the paragon of human rights, model of democracy, nor the free market capitalist model that drives the world economy. America falls short morally and economically far too often—but has maintained its aspirations. That's what was at stake in 1800. This was first great test of a republic. America passed the test and the world should be grateful. There will never be a more important presidential election.

As for the cast of characters, Jefferson's shaky victory from 1800 was validated by an 1804 electoral landslide over Charles Pinckney, who would be the Federalist standard bearer twice more, and lose each time to Madison.

Hamilton, the supposed kingmaker, would be dead after a duel with Burr. Despite killing a man, Burr was able to finish his term as vice president, but by 1807, Burr was brought to trial for conspiracy for leading a charge against Spanish territory and for seeking to separate from the United States. Chief Justice John Marshall acquitted Burr on the treason charge, but the scandal destroyed the political career of the man who came very close to being president.

All of this of course would have been very different had there been a President Burr ...

CHAPTER THREE

President Burr

THE FEDERALISTS IN the House of Representatives chose not to listen to their intellectual leader. It seemed Alexander Hamilton's aggressive advice was a little too principled. Besides, had Hamilton not gone after Adams more viciously than Jefferson, Federalists would not have to decide on a lesser of two Democratic-Republican evils.

The former Treasury secretary's assertion that, "I trust the Federalists will finally not be so mad as to vote for Burr," comes across a bit too condescending.

Moreover, the paltry concessions Bayard brought back to the Federalists aren't convincing. Alas, Burr actually had the guts to leave Albany for Washington and contest the presidency.

After losing the Congress in the 1800 election, the party of Adams is presented with a way to at least have a strong influence on the executive that they are certain wouldn't be there if the enemy—Thomas Jefferson—became president.

Aside from Hamilton, that walk and talk between with President Adams and Vice President Jefferson was also key. Though Jefferson was coy, he essentially ensured Adams he would not be a wild-eyed radical. What if Adams were more bitter at his

Tainted by Suspicion

loss and was unsatisfied with Jefferson's assurance? Adams cannot reassure his party that Jefferson would be reasonable. The Federalists step back from the ledge of a constitutional crisis of seizing the presidency for a party member. They instead side with Burr—a compromise within the parameters of the Constitution.

All or any of the scenarios could have tipped the scales in favor of Burr during the House vote.

Is it not reasonable to ask: Why, Mr. Hamilton, are no principles worse than the wrong principles? It seems quite the contrary. Burr could be shaped and molded if it was beneficial for him. Jefferson might well be unmovable. Who among the Federalists could have projected Jefferson's triangulation? It could probably well be rationalized that ensuring the radical pro-French, godless Jacobins from having a monopoly over the American government.

Federalist Congressman James A. Bayard of Delaware finds no reason to switch his vote from Burr to no vote. He certainly doesn't encourage other Federalist to vote a blank ballot, and upon either scenario—ignoring the overbearing Hamilton or a not so cordial meeting with Adams and Jefferson—Burr gains votes, winning the necessary majority to be the third U.S. president.

Had Burr won the presidency, two things are near certain. Burr's life and legacy would have turned out far better, and Hamilton would have lived longer.

But beyond that, very few things are certain. A Burr presidency would assuredly not have been identical to a Jefferson presidency. The political atmosphere would have been different with Burr the New York politician as opposed to Jefferson the Virginia philosopher, and it might have overturned the entire political chain of events for centuries.

Federalist Loyalty?

As president, the ever pragmatic Burr would have only one option about where to cast his lot, said Edward J. Larson, the Hugh & Hazel Darling Chair at the Pepperdine University School of Law, and Pulitzer Prize winning author who wrote *A Magnificent Catastrophe: The Tumultuous Election of 1800, America's First Presidential Campaign*.

> *I don't think he would have had any choice but to side with the Federalists. They would have been the ones who lifted him to office.* [49]

Larson continued:

> *Burr was driven, power hungry and a crafty, brilliant politician. He would have been crafty enough not to have been a tool. He would have tried to craft coalitions to focus on self interests of various Republican members.*

Then again, the Federalist lawmakers that made him president were in the minority. So attorney David O. Stewart, author of *American Emperor: Aaron Burr's Challenge to Jefferson's America*, and former recipient of the Washington Writing Prize for Best Book, doesn't think the Federalists would have gotten the president they were seeking:

> *They [the Federalists] would have found that President Burr was profoundly ungrateful.* [50]

Also characterizing Burr as a crafty and pragmatic politician, Stewart believes he would have known the Federalists days were numbered. He said:

> *The Federalist might have been able to remain a viable party a little longer if they had orchestrated a Burr victory. But they were doomed. They were an aristocratic party and this was not going to be an aristocratic nation.*

Above all, Burr would have sought the best deal, which would not have been with the Federalists in the near term but possibly the majority Democratic-Republicans in the long term, said Adam Carrington, a professor of politics at Hillsdale College. That said, Carrington believes a deal in favor of Burr might have extended the party's life. He said:

> *The 1800 election killed the Federalist Party and they were never competitive again. This is partly because Thomas Jefferson was leading the other side. That destroyed the Federalists. It's possible the Federalists would have had a longer life in the absence of Jefferson. Because of how unprincipled Burr is, it might have extended the life of Federalist Party and you would not have had one-party rule until the age of Jackson. But I don't think Burr would have done much to repay the favor to the Federalists for making him president. Given that the Democratic-Republicans won majorities in both the House and Senate, he would have seen where the winds were blowing.* [51]

Politicians were fickle even in those days.

It might well have been that their loyalty to Jefferson—subjugated to the vice presidency for another four years—would have been fleeting. Do not forget, the Democratic-Republicans could not have won the 1800 elections without Burr's clever work to ensure his party won the New York state legislative races. Absent that, Adams would have won a second term. Democratic-

Republicans knew this. Would President Burr have been able to mend fences with the party faithful? Or would the Democratic-Republican majority in the House retaliate with the political noose of impeachment to move Jefferson up?

Impeachment?

Historians have a different verdict on whether the Jeffersonians in Congress could have moved so early to impeach a president.

Stewart, the Burr biographer, said:

> *If he had won the 1800 election, then he certainly would have been given some sort of a honeymoon period in office prior to an impeachment. A few months at least. Burr would have put that time to good use in binding up wounds with the Republicans, not least by buying them off with patronage. Thomas Jefferson was always shy of direct confrontation. I wouldn't consider the risk of impeachment very high.*

Stewart added:

> *Being far more of a pure politician than Jefferson, Burr was a big fan of patronage and showing gratitude to friends and political allies looking for plum government jobs. Jefferson, on the other hand, had been critical of Adams for nepotism and cronyism. So he wasn't eager to throw government workers out to bring Democratic-Republicans in. Even then, presidents cared about optics. The spoils system that truly came into effect under President Andrew Jackson would have likely ballooned nearly three decades earlier had Burr become president.*

Other historians think the political weapon of impeachment might have been very likely. University of Dayton history professor Larry Schweikart said:

> A Burr presidency would have been a disaster. Burr was out for Aaron Burr. He had no loyalties, no principles, no philosophy and almost no friends. He might have been impeached. If either side proposed it, the other party would probably say 'fine by me.' [52]

The ill will that would have been established from a Burr victory should not be underestimated, said Ronald Feinman, an adjunct history professor with Florida Atlantic University and author of *Assassinations, Threats, and the American Presidency: From Andrew Jackson to Barack Obama*. Feinman, a presidential historian, believes a President Burr would face a significant risk of impeachment:

> There would have been a lot of anger over a stolen election. Thomas Jefferson was much more respected. The chances of a second term for Burr would have been unlikely. He could have even been impeached by a Democratic-Republican majority. Burr could not have united the country. He almost certainly would have been a one-term president and one-term presidents don't unite the country. [53]

Burr and Slavery

There is one area where Feinman thinks there is at least some slight possibility that Burr would have made a difference—a very, very big area. Burr opposed slavery, though he was somewhat squishy about the matter, having owned slaves in the past. Feinman said:

> *As president, Burr might have been more open minded than Jefferson to opponents of slavery. It was an issue that caused trouble for the Democratic-Republicans. There might have been more turmoil if there had been a northern president.*

Joshua Spivak, Senior Fellow at the Hugh L. Carey Institute for Government Reform at Wagner College, believes a northern president would have expedited the end of slavery at least to some degree:

> *I have to imagine it would have made a difference. It's hard to claim one president would have ended it. But with Burr, maybe the country would have moved away from it. Burr is a more merchant based politician on his economic views, as opposed to the more agriculture based Republicans. Also, with Burr, maybe southerners Madison and Monroe would not have been president.* [54]

The Virginia Dynasty that typically includes George Washington's two terms with a four-year interlude before the three consecutive two-term presidencies of Jefferson, James Madison and James Monroe certainly gave the South significance influence during 32 of the nation's first 36 years.

Stewart, author of *American Emperor*, said:

> *The Virginia dynasty was a consequence of the 1800 election. There had very much been a battle between Virginia and New York, with the Clintons, George and DeWitt Clinton that is, seeking prominence. There was a strong regional split.*

The first Clinton family to impact American politics was a leading New York dynasty. George Clinton, who ended up replacing Burr as vice president during Jefferson's second term, had been the leading Democratic-Republican in New York. His nephew, DeWitt Clinton, would follow in his uncle's footsteps becoming both governor and U.S. senator. George Clinton and Burr detested one another, even though Clinton as governor appointed Burr to the U.S. Senate and Burr later encouraged Clinton to come out of retirement to run for governor again.

A Burr presidency might have upended the line of presidential successors that we know by shifting the balance of power away from Virginia to New York, or at least to the northeast. Would that regional shift alone—pushing the Democratic-Republicans into a more industrial focus, away from an agriculture-based economy—have been enough to hasten the demise of the worst historical scourge on America?

Probably not, experts say. Stewart asserted:

> *There was no social or political pressure to deal with slavery. Burr was antislavery personally but occasionally owned a slave or two for his personal convenience. No reason to expect any effort from him on slavery if he were president.*

Larson of Pepperdine University believes there might well have been a long-term political shift, but that would not have altered the debate over slavery in a meaningful way. Larson was doubtful that Burr could have gained support for a second term. He said:

> *The next Republican candidate would have been either Jefferson or Clinton. Jefferson, if he had lost the presidency for a second time in 1800, might have been frustrated and walked away from running. So it could have been Clinton from New York. Clinton would have won. It might have sped up the decline of slavery. But I don't think so. I view all politicians of that time—with*

> the exception of John Quincy Adams—as such compromisers. The Federalists were fairly strong in the South. In fact, in 1804, they nominated Charles Pinckney, who was one of the largest slave owners in the country. So there was no party breakdown.

Being the consummate politician, it seems highly unlikely Burr would take such a politically risky stand, said veteran New York political consultant Luis Miranda, whose son Lin-Manuel Miranda wrote Broadway musical *Hamilton*.

Miranda said:

> I see Burr as such a pragmatist. He sympathized with ending slavery. But I don't believe he had enough principles to do anything that might sacrifice his political future. [55]

Burr and the Louisiana Purchase

But Miranda, who has worked for New York politicians Hillary Clinton, Charles Schumer and Edward Koch, is enamored by the political skills of one of New York's first notable political giants. He said:

> Burr was actually a better retail politician than Jefferson. Burr could run a campaign like campaigns are run now. He was a get-out-the-vote candidate. He was far better at that than Jefferson. Had Burr gotten elected, he would have been more deeply involved in the intrigue and machinations of politics than Jefferson.

Burr's political instincts likely would have been enough to lead him to also make the Louisiana Purchase, Jefferson's greatest and most farsighted accomplishment as president, Miranda believes:

> *He was a bit less intellectual than Jefferson. Jefferson not only ran the country, but he helped create a structure for the nation to continue to run generation after generation. Burr didn't have that foresight. But he doesn't pretend to be a nice guy. Burr saw which way the wind was blowing and he knew better than most how to harness it. He would make a deal with whoever continued to deal with him.*

The 1803 deal between the Jefferson administration and Napoleon Bonaparte's France saw the U.S. acquire about 827,000 square miles of land west of the Mississippi River for $15 million, a mass expansion of the still young country.

Larson, author of *A Magnificent Catastrophe*, said:

> *The Louisiana Purchase never would have happened under Burr or Adams. Only Jefferson could have pulled that off. The French loved Jefferson. There is no way Napoleon would have sold it to Burr.*

But others strongly disagree, arguing that it was nearly a given. Eric Patterson, dean of the Robertson School of Government at Regent University, said:

> *The only reason they wouldn't make the purchase would be out of a very small minded partisan interest, maybe if the Federalists were afraid a western expansion would grow the Democratic-Republicans. But that's not very likely. I think any of the candidates, Burr, Adams, Pinckney would have made the purchase.* [56]

Jefferson, as a Democratic-Republican, favored greater congressional authority and a weak executive. Yet he made the decision on the Louisiana Purchase when Congress was out of session, determining he wouldn't let the opportunity for the country pass.

Believing Burr wouldn't have been the least bit concerned about separation of powers, Stewart asserts:

> *Jefferson's biggest accomplishment was the Louisiana Purchase. Burr absolutely would have done that and he wouldn't have given it any second thoughts.*

Burr's Real-Life Presidency

One assessment of Burr as president could be based on what he actually presided over. In those days, like Adams and Jefferson before him, the vice president regularly presided over the Senate. Today, the vice president might show up for a ceremonial occasion or to cast a tie-breaking vote.

New Hampshire Federalist Senator William Plumer once said:

> Mr. Burr, the Vice President, presides in the Senate with great ease, dignity & propriety. He preserves good order, silence and decorum in debate—he confines the speaker to the point. He has excluded all spectators from the area of the Senate chamber, except the members from the other House. A measure which contributes much to good order.

Keeping the riff raff out of the Senate might seem a natural liking for the aristocratic Federalists, but Burr had some support within his own party as well. However, many in his own party believed him to be a bit too chummy with the enemy—even an apostate.

On Jan. 27, 1802, Burr cast a tie breaking vote in favor of the Federalist on an issue quite important to the Jeffersonians—repealing the Judiciary Act of 1801. The law was passed by the lame duck Federalist Congress and signed by lame duck President Adams.

As mentioned in the previous chapter, the law relieved the U.S. Supreme Court justices from working on circuit courts. It also reduced the number of justices from six to five, effective with the next vacancy. Adams was able to appoint Federalist judges to the lower courts, and it looked unlikely that Jefferson could name any Supreme Court justices.

Kentucky Sen. John Breckinridge, a Democratic-Republican, introduced legislation to repeal the Judiciary Act. One Democratic-Republican senator was absent and another had resigned. Still others in Jefferson's party weren't keen on changing the laws governing a co-equal branch of government. So it was important that leadership be able to rely on Burr's vote.

When the Senate tied on the Judiciary Act, the Democratic-Republicans felt assured they could count on the vice president's support. What they didn't know is that Burr had worked out a deal with Federalists to add amendments to the law acceptable to moderate Democratic-Republicans. New Jersey Federalist Senator Jonathan Dayton referred the bill to:

> ...a select committee, with instructions to consider and report the alterations which may be proper in the Judiciary system of the United States.

The wily Burr expressed his reason for voting against the repeal—to allow the select committee to do its work.

Burr told the Senate:

> I am for the affirmative, because I never can resist the reference of a measure where the senate is so nicely balanced, when the object is to effect amendment, that may accommodate it to the opinions of a larger majority; and particularly when I can believe that

> *gentlemen are sincere in wishing a reference for this purpose. Should it, however, at any time appear that delay only is intended, my conduct will be different.*

Burr announced the five members of the committee would be three Democratic-Republicans and two Federalists. The problem his party had is that he chose a Democratic-Republican who had voted with the Federalists against the repeal—John Ewing Calhoun (a cousin of future vice president John C. Calhoun).

Burr said he was disturbed at the thought of "...depriving the twenty-six judges of office and pay." He also is believed to have been laying the groundwork to build up a coalition of his own party and Federalists to start a separate party.

The Judiciary Act would also indicate that Burr was ready to cut a deal with the opposing party should there be potential gain. Whether for principle or politics, he did oppose encroachment on the judiciary for short term partisan gain—which might represent a difference between himself and Jefferson beyond just style.

The notion that Jefferson was a superior statesman to Burr should not be necessarily a given. Burr would have been an unprincipled but potentially effective president, said Spivak of Wagner College:

> *I don't know that Thomas Jefferson would have been a greater president than Burr. It's not clear that Burr would have been so much worse. Burr was more transactional than Jefferson, more into making deals. Burr would be comparable to Mitt Romney, not particularly strong on principles, but a technocrat, a dealmaker.*

Clearly, had he been president, he would not have made the unsuccessful run for governor of New York—an office he sought as a sitting vice president because he was well aware Jefferson would not run with him again, as someone already shut out of decision-making in the administration.

The ambitious pragmatist considered joining the Federalist Party in New York, but instead launched an independent campaign, with stealth Federalist backing, for New York governor in 1804. Jefferson and the Clintons covertly pushed attacks against Burr. Hamilton, for some of the same reasons he didn't want Burr to become president, also didn't want him to be governor—feeling it was time to snuff him out once and for all, politically speaking, declaring he had a "despicable opinion" of Burr.

After Burr lost that election, he focused his blame on one person. He challenged Hamilton to the duel held on July 11, 1804 in Weehawken, New Jersey. It was Burr, of course, who snuffed Hamilton out once and for all, not politically but literally, killing one of the country's greatest economic minds on what was often called in those days, the "field of honor." Dueling was illegal, but Burr had immunity from prosecution in Washington, D.C., where he returned for what was interestingly enough one of his finest moments.

Burr presided over the Senate for the impeachment trial of U.S. Supreme Court Justice Samuel Chase—a role where he demonstrated some leadership after the most awkward of circumstances.

Stewart, author of *American Emperor*, said:

> *After he killed Hamilton, he remarkably came back to Washington to preside over the impeachment trial of a Supreme Court justice. He did a bang up job and was extremely fair. On the occasions Burr had power, he was surprisingly responsible. There was an extensive fear of what he would do if he had power. He was more dangerous out of power. He was moderate and fair minded. He was not an ideologue and that was a hindrance to him in some ways.*

The House of Representatives impeached Chase for judicial misconduct on March 12, 1804—an election year. It was also a year when Burr knew he would not be on the ticket with Jefferson again. Chase was a Federalist judge named to the court by President Washington and accused of bias against defendants charged with violating the hated Alien and Sedition.

Chief Justice William Rehnquist profiled the Chase impeachment along with the impeachment of President Andrew Johnson in his book, *Grand Inquests*. As was the case with the impeachments of Johnson and Bill Clinton, and near-impeachment of Richard Nixon, the Chase impeachment was tied up in a political and cultural war at the time. Like the Judiciary Act, Chase also represented to Democratic-Republicans the fear of a Federalist controlled court system.

Despite the rift between the Democratic-Republicans and Burr, the Senate majority didn't want to offend the vice president presiding over the trial. So the frosty relationship thawed a bit.

Burr ran a disciplined trial, as one newspaper reporter said "with the dignity and impartiality of an angel, but with the rigor of a devil."

Manasseh Cutler, a clergyman and congressman from Massachusetts, reported that the trial was:

> ...conducted with a propriety and solemnity throughout which reflects honor upon the Senate. It must be acknowledged that Burr has displayed much ability, and since the first day I have seen nothing of partiality. [57]

Though, it wasn't to every one's liking. It was, after all, a political setting.

Federalists didn't like the way the vice president treated Chase. Pleasing to his party compatriots, Vice President Burr frequently interrupted the aged Justice Chase, who actually broke into tears. Also, Burr lectured the Senate on proper judicial etiquette—scolding some for walking in the Senate chamber during witness testimony, or eating apples while the trial was occurring. Senators on both sides of the aisle resented being lectured about decorum from a man who recently killed a former cabinet official in an illegal duel.

Democratic-Republican Rep. John Randolph of Virginia led the impeachment managers, essentially the prosecution team. But Burr—as essentially the trial judge—would often intervene with questions for clarification. As the Senate Historical Office writes of the trial:

> *When either side objected to a question posed by the other, Burr took careful note of the objection, ordering that the offending question be 'reduced to writing' and put to the Senate for a determination.*

In the broader sense though, the Chase trial might have demonstrated how Burr could have risen to the occasion as commander-in-chief.

Burr's insistence on decorum for the trial that certainly involved raw partisan emotion helped further the Senate's reputation as the "World's Greatest Deliberative Body." Burr's Federalist fan, Sen. Plumer observed Burr:

> *...certainly, on the whole, done himself, the Senate and the nation honor by the dignified manner in which he has presided over this high and numerous Court.*

Only two articles gained a slim majority—well short of the two-thirds required for removal. The Senate voted unanimously to acquit on other articles. On March 1, Burr announced after a tally of the votes:

> *It appears that there is not a Constitutional majority of votes finding Samuel Chase, Esq., guilty, on any one article. It therefore becomes my duty to declare that Samuel Chase, Esq. stands acquitted of all articles exhibited against him.* [58]

Burr also presided with dignity over a joint session of Congress on Feb. 13, 1805, where he announced that Jefferson had been re-elected president and his nemesis, one of many, George Clinton, would be replacing him as vice president, which Sen. Samuel Mitchill described as:

> *...so much regularity and composure that you would not have seen the least deviation from his common manner, or heard the smallest departure from his usual tone.*

Of course, he didn't really have a choice. It's not so different from what future vice presidents, such as Richard Nixon and Al Gore would have to do in 1961 and 2001. Both managed to handle disappointment without mounting an insurrection. Larson, of Pepperdine, said:

> *Whatever he did, he did well. He did well as a soldier in the Revolution. He did well as an attorney. He did well as a politician, nearly becoming president. He did a fine job presiding over the Senate. Burr would not have gone off the rails had he not lost the presidency and then not lost the New York governorship.*

Burr biographer Stewart had a near identical assessment:

> *His crazy trip out west is because he was finished politically. He was looking for a way to be great. It*

> *wasn't happening. He was just a regular politician and was damaged.*

That "crazy trip" was of course Burr's drive to take over much of Jefferson's signature accomplishment, the Louisiana territory. Burr thought he could redeem himself by taking over the territory and essentially making it his fiefdom. It seems beyond absurd by today's standards that Joe Biden, Dick Cheney, Al Gore or Dan Quayle—all colorful vice presidents in some form—would engage in such a bizarre adventure.

Feinman of Florida Atlantic University said jokingly:

> *There were two villainous vice presidents, Aaron Burr and Spiro Agnew and there were also two sitting vice presidents who shot someone, Aaron Burr and Dick Cheney.*

Even placing this in the context of the times, Burr's move was truly outrageous. In 1807, he conspired with James Wilkinson, U.S. Army commander and governor of Northern Louisiana Territory. The two coordinated a plan to conquer some of Louisiana and potentially expand into Mexico, where Burr would declare himself the emperor of a newly carved out territory. The two even trained forces for the plan. Then Wilkinson got cold feet, wisely, and ratted out his co-conspirator before the invasion was ever launched. Burr was arrested and charged with treason. His trial was held in Richmond, Virginia, with Chief Justice John Marshall presiding.

Marshall instructed the jury that two witnesses must testify to a specific, overt act to convict of treason. The prosecution could not provide a second witness. After just 25 minutes of deliberation, the jury foreman read the verdict:

> *We the jury find that Aaron Burr is not proved to be*

> *guilty under this indictment by any evidence submitted to us. We therefore find him not guilty.* [59]

Burr was acquitted, but whatever miniscule chance he had of a comeback was obviously dashed. He fled the country fearing additional charges might arise.

Burr Re-Election

Burr's megalomaniacal attempt to become an emperor came in the middle of what could have been his theoretical second term of his presidency. As unlikely as most historians consider a second term, one can recall at various points where conventional political wisdom shunned the prospect of a second term for Barack Obama over the economy, George W. Bush over the Iraq war or Bill Clinton after losing the Congress in 1994.

There are so many factors. First, if Burr had managed to win in the House over Jefferson in 1800, would he really have "stolen" anything?

Certainly Jefferson was supposed to be at the top of the ticket. But pre-Twelfth Amendment, there were no tickets. Burr in fact ran for president. He declined to step aside. For Jefferson, this was unforgivable, but in reality, Burr violated no constitutional or legal rules. The fact he pulled off a herculean effort to deliver New York for the Democratic-Republicans, put the party in presidency for the first time in the nation's history. Had Burr become president, regardless of the unusual circumstances, he might have gained some party loyalty by virtue of being its first president. Judging by his Senate leadership, Burr might have been able to reach out to Jefferson loyalists and co-opt enough of the Federalist agenda to keep public support. If he could overcome a Vice President Jefferson trying to undermine him, and secure the Louisiana Purchase, a second term might have been very feasible.

Jefferson established the embargo against British ships during his second term. Burr might have handled things differently. Stewart said:

> There was a struggle with Britain at sea and the British were really mistreating our sailors. British warships were openly firing on American ships. Jefferson chose not to go to war when a lot were demanding we go to war with Britain. Jefferson left it to Madison to clean up. If Aaron Burr had been president, he would have gone to war. He was more militaristic and he might have gotten public support. America was no less ready to go to war then than in 1812. It is a war the United States might have won. Burr was a very good military leader.

However, there is the domestic political situation to consider.

If President Burr was beholden to the Federalists, a pro-British party, he might have been very reluctant to lead the country into combat, Larson argued:

> He would have been aligned with the Federalists. He might have been prone to go to war to boost his credibility domestically. If so, he would have gone after France. He would have cut a deal with the British.

***

It's difficult to imagine a more tragic figure than Burr. If raw ambition were a weakness, half the presidents would have never made it to the White House, so that wasn't his Achilles heel. Burr had all the tools to become president: a crafty politician whose ultimate principle was Aaron Burr. Again, not so unusual for many politicians. He became unhinged when the presidency had permanently slipped away—first killing Hamilton and following years later with his boneheaded conquest plot.

He could have made two choices after the 1800 Electoral College tie.

Step forward and publicly declare his allegiance to Jefferson, winning the president-elect's confidence. He might have been an active member of the Jefferson team and might have been on path to take Madison's place as the fourth president of the United States.

The alternative, a logical one if he wasn't going to endorse Jefferson, would have been to actively lobby House members—presumably Federalists—to give him the job. Known as a dealmaker, he apparently never even made an attempt when it mattered most. Burr likely would have found a way to be discreet and his actions might have been enough to counter Hamilton's influence.

Instead, he chose neither, which did not demonstrate principle or ambition.

Choosing to straddle the fence, he seemed to presume that the Jeffersonians wouldn't be upset with him so long as he didn't publicly campaign. He also seemed to think that he could somehow overcome Hamilton by standing on the sidelines. A politician who wants greatness—as Burr clearly did at some point—cannot wait for it to be thrust upon them.

It was Hamlet-style indecision after the pivotal moment in life that lost him the presidency forever and sent him on a downward spiral career wise—and perhaps mentally, sealing his fate as the most disreputable and villainous founding father.

PART II

John Quincy Adams vs. Andrew Jackson

Tainted by Suspicion

CHAPTER FOUR

Democracy Arrives

A CONTROVERSIAL ELECTION battle occurred between an aristocratic New Englander named Adams and a southern slave-owning plantation owner claiming to speak for the people was ultimately decided by the House of Representatives.

It sounds a lot like 1800, but 1824 was still very different.

It was the second time in 24 years an election would be thrown to the House. What might be a bigger question is why did it not happen more often? The Founders did not envision political parties initially. In the absence of parties, it might be presumed that some Founders envisioned the possibility of the Electoral College being a nominating process, selecting between a large group of regional candidates, and the House would decide on the winnowed field.

As Donald Ratcliffe wrote in *The One-Party Presidential Contest: Adams, Jackson, and 1824's Five-Horse Race*:

> Only if one candidate stood head and shoulders over his rivals—as Washington did in 1788 and 1792—would the Electoral College normally be able to make the decision. The Founding Fathers had not anticipated

> the emergence of two national party formations in the
> 1790s that effectively reduced the number of candidates
> to two in election after election between 1796 and
> 1816, and so guaranteed that (barring a tie) one of
> them would have a majority in the Electoral College. [60]

The modern Democratic Party celebrates Jefferson-Jackson Dinners across the United States, whom the party sees as the dual founders. Although a southern plantation owner, Thomas Jefferson was a towering intellectual who structured the overarching ideology of America. While framing much of his campaign as the people vs. the elite, Jefferson himself was very elite with a mindset filled with complexities and nuance. Jackson was very wealthy, but he was neither very complex nor nuanced.

'Good Feelings' Fade

The candidate pool was wide in 1824, with Speaker of the House Henry Clay of Kentucky—who would go on to play an outsized role in the campaign; Secretary of Treasury William H. Crawford of Georgia; and for a time, Secretary of War John C. Calhoun of South Carolina, all vying. At one point in January 1822, it appeared 17 people were jockeying for the job. But most fizzled away.

Andrew Jackson, "the friend of the common man" by contrast, was the first true populist-style politician to rise to the presidency through an insurgent candidacy, or as historian Paul Johnson referred to him in *A History of the American People*, Jackson was "the first case, in fact, of presidential charisma in American history."

He was almost the Donald Trump of his day, though not as wealthy. He could also be compared to a class-oriented populist such as Bernie Sanders. Jackson excited the electorate with plain talk. He knew how to channel anger, anger that was largely justifiable toward an out of touch, unproductive elite in Washington. While in those days, surrogates would generally sling mud in presidential campaigns, the candidates themselves would—gentlemanly—avoid mixing it up, Jackson had no such constraints and called the banks, the War Department and Washington in general, "The Great Whore of Babylon." [61]

Willard Randall, an award winning journalist and historian, who is the author of 14 books on U.S. history and a professor emeritus at Champlain College, said:

> *Andrew Jackson would be a very strong candidate today. He would deliver ripping speeches about the 2008 recessions, how the big banks were bailed out, but how the working people lost their homes. It's the kind of thing Bernie Sanders would also say. Jackson called the National Bank the 'hydro-headed monster.' It's the kind of thing Trump would say.*

Jackson would say what was on his mind, but he also knew how to be coy. Asked in 1821 if he would seek the presidency, he responded:

> *I can command a body of men in a rough way, but I am not fit to be president.* [62]

The Monroe presidency was called the "Era of Good Feelings," because the War of 1812 was over, the Missouri Compromise had temporarily solved the slavery debate and the country was experiencing growth and prosperity. The same party controlled the White House for six straight elections, a very good feeling for Democratic-Republicans, and Monroe wasn't even challenged for a second term in 1820. But the country was also experiencing corruption, and the public was angry about it.

Both Calhoun, running the War Department, and

Crawford, running Treasury—while angling to be the next president—openly accused the other of abusing their office for personal gain. Members of the administration and members of Congress allegedly accepted loans from federal contractors that they were never expected to pay back. Newspapers denounced the corruption, as the *Baltimore Federal Republican* announced bribers were guilty of "enormous defalcation," only "one of innumerable instances of corruption in Washington."

The New York Statesman newspaper bemoaned the...

> ...scandalous defalcation in our public pecuniary agents, gross misapplications of public money, and an unprecedented laxity in official responsibilities.

All of this presented an opportune time for a charismatic outsider to enter the fray, as Jackson called for a "general cleansing" of the nation's capital.

Jackson perhaps had an easy target in Secretary of State John Quincy Adams. Not corrupt, but still the son of a president, the embodiment of entitlement—part of a legacy of Jefferson, Madison and Monroe, all former Secretaries of State who became president as if it was the natural stepping stone.

In fact, Jackson, by contrast, was the only major candidate with no vast administrative experience in the federal bureaucracy. Whereas the other three candidates were multi-lingual, Jackson only spoke English, and not the King's English. He didn't even write English that well. Post-George Washington, every president had held a cabinet post. But like Washington, Jackson was revered by the public for his time as a heroic general on the battlefield.

In a good bit of irony, in 1818 it was Secretary of State Adams who pressured President Monroe to support General Jackson's undeclared war against the Spanish forces by invading Florida. Thanks in large part to Jackson's bravado, Spain conveyed the Florida territory to the United States in July, 1821. Jackson became the governor of the Florida territory. [63]

Jackson and Adams were both supporters of the Monroe administration. Though a member of the cabinet, Crawford didn't back administration policies, nor did Clay.

Adams even wanted Jackson to be his vice president, which would have altered history considerably. Adams thought Jackson's large personality would liven up the office of the vice presidency, and "would afford an easy and dignified retirement for his old age." He also added that the vice presidency was "a station from which the General could hang no one." Supporters of an Adams-Jackson '24 ticket came up with a slogan. "John Quincy Adams who can write; Andrew Jackson who can fight." [64]

For the 1824 election, there was an undercurrent of that reoccurring "time for a change" theme that surfaces in every few presidential elections to the current day. To put this in modern perspective, the old Republican guard continued to say throughout 2015 that the 2016 campaigns of outsiders Trump, Dr. Ben Carson, Carly Fiorina, or even Sen. Ted Cruz were doomed to fail. That's what history tells us, since insurgent candidates on the Republican side always eventually succumb to the frontrunner. Unlike the Democrats, who historically nominates surprises. But the rules completely changed in 2015 leading up to the first primaries.

Likewise, the rules completely changed in 1824. Adams was the heir apparent to the presidency less because his father held the job, than because he was the Secretary of State, the instant springboard. That was the political rule for the last three presidents. It would be called a kick-the-bums-out voter mood today.

Voting Boom, Caucus Collapse

There were 24 states by this point and an expanded pool of voters. A quarter of the states still did not allow voters to choose presidential electors—New York, Vermont, Delaware, South Carolina, Georgia, and Louisiana. The rest allowed the public to vote, or at least allowed white males to vote. [65]

It's understandably tough to get excited about expanded white male suffrage—hardly liberty and justice for all by any modern understanding. But, when states liberalized their voting rules by lifting the property-owning requirement, it was a massive enfranchisement for the time. Universal white male suffrage had not arrived by 1824, but was practiced in every state except for Virginia, Rhode Island and Louisiana. [66]

Although the King Caucus system kept the public out of the nominating process, it was a strong party system that steered popular voting. During Jefferson's time, some northern states got 60-80 percent turnout from the eligible white male voters. Even for the six states that did not allow voting for president, voters in those states did elect state legislators. Since state legislatures in those states chose electors, these races were indirect votes for president. Given this move toward more popular democracy it shouldn't come as a surprise that by now the faction horrified by too much direct democracy—the Federalists—had withered and died.

By 1824, the Democratic-Republican Party had become too dominant for its own good and engaged in infighting and splintered mostly along regional lines. The fractured party is one reason why the Democratic Party's claim of direct lineage to Jefferson is dubious at best.

It should also be noted that in the 18 states that allowed popular voting, only six of those states had all four major candidates on the ballot. [67] Voters in New England states chose between Adams and Crawford. In Atlantic states the voting was between Adams, Jackson and Crawford. In the Southeast, it was Crawford and Jackson. In the old Northwest and Louisiana, the choice was Adams, Clay and Jackson. So the will of the people was not as easily determined as the Jacksonians would later claim.

Ratcliffe wrote:

> One of those states was New York, which in 1824 contained one-seventh of the nation's population and cast more votes in its state election in November than even the most successful candidate had won in the popular-vote states. All the indications are that Adams had the backing of about 40 percent of the votes cast in New York, while Jackson had failed to register any significant popular support there at all. That is sufficient to have given Adams a nationwide lead of at least 34,000 votes. In no way was Jackson the clear choice of the people in 1824. [68]

This enfranchisement caused the collapse of the congressional caucus system, in which party caucuses in Congress would nominate candidates for president and vice president. It suited the parties just fine since 1804. It didn't suit some of the new Western states being admitted into the union. The rage against Washington didn't begin with Jackson, but had started as voters began electing new members of Congress and state legislators who favored allowing the voters to elect presidential electors from their state. The caucus system collapsed in 1820 when it became unresponsive to the demands of an empowered public. [69]

Imagine this system in the modern era. The aforementioned outsiders Trump, Carson, Cruz or Fiorina would not even be in contention if Senate Majority Leader Mitch McConnell and Speaker of the House Paul Ryan rallied their caucuses to choose a presidential nominee. It's a near certainty that if Democratic House and Senate leaders Nancy Pelosi and Harry Reid were leading their troops to choose the Democratic nominee in 2008, Barack Obama would have not gotten a second look against the establishment favorite Hillary Clinton. The famed smoke filled rooms by party bosses would actually be a further evolution in the democratization of the nominating system.

So loathed was King Caucus, that Hezekiah Niles, publisher of the *Weekly Register* believed it would be preferable to the halls of Congress be "converted into common brothels," than used for selecting the future chief executive of the country.

Primaries? Let's not get crazy. When William Duane of Pennsylvania, considered a radical then, proposed a convention of delegates made up of people who were active in the party, the notion was shunned. National Party conventions? That might be a little too close to direct democracy. Parties, as we know them, had not fully developed yet. In place of a caucus would be regional endorsements of candidates by state conventions or state assemblies—sort of a state primary, only with legislators casting the votes. This nonetheless brought the public closer to the nominating process.

It was the absence of Parties that year that prompted some of the out-of-the ordinary campaigning and even public opinion polling—yes, polls in 1824. Generally, these were straw polls. Sometimes polls were taken at barrooms, Fourth of July celebrations, among members of grand jury proceedings, aboard boats, in marketplaces. In some cases, women—ineligible to vote—participated in the surveys. These were hardly scientific, but did provide a sampling of public opinion for curious political observers. [70]

The Proud Democrat

The 1824 campaign was a disputed election from the beginning, as a single party would have four nominees, each claiming to be the rightful Democratic-Republican nominee. Because of this, ballots did not reference parties.

In lieu of Congressional caucuses, the Tennessee state legislature sought a jumpstart on the campaign by nominating Andrew Jackson for president in 1822, putting his hat firmly in the ring before any other viable candidate. The following year, the legislature named him to the U.S. Senate seat. His campaign was far more supportive of calling him General Jackson rather than Senator Jackson.

Jackson shunned some of the old rules in political language. In the elections of 1796 and 1800 the only folks using the term "Democrat" were Federalists smearing the Jeffersonians. There is a reason the Democratic-Republicans typically referred to themselves as Republicans. Democracy had connotations of mob rule, which had connotations of France.

Jackson used his words that year to promote the move toward more voting rights, unapologetically calling himself a democrat, as the fear of a tyrannical mob had faded from the public's mind with distance from the French Revolution. Jackson affirmed that those subject to rights, and laws and punishment, "ought to be entitled to a vote in making them." He believed every state legislature must allow the presidential vote for "the happiness, security and prosperity of the state" and that:

> The great constitutional corrective in the hands of the people against usurpation of power, or corruption by their agents, is the right of suffrage; and this when used with calmness and deliberation will prove strong enough—it will perpetuate their liberties and rights.

The public was willing to forgive much from Jackson. He was known for a temper, engaged in brawls and killed a man in a duel for slurring his beloved Rachel.

While Madison and Monroe were mostly in the Jefferson tradition of standing for the common man, they were not of the common class. Neither was Jackson. But, he knew how to speak their language and came along at just the right time when the electorate was expanding. He was the outsider who didn't serve his country by sitting in a comfortable office in Washington, but by risking his life in battle for the United States, very appealing at the time. Experienced politicians and writers of the day did not believe Jackson could be president. For one, it seemed unlikely he would draw cross regional appeal in New England, the South and western states. [71]

Jackson, born in 1767 a few days after his father died, experienced much loneliness in his life. His oldest brother was killed in the Revolutionary War, while he and his surviving brother were taken prisoner by the British. His brother and mother died of smallpox leaving Jackson an orphan at age 14. He was self-educated and became a successful lawyer and an even more successful soldier.

There was some marital confusion after he married Rachel Donnellson before her divorce had been finalized. This did not surface during his first run for the presidency, but it was a major headache in his subsequent campaign.

His assertion of an outsider status was based more in attitude than on resume, as Jackson held a very enviable string of public offices. In 1796, he attended a convention where the state of Tennessee is established, and served in Tennessee's House of Representatives from 1796 to 1797 before he was elevated to the U.S. Senate, serving there for another year. Not particularly fond of working in Washington, he returned home to serve as a Justice on the Tennessee Supreme Court from 1798 through 1804. Then he entered the military as a major general of the Tennessee militia in 1803, while still serving on the court.

Jackson supporters called him:

> ...*the soldier, the statesman and the honest man; he deliberates, he decides and he acts; he is calm in deliberation, cautious in decision, efficient in action.*

Jackson said:

> *The office of Chief Magistrate of the Union is one of great responsibility. As it should not be sought by any individual of the Republic: so it cannot with propriety be declined when offered by those who have the power of selection.* [72]

In another long political tradition, Jackson was among the first politicians to act as if the job of the presidency was seeking him. Though, he seemed to work hard at seeking it.

He was an Army general in 1815 when he led soldiers to soundly defeat the British in the Battle of New Orleans during the War of 1812. This turned him into a national hero, even though the battle occurred after a peace had been negotiated. News traveled slowly in those days. Supporters, quite hyperbolically, touted him as another George Washington. He was also known for battling the Creek Indian tribe in 1813 and established a reputation as an Indian fighter in the Seminole War in 1818 and proponent of expanding the United States westward.

As for his ownership of slaves, Jackson never betrayed any conflicting emotions the way Jefferson had. Jefferson believed it to be a morally and economically bankrupt system, yet kept slaves at Monticello and did not free them in his will. Jackson was not one to speak up on the slave trade, but seemed to have no qualms with keeping them at his Tennessee plantation, the Hermitage.

Jackson didn't talk about a lot of issues other than vague

references about the common man. One specific was closing the Bank of the United States.

Caucusing for Crawford

In the summer of 1824, in a weak attempt to salvage the caucus system, less than one-third of Congressmen eligible to attend voted to nominate William H. Crawford for president for the Democratic-Republicans, the second major candidate in the race.

New York Sen. Martin Van Buren used his influence to ensure the nomination, but the caucus selection actually harmed Crawford's chances, being identified with the system that was scorned by most Americans. There was reason to believe he would be a frontrunner—largely because he was seen as Monroe's choice at one point. The president believed early on that he would win the caucus, even a real one.

The *Baltimore Morning Chronicle* wrote of the caucus:

> *The poor little political bird of ominous note and plumage, denominated a CAUCUS, was hatched at Washington on Saturday last. It is now running around like a pullet, in forlorn and sickly state. Reader, have you ever seen a chicken directly after it was hatched creeping about with a bit of egg shell sticking to its back? This is a just representation of this poor forlorn Congressional caucus. The sickly thing, is to be fed, cherished and pampered for a week, when it is fondly hoped it will be able to cry the name of Crawford, Crawford, Crawford.* [73]

Crawford, of Georgia, was born in 1772. Before serving in the cabinet, he was a U.S. Senator, then minister to France. President Madison named him as Secretary of War and later Secretary of Treasury. The nation's finances were in disarray after the War of

1812. Monroe kept him at Treasury in order to have an experienced hand.

Under Monroe, Crawford initiated the Reform Bill of 1817 that gave the Treasury Department the responsibility for settling financial accounts of all other federal departments. The new law altered the department with new duties. Crawford also oversaw infrastructure improvements such as coastal fortifications and construction of the Cumberland Road leading westward.

Van Buren's backing seemed promising for appeal in the North and South. One political liability was a legendary temper that made him not so likable around other politicians. [74] The temper reportedly caused him to come to a near fist fight with President Monroe during a cabinet meeting, until Crawford took control of himself and apologized. Still, the president and his secretary of Treasury rarely spoke to one another after that.

Another liability was a stroke he suffered in 1823, which caused him to be partially paralyzed, partially blind and unable to speak. He was still persuaded to run for president by several politicians that mounted the caucus effort. At a time when most candidates didn't do their own campaigning, the stroke was not in and of itself a deal killer. Crawford was able to return to his cabinet job after the illness. [75]

It was during the presidential campaign that some of Crawford's friends and close operatives feared for his life and wanted to turn to a replacement candidate—most likely Clay. Cabinet officials even debated whether he was fit to serve, and whether the Treasury Department was being properly run. It was Adams who provided reassurance that his opponent could continue in his cabinet role. [76]

A President's Son

It fell upon the Massachusetts state legislature to formally nominate Adams for president of the United States, designating him as the true (in their eyes) standard bearer of the Democratic Republican party 28 years after his Federalist father defeated the party he now belonged to.

John Quincy Adams had joined the Democratic-Republicans when Jefferson was still president. He saw the political realities, and there was really nowhere else to go for someone with political ambitions. But more to the point, like his father, Quincy Adams was a pragmatist. Just as his father was seen as a moderate, so too was Quincy Adams, even more so. He was sometimes known as a "Jeffersonian Federalist" by Democratic-Republicans that didn't trust him because he was a New Englander and the son of John Adams. Many blamed Adams for morphing the party of States rights into a "National Republican" party, or a covert Federalist party.

Moreover, he had not been silent about his moral revulsion toward slavery, which worried southern voters. He had criticized the Missouri Compromise of 1820 for being a pro-slavery conspiracy, a phrase he used interchangeably with slave power. Adams also tried to include language opposed to international slave trade in the Treaty of Ghent in 1815, which brought the War of 1812 to an end, but he was unsuccessful. [77]

Similar to his father, the younger Adams, born in 1767, was sometimes mocked for his physical appearance. He was a short, bald man who really couldn't capture the public's imagination. He jokingly described himself as, "a man of reserved, cold, austere and forbidding manners." His opponents basically agreed, calling him a "gloomy, misanthrope." [78]

The man who would go on to be known as "Old Man Eloquent" was secretary to his father in Europe and became an accomplished linguist. While being the son of a president clearly gave him a leg up in life, Adams paid his dues. While his father was Vice President, the young Adams was named as minister to Holland in the Washington administration from 1794 to 1797. It was a political controversy when his father as president named him minister to Prussia, inviting denouncement for nepotism, which it of course was. But the first President Adams was certain his son was the best man for the job.

Quincy Adams stood on his own after the single-term Adams administration had ended. The Massachusetts legislature named him as the U.S. Senator in 1803, a post he held for five years, before moving to the job of minister of Russia for six years. Adams was in Russia through most of the War of 1812, but was named as minister of Britain in 1815, where he worked out a deal with the British to bring the war to an end with the Treaty of Ghent. His diplomatic record during the Madison administration paid off.

As Secretary of State under Monroe, Adams worked out an agreement for joint occupation with England for the Oregon country, obtained Florida from Spain while taking his pro-General Jackson stance. He also formulated the Monroe Doctrine. Adams ultimately had to prove himself enough to the party that opposed his father, but which realized he would be a powerful ally, and for the most part was successful.

The Great Compromiser

The Kentucky state legislature was next to act in also nominating its favorite son, Henry Clay, to be president.

If there was going to be a viable challenger to the heir apparent Adams, the safest money was on the Speaker of the House, a man with deep connections and deep respect across the country. His Missouri Compromise, he thought, would prevent a North-South conflict over slavery, when it fact it only kicked the can down the road. Despite that, he would be Abraham Lincoln's political hero. For Clay, born in 1777, compromise was a reality of government and he built a reputation for being a great compromiser and cutting deals.

It fit in to his vision of the American System, finding common ground among parochial interest between House members looking out for their own districts, and framing something for the greater national interests. The American System was based on tying the nation together through economic interests and by buildings roads and harbor entries, supporting the Bank of the United States and maintaining protective tariffs for southern sugar and northern textiles and iron. Clay envisioned himself as president as early as 1817, the year he talked Monroe out of naming Crawford secretary of state, fearing it would endanger his own presidential ambitions. Considering the rapport later developed between Monroe and Crawford, the president likely appreciated the advice. [79]

Still, it's hard to discern an ideology other than unity and compromise. Clay wanted to keep the country united as one nation, not a small goal for the time. Similar to Jefferson, Clay opposed slavery personally, though he owned them and never set them free. Moreover, it seemed too divisive a political issue for a Speaker who feared polarization might interfere with important deals. He believed that slavery was such a weak economic system, that the South would drop it voluntarily if it had to compete in a national economy. [80] If Clay viewed the American System as a backdoor abolitionist movement and avoiding division and war through economic incentives, it doesn't seem to have worked. On the other hand, his full vision was never brought to fruition. Even if his theory were true, it might have well meant slavery would have continued well into the 20th century before reaching a natural death. The pinnacle of Clay's career in Congress might have been avoiding a Civil War until one was unavoidable.

The Missouri Compromise of 1820 settled the tension between the North and South over slavery. Of the 22 states at the time, half were free and half were slave. The Missouri territory's request for admission into the union as a slave state had the potential to upset the balance. Clay, still a senator at the time, brought the sides together with the agreement to allow Missouri to be admitted as a slave state if Maine—previously a part of Massachusetts—could be admitted as a free state. Further, Missouri would be the single exception, but slavery would be banned in the Louisiana Purchase lands. Like any compromise, neither side was happy. The South thought it set a precedent of allowing Congress to decide on slavery, while the North thought Congress had caved to slave power.

With his eye on the presidency, Clay made a play to be Monroe's vice president in 1820, which he didn't achieve. Adams thought Clay had "disclosed his designs too soon" before assembling a coalition. [81]

Clay thought it to his advantage to have a crowded field in 1824—better to send the election to the House of Representatives where he was confident he'd be a lock to win.

To put Clay in the context of modern elections, think of the candidate who checks all the boxes and looks good on paper, starts strong in a primary—appears to be a likely frontrunner—then unexpectedly fizzles because he—or she—can't connect. There is one of every four years. That might well describe Clay in 1824.

He was first elected to the Kentucky General Assembly in 1803, and mostly advocated Jeffersonian ideas even though he would gravitate towards nationalism. He bounced back and forth in both houses of Congress. In 1806, he was briefly hired to the unenviable task of being the attorney for Aaron Burr. It's a task he abandoned when he was appointed to the U.S. Senate. In two years, he was elected to the U.S. House, and became Speaker, then returned to the Senate in January 1810 through an act of the legislatures before he was elected again to the House that August by voters. He would remain in the House as Speaker for the twelfth, thirteenth, fourteenth, fifteenth and sixteenth Congresses.

Clay was uncompromising on foreign policy. This nationalism on domestic issues led him to be very hawkish during the War of 1812. Even though he championed the War of 1812, he was part of the treaty delegation for the joint American-British peace negotiations in Ghent, Belgium in 1814, so Adams would not be the only candidate with a claim to credit for this diplomatic feat. However, on a few points he clashed with Adams, opposing the Adams-Onis Treaty that renounced any claim the United States had to Texas and locked in a western boundary of the Louisiana Purchase. [82]

Clay loathed Jackson and thought him a demagogue who might very well become a dictator if he were to become president.

Clay wrote:

> *I cannot believe that killing 2,500 Englishmen at New Orleans qualifies for the various, difficult and complicated duties of the First Magistracy* [83]

Clay was a gifted orator, with national name notoriety that would seem to make him a good candidate for appeal across regions. A smooth politician, so much that Calhoun said, "I don't like Clay...but by God, I love him." [84]

Still, although a Kentuckian (a western state on the U.S. map then), Clay was weak in the South, where voters didn't want nationalism—still preferring the Jeffersonian tradition of States rights and a farm economy. Slavery, of course, played a big role on this front as well.

Second Thoughts

Among the most colorful characters in American political history might be John C. Calhoun of South Carolina, who wanted to ascend to the presidency after serving as Secretary of War under President Monroe. He proclaimed slavery to be a "positive good," and had solid support among slave owners.

However, he had little backing outside the South. After initially entering the race for president, he dropped out to announce he was running for vice president instead. He decided to back Jackson, whom he believed would have southern interests at heart. But Calhoun did have enough appeal that both Adams and Jackson supporters endorsed him for the vice presidency on their ticket—meaning he was all but in.

Conservatives and Liberals

The partisan press did not let up during the race, praising their own candidates and seeking to destroy the oppositions with less than provable accusations, to say the least. Newspapers attacked Adams for how he dressed and for having an "English" wife. Other broadsheets accused Jackson of murder. Clay was called a "drunkard and a gambler," while Crawford was just accused of simple corruption in office. [85] One politician is reported to have commented, that if all these charges are true, "our presidents, secretaries and senators are all traitors and pirates." [86]

On the ideological scale, it again is always tough to impose the standards of that era on today, but there are broad generalities.

Like his father, Adams would probably be seen as a conservative, a man dedicated to defending American institutions and social order. Yet, he was quite dovish and always preferred diplomacy to war, which could theoretically put him on the left regarding foreign policy. He also believed in a strong national government.

Jackson—though with his opposition to the National Bank might seem to fit well with libertarians and tea partiers today in some aspects—would still be more of a liberal for that time because of his rabble rousing populism and class war rhetoric.

Further, his adoration of federal patronage fits in the frameworks of a big government philosophy even if he did favor states rights. His fervor for more direct democracy, which conservatives at the time believed could lead to mob rule and eventual tyranny, would also make him a liberal for his time. So, while he might very well fit with the right on an array of issues, he was too non-conventional to be viewed as conservative.

The other candidates are even more complex.

Clay was definitely someone who believed in a strong federal government, but he was also a hawk on military matters. A strong federal government and big government are not necessarily the same. Whether Clay would have approved of the current federal leviathan today is unknowable, but it's not likely he or any of the staunchest Federalists from a generation earlier ever envisioned it.

Thus, support for internal improvements in that era doesn't make one a New Deal liberal. Building roads and canals was starting from scratch. Further, Clay wasn't a Jefferson-style agrarian and veered toward the Hamiltonian economic view.

Clay was ultimately a pragmatist who wanted to finish the job and believed cutting deals was the way to do that. However, history tells us there are core issues that can't be compromised and Clay tried his best to find middle ground on one of those.

Crawford's signature issues are even more difficult to assess on today's ideological scale. He backed the National Bank, considered a conservative financial view for that day, but he pushed to limit the term of many federal officials to four years, which helped create a spoils system.

Contrary to some self-styled Jeffersonians, Crawford

preferred calling a constitutional convention to having states nullify federal laws. After the election, he would join a faction calling themselves the Liberal Democrats. Yet, even then, 'liberal' generally had a connotation closer to libertarianism. [87]

Ideology was not the defining factor. Many voters were driven by emotion, and that could only help one candidate.

CHAPTER FIVE

'The People Have Been Cheated'

DESPITE THE EARLY predictions of experts, Jackson seemed to have the wind of public sentiment behind him. Pro-Jackson rallies were drawing enormous crowds in the important swing states of Illinois, Indiana, New Jersey, New York and Pennsylvania.[88]

Old Hickory seemed to have already won the popularity contest. Though Van Buren backed the Crawford campaign at that point, Jackson closely followed the Van Buren model of speaking in generalities and avoiding commitment on any issue—most of all, not talking about slavery.

Adams was the only viable alternative, and Clay and Crawford voters who didn't want Jackson as president, closed ranks around the New Englander.

After the popular vote was cast in the 18 states, it seemed clear who would win. Jackson won 152,901, while Adams won 114,023. There was a significant drop off for third and fourth place in the popular vote, but a near tie. Clay received just 47,217 votes and Crawford got 46,979.

Jackson believed the presidency was his. He clearly made the most impressive showing, carrying a majority of electoral votes in 11 states—Alabama, Illinois, Indiana, Louisiana, Maryland, Mississippi, New Jersey, North Carolina, Pennsylvania, South Carolina, and Tennessee. In an election defined by regional preference, Jackson was the only national candidate.

Adams won the formerly Federalist strongholds of the six New England states, plus New York. Crawford carried only Delaware, his home state of Georgia and Virginia. It was enough to put him in third place.

On Dec. 1, the Electoral College announced the results. Jackson won the most Electoral College votes, winning 99 votes to the 84 votes for Adams. However, he didn't have a majority, or 131, of the electoral votes that he needed. Despite coming in last place in the popular vote, Crawford would actually beat Clay in the Electoral College, 41 voters to Clay's 37 votes. Clay, the candidate believed to benefit the most from a crowded field, would no longer compete for the presidency in the House of Representatives, because as the Twelfth Amendment states, the House decides only among the top three candidates.

The memory of the election 24 years earlier was still fresh for many at the Capitol. Officially, Crawford was in contention in the House, but it was really a contest between Adams and Jackson. Had Clay still been in contention, it's very possible he would have had the political clout to get himself elected in the House chamber that he ran so effectively.

Still, he did have the chance to be a kingmaker in a far more direct way than Hamilton in 1800. It was no secret he was not a fan of Jackson and considered him a threat to the American System of internal improvements, whereas Adams generally backed internal improvement, though not necessarily Clay's vision.

One Virginia newspaper harkened back to 1801, asserting the election in the House was "the severest trial to which our individual constitution can be exposed." As chaotic as 1801 was, this time, there would be no party allegiance, and with three candidates, numerous deals could potentially be made. The horse race phase was over, but the horse trading could begin. [89]

'Political Weathercocks'

After arriving in Washington on Dec. 7, 1824, Jackson wrote a letter to political supporter and former military ally John Coffee in Tennessee informing him of rumors that Adams and Clay had struck a deal, or would do so if they haven't already.

Adams invited Clay to his home in early January 1824 in a meeting that lasted for several hours, but the topic is not known. It certainly fueled suspicion.[90] Before the vote, a Philadelphia newspaper, the *Colombian Observer*, published an anonymous letter on Jan. 28 claiming Clay would back Adams in return for being named Secretary of State. Clay strongly denied this.[91]

In fact, there were two meetings between Adams and Clay, on Jan. 9 and Jan. 29, 1825.[92] Nevertheless, there was not a lot of reason to believe Clay was divided. He and Adams saw eye to eye for the most part on infrastructure, on tariffs and the National Bank.

Jackson wrote a letter from the Senate floor on Jan. 24, 1825 insisting that the House had a responsibility to abide by the choice of the people.

Jackson wrote:

> It shows the want in principle of all concerned. It will give the people a full view of our political weathercocks here and how little confidence ought to be reposed in the professions of some great political characters.[93]

Before the House voted, Adams, Jackson and Clay were at a dinner party in Washington, where Clay perhaps reveled in his clout and showed he couldn't resist the metaphor. Jackson and Adams were both sitting near the fireplace with one vacant chair between them. Seeing this from across the room, Clay strolled over and plopped down in the middle seat, where he amused the other attendees saying:

> *Well gentlemen, since you are both so near a chair and can neither occupy it, I will step in between you and take it myself.* [94]

The House convened on Feb. 9, 1825, each state having a single vote that would be determined by a majority vote inside the delegation. This time it was less dramatic than 1800—it didn't take 36 ballots, but just one ballot. And this time a candidate named Adams prevailed.

Clay directed Kentucky, Missouri and Ohio—the states he won—to the Adams camp. Most of Clay's supporters, as well as the remaining Federalists, backed Adams in the House, enough to give him a single vote victory. The House delegations of three states that Jackson carried, Illinois, Louisiana and Maryland, went to Adams. This gave Adams a majority of 13 out of 24 states. [95]

Clay announced the newly-elected President of the United States and formally notified the Senate and arranged for a committee to let Adams know of the victory. Though not the first president elected after a drawn out process, Adams was the only president to assume office without a majority of the electoral votes. In a dour response, Adams said he regretted that there could not be a do-over for submitting the "decision of this momentous question" again "to obtain a nearer approach to unanimity."

Alleged Deal

A day later, President Monroe held a White House party for his successor, which interestingly enough, Jackson attended. It was in the East Room that the two men came across each other, and stared for a few awkward seconds. The other attendees of Washington elite reportedly stopped their conversations to stare. Jackson was the first to extend his hand. "How do you do Mr. Adams?" the Tennessee senator said to the president-elect in a friendly manner. "I give you my left hand, for the right, as you can see, is devoted to the fair. I hope you are very well, sir."

Adams shook his rival's hand. "Very well sir. I hope General Jackson is well," Adams said.[96]

Those in attendance were said to have been impressed with Jackson's friendliness, appearing to be a good loser, and Adams reserve. The Jackson grace wouldn't last long. Adams had actually wanted to name Jackson as Secretary of War, but Jackson had other plans for the next four years—running for president.[97]

On Feb.14, Clay accepted the offer of the President-elect Adams to serve as his Secretary of State—presumably making him the next heir apparent since the last four men to lead the State Department became president.

Jackson and his supporters immediately called this a "corrupt bargain" between Adams and Clay. The caucus system was supposed to be gone, but Jackson and his supporters claimed Clay essentially resurrected it to thwart the will of the people and install Adams.

Jackson said referring to Clay:

> *The Judas of the West has closed the contract and will receive the thirty pieces of silver. His end will be the same.*[98]

The enraged Jackson said Speaker Clay approached him with a

similar offer—to make him president in exchange for Jackson appointing him as Secretary of State. As Jackson told it, he had too much character to accept such an offer. So Clay went to Adams with the same offer and received a different answer. [99]

Clay and Adams denied the any deal was made. Clay even demanded a congressional investigation into the allegations, which found no proof. It is one of those things that can be difficult to prove or disprove if no witnesses were present for those meetings. Above all, having those meetings to start with seems a miscalculation on the part of Adams who should have known it might look suspicious.

That said, there is no question who Clay preferred between the two. The only real question is who was telling the truth, Jackson or Clay, on the charge that he made the same offer to both rivals. Clay considered the optics of becoming secretary of state as well, he later told friends, but thought he couldn't reject the nomination because:

> *It would be said of me that, after having contributed to the elevation of a president, I thought so ill of him that I would not take first place under him.* [100]

Public sentiment had turned against Adams even before his inauguration. He and wife Louisa Catherine Johnson Adams went to the theater one night and the actors on stage began mocking him and the means by which he rose to power. Then the audience began singing the "Hunters of Kentucky," a pro-Jackson campaign song that commemorated the general's war heroism. [101]

Jackson resigned from the Senate and set out on what would essentially be a four-year presidential campaign to topple Adams. The Tennessee state legislature nominated him in October 1825 for the 1828 presidential race. So, no, presidential elections are not starting unusually early in our modern era.

The 1828 election established a new party system. This

time, Jackson would have the backing of Van Buren and the machine the New Yorker helped create. The Jacksonian Democrats, favoring more direct democracy and unapologetically using the phrase that seemed dangerous a generation ago, eventually became what today is the Democratic Party.

As for Crawford—citing disagreements with the president's policies—he declined the offer from Adams to serve again as the Treasury Secretary.

As many other politicians would do later, Jackson told all who would listen that this great cause was not only about him:

> *The people have been cheated. The corruptions and intrigues of Washington...defeated the will of the people.* [102]

Vice President Calhoun, meanwhile, worried about his own fortune with an Adams-Clay alliance, so he united with Jackson's Democratic Party. There was a strong coalition with powerful leaders seeking to undermine the Adams presidency—which was cast as illegitimate. A three-headed political monster of sorts in Jackson, Van Buren and Calhoun all sought to destroy the Adams presidency.

By breaking down House members, how they voted and who their second choice would be based on their ideology, an analysis by two University of Illinois Urbana-Champaign professors determined there was no "corrupt bargain." The professors, Jeffery A. Jenkins and Brian R. Sala used a "spatial voting theory," which means each member of the House should most prefer the alternative closest to his owner position.

The 1998 analysis said:

> *We found no evidence to support the allegations of vote-buying leveled against Adams, as he captures a majority of states via sincere voting. Voting errors involving*

> Adams lie systematically closer to the cutting line than did 'correct' votes. Additional evidence from an examination of 'lame-duck' MCs' [Members of Congress] subsequent careers and an analysis of the congressional elections of 1826 support our findings. [103]

Days of Trial

In the midst of constant hammering by political opponents and opposition press, Adams tried to reach out to the common man, but always came off as aloof, not so different from how New Englanders Mitt Romney in the 2012 election and John Kerry in the 2004 election just couldn't make regular people like them. During his first address to Congress Adams made what might have seemed like a fatal political flaw. He said:

> While foreign nations less blessed with that freedom which is power than ourselves are advancing with gigantic strides in the career of public improvement, were we to slumber in indolence or fold up our arms and proclaim to the world that we are palsied by the will of our constituents, would it not be to cast away the bounties of Providence and doom ourselves to perpetual inferiority? [104]

It was criticized as a condescending, elitist speech in which the president not elected by the public lectured the elected people's representatives in Congress against abiding by the wishes of the public. Jackson could have almost written the line for his rival to speak.

The anti-Adams newspapers, of which there were many, consistently called the president a Yankee elitist, and he was mercilessly mocked for proposing an astronomical observatory—

noting that Europe had 130 to America's none. The newspapers ridiculed him for wanting to appropriate public money for such a bizarre notion as exploring space. Though he subscribed to Clay's American System of internal improvements, Congress blocked all his proposals to promote a canal system and western expansion—things that Jackson supporters weren't entirely against but something they didn't want to grant an illegitimate president a victory on. Adams did manage to get the Cumberland Road, the nation's first federal road, expanded into Ohio.

After Jacksonians increased their numbers in the 1826 congressional midterm elections, Adams wrote, "days of trial are coming again," and that Washington was populated with "thousands of persons occupied with little else than to work up the passions of the people." [105] Like his father, he feared the wild passions of the populace and felt the need to do what's right rather than what is popular. He had enough of a conscience that he fought for land rights for American Indians, something Jackson would attack him for in 1828, claiming he was "pro-Indian," an epithet at the time. Still, when Georgia, Mississippi and Alabama violated treaties with Native Americans, Adams pondered but opted against using federal force to enforce the treaties. When he didn't act, it was taken as a sign of weakness. He was essentially ineffective and lacked authority to truly show leadership because the cloud of the people's will was still hanging over his head for his entire presidency.

It should be noted that for all the wailing about thwarting the will of the people, in Adam's own Massachusetts, among the 18 states that could vote, just 37,000 voted in the presidential race, compared to 60,000 for governor in 1823. In Ohio, a Clay stronghold, just 59,000 showed up to vote for president—a decline from 76,000 who showed up for the governor's race earlier in the year. Virginia—home of every president except one up to that point—was faced with the harsh reality that one of their own wasn't going to president, and only produced 15,000 voters.

In Pennsylvania, the state where the nation was founded with every reason to perform their patriotic duty, just 47,000 bothered voting.[106]

Further, six state legislatures gave Adams more than half of their electoral votes, 36 votes compared to 16 for Crawford, 15 for Jackson and four for Clay.[107]

The polarization over the alleged deal was illustrated in 1826 when Democratic Senator John Randolph of Virginia, a firebrand, delivered a speech on the Senate floor accusing Clay of rigging the election, referring to him as a "blackleg," a slang term for a cheating gambler. Secretary Clay was so tired of defending against the accusation of the deal, that he actually challenged Randolph to a dual—believing it would be a way of defending his honor once and for all. They met near the Potomac River. Fortunately for both, it would not have the historic enormity of the Burr-Hamilton duel. Rather, they were the duelers who couldn't shoot straight.

Randolph accidentally discharged his weapon, and had to be given another gun. Then both men shot at each other and missed. They reloaded and Clay fired a bullet that only pierced Randolph's case. Randolph fired his gun in the air as a means of calling a truce, saying, "I do not fire at you, Mr. Clay." They shook hands and were reportedly on friendly terms thereafter.[108]

After being a perennial presidential candidate, Clay would pull off another legislative feat to delay an inevitable civil war. Clay brokered the Compromise of 1850 which upset all sides of the slave debate, by admitting California as a free state, admitting the territories of New Mexico and Utah with the option of legalizing slavery and stronger fugitive slave laws. The compromise abolished the slave trade in Washington, D.C. even though slavery itself remained legal.

However, much of Clay's work was undone by Senator Stephen Douglas of Illinois in the Kansas-Nebraska Act of 1854 that completely repealed the Missouri Compromise in favor of "popular sovereignty" or allowing each new territory to decide on its own whether to allow slavery.

This not only undid much of Clay's legacy of putting on the brakes for civil war, but Douglas's leading role on "popular sovereignty" slammed a foot on the accelerator toward the conflict.

***

The 1800 election—aside from one's preference of the senior Adams or Jefferson—ended in the best way. In 1800, the young republic was an inspiration to the world by resisting the temptation to tear itself apart over who controlled the executive branch. Within 24 years, the high ideas of those founders had degenerated into a deep cynicism of politicians and the political system. Democratization had taken root for the first time in a presidential race only for the public to feel their vote didn't count and was still being controlled by a cabal in Washington.

Jackson, with the help of Van Buren, built a new party, the Democratic Party, whose supporters believed it had the most legitimacy of the four Jeffersonian factions because it carried the popular vote. Supporters of Adams and Clay, as the winning team, believed they were the legitimate faction, and called themselves the National Republicans.

In 2004, the party of Jackson would use the slogan "Like father like son, one term and he's done," to describe George W. Bush—wrongly as it turned out. In 1828 it would have been a fitting slogan for John Quincy Adams who lost soundly to Jackson, legitimizing the Jacksonian Democratic movement. Though Adams left the White House with seemingly little to show for it, he would go on to become one of the great members of the House of Representatives—something no modern ex-president would ever run for—where he dedicated his life to ending slavery.

When Jackson reached the White House, he had a tumultuous eight years himself, with the trail of tears, killing the

National Bank and his own battles with Calhoun. All significant. The question is: What would have been the historical significance of Jackson becoming president four years earlier?

CHAPTER SIX

President Jackson—Four Years Early

SO, IF ANDREW Jackson had won four years earlier, would that simply mean much of what happened after 1828 would have happened earlier?

That's partly true, but it's not that simple.

On many levels, what Jackson considered a "Corrupt Bargain" turned out to be a blessing with regard to his presidency. In 1828, he won with a clear mandate. Had Jackson carried the day in the House of Representatives in 1824 after winning a plurality of the votes, he would have very little mandate.

That could have meant Jackson would not have issued more vetoes than any other previous president combined to that point. This could have meant a less confrontational stance with Congress on many fronts. This could have placed obstacles to his war with the bank. This could have even meant less patronage if he didn't believe he was installing a new government at the people's will.

Willard Randall, professor emeritus of history at Champlain College and author of *1814: America Forged by Fire* said:

> *I don't think if he had been elected in 1824, he would have been able to grab so much power for himself. I don't think he would have swept everyone out of federal office and installed his own people.* [109]

He added:

> *His election in 1828 was a big breach to the social order. Boston was thrown out.*

That 1824 election also created a profound regional divide that intensified hostilities from the South toward the "Yankee elitist" president.

Again, Randall:

> *We might not have had the sharp North-South divide so early. The country was so divided after the election. Adams was booed when going to the theater.*

The power of New England had clearly eroded with the first president from the West who set out and succeeded in shaking up Washington.

Much of Jackson's overwhelming popularity in the lead up to the 1828 election was fueled by the public discontent and anger over the perception of an Adams-Clay deal that installed Adams into the White House over the supposed people's choice in return for making Clay the secretary of state. While it was a bit of a stretch to say Jackson was the absolute people's choice in 1824, the bottom line is that he won more popular votes than any other candidate. This provided wind to his sails going into 1828.

Jacksonian democracy, also called popular sovereignty, was a concept that gained immense steam after Jackson's 1824 loss, based largely on the view that the election was somehow stolen from him. The election result worked the nation into a bit of a fit.

Tainted by Suspicion

Even though popular voting was not universal for presidential races, the result gave many the feeling that their vote didn't count. Jackson, whom they considered the rightful president, made many promises and galvanized the masses. Without the 1824 election going to Adams—at least in the fashion that it did—there might not have been a charismatic leader to push the notion of popular sovereignty.

Adam Carrington, a professor of politics at Hillsdale College, said:

> *Just as today, some people never forget Florida in 2000, their political conscience was formed by it, there were many people then whose political conscience was formed by 1824. Had Jackson been elected in 1824, he may have been more tempered, but he still had tendencies to vote for the public and move things in his direction. He always opposed the National Bank because he thought it prioritized business interests.* [110]

Others don't believe Jackson needed a mandate.

"The personality of Jackson might not have required a large public outpouring," said Eric Patterson, dean of the Robertson School of Government at Regent University and author of *Ending Wars Well: Just War Thinking and Post-Conflict*. He continued:

> *I think he would have had a western-style national and foreign policy. He would have made war on the Bank of the United States and on the American Indians if he had been elected in 1824. Andrew Jackson didn't need a mandate. He was going to be Andrew Jackson regardless.* [111]

Patterson also saw the parallels between the Jackson candidacy and that of Donald Trump, as well as Ross Perot and other outsiders. Patterson believes that Jackson could have channeled that sentiment effectively if he entered the presidency earlier:

> *They were appealing candidates because they knew how to tap into frustrations across the electorate in a way other candidates had not caught on to yet because other candidates were slow to realize the country had changed.*

Ultimately, Jackson's governing style would have relied most on who sided with him in the House. If Clay—who personally disliked him—saw some political advantage to siding with Jackson, it might have brought about considerable change to Jackson's legacy, said Donald Ratcliffe, a teaching fellow at the Rothermere American Institute at the University of Oxford and author of *The One-Party Presidential Contest: Adams, Jackson and 1824's Five Horse Race*. He said:

> *Much would have depended on who elected Jackson and who he placed in his cabinet. If he had been elected essentially by Clay's Western supporters, he would have faced severe problems in reconciling their demand for the American System with his southern supporters' opposition to it. He had a similar problem in 1829-30 and then he risked his Western support in order to satisfy southern discontents.* [112]

No Democratic Party

Perhaps the biggest change would be no Democratic Party being created, or at least not what evolved into today's party.

After the 1824 campaign, what remained of Jefferson's Democratic-Republican party divided into the Jacksonian

Democrats and the Adams-Clay National Republicans. The National Republicans went the way of the Federalists before the 1836 election, replaced by the Whigs.

Though Democrats celebrate Jefferson/Jackson Dinners, it's Jackson—with the help of Martin Van Buren and other top political operatives among his staunch supporters—that started what is today the Democratic Party.

Paul Haynie, professor of history at Harding University in Arkansas, said:

> Had Jackson won in 1824, you never would have had the modern Democratic Party. That would have meant a massive shift in politics. The Democratic-Republicans Party might have been able to maintain party unity, or reunite its factions for a while after the 1824 election. But somewhere down the line, there would have been a break. [113]

That change could be cosmetic. There indeed would have been some party to emerge that stuck with a Jacksonian view or at least rhetoric of championing the common man. Such rhetoric would have produced a tendency to veer toward the populist and progressive movements of later generations. It might not have been called the Democratic Party.

Larry Schweikart is a professor of history at the University of Dayton and the author of *Seven Events That Made America America*, where he wrote about the Democratic party's creation. He said:

> The aftermath of 1824 was significant because Martin Van Buren used the time between then to create the Democratic Party with the spoils system, the patronage, bribes and rewards to make sure people turn out for Andrew Jackson in 1828.
>
> It was in fact the Jackson presidency, along with

> the political machinery established by Van Buren that created the framework for big government.
>
> The spoils system causes government to grow. With every election one candidate promises more government jobs and the other candidate feels he has to promise more.[114]

Jackson's popular sovereignty was based largely on giving the masses what they want, which fit well with the spoils system. Though he isn't often associated with big government, under Jackson, the federal workforce expanded significantly. One anecdote demonstrating this was Jackson friend and political operative William Lewis. So grateful for his friend's help for orchestrating his political successes, Jackson first offered Lewis a cabinet position of his choosing. Lewis turned him down. Lewis said he would prefer a well-paying government job that required no work. Jackson appointed him as a Treasury Department auditor.[115]

This would be the case before civil service reform—as we'll see in a later chapter—became a popular political issue. It's a view that government could be used to reward friends and punish enemies. Carrington of Hillsdale contends it might not be entirely fair to blame big government on Jackson:

> *If a progressive is to be defined as amassing power into the executive branch, then Jackson would be a progressive, but so much of the progressive movement was an overreaction to the spoils system. The spoils system was replaced with a bureaucracy of permanent civil servants that took government out of the people's hands. At least in a spoils system, voters could keep a corrupt system in check. Jackson had excesses. But he vetoed the national bank and national improvements. He thwarted the expansion of big government.*

Trail of Tears Earlier

Some historians have described the presidency of John Quincy Adams as stillborn, despite an ambitious national agenda. Adams advocated internal improvements and Clay's American System for federal spending on roads and canals to increase commerce from within the United States. In those days, to their credit, politicians actually looked for ways to pay for their grandiose initiatives. Under the American System, the improvements were to be financed by heavy tariffs on imported goods. Adams also called for a national university and a national astronomical observatory.

Haynie said:

> The Jacksonian Democrats in Congress opposed and blocked most of what Adams wanted to do, so in some ways not that much would have changed. Adams had a quiet administration. It would be more a matter of style. Jackson was far more aggressive.

Jackson would have come in with a very different agenda, opposing internal improvements or any other remnants of the Federalists.

By 1826, the Jacksonians gained a majority in Congress and ensured the next two years of the Adams administration would go virtually nowhere. Jackson, who was always a popular president, might have been able to sweep in a similar midterm majority in 1826 to support his policies.

Adams's Vice President John C. Calhoun—with his own eye on the presidency—threw in with Jackson for 1828.

Adams made an effort to get a fair deal for Native Americans regarding broken treaties in certain states, primarily threatening to use force in the state of Georgia so the state would honor its treaty. But Democrats attacked him for being "pro-Indian." Adams threat to use force turned out to be hollow, so

Alabama and Mississippi took similar actions against Native Americans. Adams felt, perhaps correctly, that he lacked the political clout to take action. But his half measures were still the opposite of Jackson, whose contempt for Indians would have led him to wholeheartedly support what the states were doing. Arguably, these states would have acted more unjustly without some check on their power. A weak check by Adams was a greater deterrent against violating a treaty than an endorsement of such a violation by Jackson.

The "Trail of Tears" might be the most infamous aspect of Jackson's legacy. Native Americans that lived on land in Alabama, Florida, Georgia, North Carolina and Tennessee were expelled to designated territory across the Mississippi River. The Native Americans walked thousands of miles to reach the new territory. One might even view it as an early case of crony capitalism; since they were removed so white settlers could use the land to grow cotton. This was effectively federal intervention to help particular business interests. National Republicans seemed to think so, questioning the Jackson commitment to a limited national government and saying legislative branch was "the very essence of republicanism whereas Jackson represented executive government, which ultimately led to despotism."

Jackson—who first justified the anti-Indian policy as a matter of states' rights—sent federal troops into the southern states to force the tribes to move west. He went beyond the congressionally approved legislation that his own party publicly justified as a "free and voluntary" relocation. He even defied a Supreme Court ruling in the 1832 case of Worcester vs. Georgia that determined states are bound by federal treaties they enter with tribes, declaring, "John Marshall has made his ruling, now let him enforce it." [116]

The ordeal demonstrated Jackson's commitment to rule of law and a limited federal government are very selective at best. He almost certainly would have taken similar action with an earlier term in the White House. Still, this brings us back to the question of whether Old Hickory might have felt somewhat restrained from taking extra-constitutional actions were he elected by a plurality as opposed to a landslide.

The president didn't believe that whites and Native Americans could co-exist. He also became anti-Indian because he saw many tribes siding with Britain during both the Revolution and personally on the battlefield against him in the War of 1812. Some Jackson defenders have argued that the forced removal of Cherokee and other tribes was in fact based not on his desire for genocide but rather his view that it would protect the tribes from genocide from the frontiersmen. [117] Nevertheless, thousands of Native Americas died because of this Jacksonian move. Whether accusing Jackson of genocide is fair, it would be accurate to call it an ethnic cleansing policy—a forced removal of an entire ethnic group of people to be isolated to another region.

Randall said:

> It's hard to believe that Jackson worried much about the Native Americans. He was killing Indians in the War of 1812, really slaughtering some of them.

Paving the Way for President Calhoun?

During the difficult trudge of the Adams administration, one major policy that he managed to sign—which made him even more unpopular—might well have significantly changed history as well. The Tariff of 1828, also called the "Tariff of Abominations," included numerous poison pill riders tacked on by Democrats, all of which failed to kill the bill.

Southerners felt disproportionately harmed by tariffs, with high prices that wouldn't hit the pro-Adams New England so harshly. The Democratic riders increased taxes on materials used by northern manufacturers. But the bill passed nonetheless and Adams signed it. It sent consumer prices on most products soaring, and had predictable impact on Adams in an election year.

Calhoun flip-flopped on his support for Clay's American System after seeing the impact of tariffs on South Carolina and the falling cotton prices. As was apparent with his split from Adams, Calhoun was not the type of vice president to loyally serve the administration of Jackson either. The two men, similar in many ways, had a testy relationship chiefly because Calhoun drafted the political doctrine of nullification, or allowing a state to simply disobey federal laws it believes are unconstitutional or harmful to its interest. This was a bit too much for even Jackson, who championed states rights, but saw anarchy in Calhoun's view.

The two men even disagreed publicly during the famous toast, in which Jackson said to his vice president, "Our federal union, it must be preserved." Calhoun replied, "The union, next to liberty, most dear."

When South Carolina threatened to secession over the tariff law, Jackson had the public behind him when he threatened to send federal troops. A compromise bill was reached with Calhoun and (by that time) Sen. Henry Clay for a smaller tariff.

That might have been very different had Jackson been elected in 1824. President Jackson from 1825 going forward likely never would have signed tariffs. He would have championed states rights and his Vice President Calhoun would not have pushed for nullification. Aside from personal issues, the two men might have gotten along well enough to serve a full eight years together.

Haynie said:

> *Jackson wanted states rights, but was a great unionist. If he had gotten in, Calhoun would have been his vice president. It's an interesting question if Calhoun had served for eight years as vice president. There wouldn't*

> *have been a Martin Van Buren vice presidency. The real break with Calhoun did come in the second term.*

Van Buren had been a political power player who helped the Jackson comeback. With Calhoun as the vice president, Van Buren served as his secretary of state. Considering the closeness, Haynie thinks, "It's a possibility he could have squeaked in Van Buren," as his presidential successor.

For that matter, it's debatable *when* Jackson might have a successor. He took office at age 60 in 1829. He walked with a cane and suffered with pain from his war wounds and duels, while also facing severe headaches.

Haynie added:

> *Another big question is who would replace Jackson? Jackson was starting to feel the effects of age toward the end of his second term. But if he were younger, Jackson being Jackson, might have run for a third term. He liked to buck tradition.*

That would mean still leaving office by 1837.

Jackson and Calhoun had other issues, but might have overcome that, which could have changed history in a negative way, Schweikart said:

> *The two guys, Jackson and Calhoun, didn't like each other personally, but without the Tariff of Abominations they could have stayed together for eight years. Boy would that be scary if Calhoun became president. He believed in the constitutional right to own slaves in peace without criticism from the North. He was essentially the first to believe in speech codes. He would have wanted to make it a crime to speak against slavery. Calhoun didn't really care so much about*

state's rights outside the realm of slavery.

Ronald Feinman, author of *Assassinations, Threats, and the American Presidency: From Andrew Jackson to Barack Obama*, also believes a Calhoun presidency would be a possibility had the nullification crisis been averted:

> *It makes a lot of sense that Calhoun might, very well, have been able to become President in 1832 after eight years of Jackson, without any confrontation with Jackson developing, and eight years of basic harmony between them. And to have such a vehement slave owner as president would be an issue that might have made the slavery issue peak earlier.* [118]

If true, the 1824 Adams victory might well have saved the country.

Feinman added:

> *I firmly believe that any possibility of civil war before 1861 would have led to independence for the South, as the North would not have been ready earlier to win, and even with their industrialization and population growth, it took four long years to win the Civil War.*

But, all these events are unknowable, particularly with two pro-slavery presidents in the 1840s. Also, Feinman:

> *Realize that John Tyler and James K. Polk both advanced slavery interests in the 1840s, so it's very possible that the future events were much the same with or without President John C. Calhoun.*

It is still very possible that, had the nullification rift not occurred,

Jackson and Calhoun would have parted ways over Secretary of War John Eaton, a Jackson ally whom Calhoun greatly disliked and wanted out of the cabinet over Eaton's scandalous marriage. The young Peggy Eaton had been accused of adultery, which reminded Jackson of the attacks on his beloved Rachel, whose death he blamed on the political attacks by Adams supporters.

There were many similarities between Jackson and Calhoun. As abhorrent as Calhoun's views on slavery were, even by Southern politician standards at the time, he had a host of interesting political views. Like Jefferson, he believed in an agrarian economy. He was much closer to Jefferson than Jackson in believing the Constitution protected from the tyranny of a majority, whereas Jackson shunned concerns over mob rule as being the will of the people. Fear of mob rule was generally an old Federalist preoccupation with French-phobia. For Calhoun, it was based on a view of the South being the minority. It seems ironic—at least by today's linguistic standards—that Calhoun would frame his arguments in defending the rights of minorities.

As a member of the House, Calhoun was among the "War Hawks" faction with Clay that strongly supported President Madison's war against Britain. He served ably as President Monroe's secretary of war, and quite possibly would have been a hawkish president. That said, later in life as a senator, he opposed President James Polk's war with Mexico. Another irony, so did a young Rep. Abraham Lincoln, an Illinois Whig, who spoke against the war on the House floor. Both opposed for opposite reasons. Calhoun believed that it was the United States empire building that could incorporate free states and shut out slave owners, while diluting slave power in Congress. Lincoln, and others in the North, feared the opposite: that the new territory represented an expansion of slavery.

For that matter, Ratcliffe of Oxford, tempers the speculation by saying one shouldn't be too quick to assume that President Jackson would not have signed the Tariff of

Abominations. Assuming otherwise, "ignores the overwhelming pressure to increase levels of protection by the late 1820s."

Ratcliffe said:

> *The president had little to do with tariff policy—Adams never pressed it officially—and the politicking of 1827-28 over the issue would still probably have been affected by the Northern Jacksonians' determination to have both a higher tariff and Jackson's re-election. In fact, the 1828 tariff was compromised to most people's satisfaction in 1832 and only the ideological objection of the South Carolinian Calhounites brought on the crisis.*

Killing the Bank

In real life, Calhoun was of course replaced on the 1832 Democratic ticket by Van Buren as vice president, who went on to be Jackson's real-life successor after winning the 1836 election.

Van Buren, despite being a political genius, lost in a landslide to William Henry Harrison in 1840 because his presidency paid the price for the economic policies of Jackson—perhaps chief among those, killing the Second Bank of the United States.

Van Buren shared the Jacksonian ideology, but might have been practical and sober enough to seek to prune rather dismantle the bank. The more ideological Calhoun, had he been Jackson's successor, disapproved of finance capitalism—believing it was the enemy of southern planters and northern laborers, but an ally to the moneyed industrial northern interests. So, he would have taken a similar course to that of Jackson.

Had Jackson been elected in 1824, that might not have happened—barring a third term. Jackson would have likely demanded an investigation into the bank if 1825, his first year in

Tainted by Suspicion

the White House, and would have (as he did in 1829) made the case to Congress that the bank was unconstitutional—a determination Congress disagreed with. His 1832 veto of an attempt by Congress to draw a new charter for the bank would have fallen into the hypothetical eight-year window. But the body blow that killed the bank came in September 1833 during the real-life second term. That's when Jackson removed all federal funds from the bank and redistributed to various state banks, known as "pet banks." Critics say this move led to a depression and the Panic of 1837 that ruined Van Buren's chance for a second term, though more updated economic models have shown other economic headwinds than the bank closure may have had a more direct effect.

It's quite reasonable to conclude that Van Buren or Calhoun might have been able withstand the Whigs had their predecessor not carried out his war on the national bank. Van Buren and Calhoun almost certainly would have tried though, since closing the bank was a key priority for Democrats who saw it as a Whig institution and as a matter of competing patronage. Patronage was core to Jackson's strength. As historians Schweikart and Michael Allen wrote in *The Patriot's History of the Unite States*:

> The president did not intend to eliminate central banking entirely but to replace one central bank with another in continuation of the spoils system. Why was the current BUS corrupt? Because in Jackson's view, it was in the hands of the wrong people. ... According to his close associate James Hamilton, Jackson had in mind a national money: his proposed bank would 'afford [a] uniform circulating medium' and he promised support to any bank that would 'answer the purposes of a safe depository of the public treasure and furnish the means of its ready transmission.' He was even more specific, according to Hamilton, because the

> *1829 plan would establish a new 'national bank chartered upon the principles of the checks and balances of our federal government, with a branch in each state, and capital apportioned agreeably to representation. ... A national Bank, entirely national bank, of deposits is all we ought to have.'* [119]

***

As much power as he drew to himself, Jackson did not permanently alter the presidency, said Gene Healy, the vice president of the libertarian Cato Institute and author of *The Cult of the Presidency* who notes Jackson was succeeded by a line of weak presidents:

> *Andrew Jackson, on the idea the election was stolen from him, played on the claims of being the tribune of the people. He is the president that used executive powers, in some ways. Still, he was the president that took on the national bank. Whether that motivated him to have more power as president—he seems like a guy with a chip on his shoulder anyway. He ignored the Supreme Court and did advocate for strong power in some areas but I don't believe he left government bigger than he found it.*

Had Jackson won with a plurality in 1824 instead of the landslide of 1828, he might have lacked the mandate to upend the entire political system, as Randall said he did.

> *There wouldn't have been popular sovereignty, the view that there shouldn't be one class of people running things, that anybody's voice should be heard.*

Personality plays a big role in any presidency. Jackson's decisive, take-charge, larger than life leadership skills might have come away with some meaningful accomplishments from 1824 through 1832. He would have chipped away at the bank and used it as a nice political scapegoat, but he wouldn't have delivered a fatal shot he did in 1833 of withdrawing federal funds. Without the foundation of what is today the oldest political party, without killing the bank and without skillfully handling the nullification threat, the Jackson elected in 1824 might well have been a very forgettable president remembered only for infamy in a slightly earlier Trail of Tears.

PART III

Rutherford B. Hayes vs. Samuel Tilden

CHAPTER SEVEN

Reform Campaign

SO MUCH OF history can hinge on a single obscure event. In 1876, much of that hinged on a small decision by Daniel Sickles, a Civil War veteran and politician who is hardly a household name or mentioned in most U.S. history text books.

The year 1876 was supposed to be a year of healing—11 years after cessation of violence between the North and South, the country still endured the aftereffects of an assassination, an impeachment and political scandals. But Americans came from across the country to Philadelphia for the nation's Centennial celebration that lasted from May to November. After eight years of corruption and division in Washington, both parties nominated governors with strong reputations for integrity who didn't disagree on that many issues. Once the mudslinging was over and Election Day passed, it was reasonable to believe that the nation could achieve a modicum of unity whether Rutherford B. Hayes or Samuel Tilden became president.

In Hayes and Tilden, the nation had reason to feel very good about turning the page. Both of these men were heroes in their own right. Hayes on the battlefield and in fighting for the rights of freed slaves after the Civil War, Tilden for fighting and winning against the corrupt political machine running his own state party.

We are only left to wonder what might have happened had Republican operative Daniel Sickles not made the small decision late on election night to drop by the Republican National Committee headquarters in New York City after a night at the theater. He found it empty except for a clerk boxing things up. The clerk told Sickles, "Tilden's been elected." [120]

At such a late hour, it might have been easy to simply accept such fortune, but Sickles, an impassioned politico, was not convinced. His skepticism would enact a chain of events that put the nation on edge for the next four months. The post-election proved the nation was far from unity, creating fears of another civil war; and in spite of candidates with integrity, seeing accusation of fraud, chicanery and intimidation.

What made the 1876 election different from 1800 and 1824 is that it was not immediately apparent the country was headed for a dispute, and when it was, there was no constitutional remedy. When there is a tie vote in the Electoral College, or when no candidate wins a required majority of electoral votes, it's clear that the matter goes to the House. The election of 1876 more closely resembled the election of 2000. In 1876 there were four states in dispute, including Florida—which would be the only disputed state in 2000. But the issues were far more serious than butterfly ballots and hanging chads. Rather, in 1876, the issues went to the heart of whether the rights of self-governance truly extended to freed blacks or for that matter, even white Republicans in the South. Also, Article 1, Section 2 of the Constitution says that the President of the Senate shall open the Electoral College votes to be counted in front of a joint session. But it does not say counted by whom. In this case, four states presented two separate sets of vote counts.

Democrats and the Klan

Despite laws being enforced, the Ku Klux Klan still carried out acts of violence on Election Day in order to try to ensure a Democratic victory.

There were three Reconstruction amendments to the Constitution: The Thirteenth that abolished slavery; the Fourteenth providing equal protection under the law and the Fifteenth, regarding voting. Each created angst among stubborn southerners.

It was the Fifteenth Amendment, ratified in 1870, that created the controversy that ensued around the 1876 election. The Amendment simply states:

> *The right of citizens of the United States to vote shall not be denied or abridged by the United States or by any state on account of race, color, or previous condition of servitude.*

And...

> *The Congress shall have power to enforce this article by appropriate legislation.*

The Ku Klux Klan, which Columbia University historian Eric Foner called, "a military force serving the interests of the Democratic Party," and University of North Carolina historian Allen Trelease called the "terrorist arm of the Democratic Party," had already been carrying out violence throughout the South against blacks and the carpetbagger Republican governments installed through military occupation directly after the war. [121]

To reinforce the intimidation tactics, the Klan would hold public burnings of Republican ballots in southern states. The result in several elections was that turnout in the Union strongholds of many southern states dropped dramatically.

After the passage of the Fifteenth Amendment, the Ku Klux Klan swept in to prevent blacks from voting. This forced President Ulysses S. Grant to push bills through a sometimes reluctant Congress, including what became known as the Ku Klux Klan Act, that would require federal supervision of election. The Ku Klux Klan Act made it a crime to conspire to prevent people from voting, holding office or having other basic equal protections of the law. Grant signed it in April 1871, and the bill succeeded in at least reducing Klan violence, though not stopping it. [122]

Democratic Tide

The South was not the only division point in the country in the years leading to the nation's Centennial. In a post-war recovery, the economy wasn't moving as fast as the public wanted and many came to view the occupation of the old Confederate states as unnecessary. The North, even some Republicans, were already growing weary of Reconstruction. This was true even of some of the most ardent opponents of slavery, the highest profile being New York Tribune Editor Horace Greely.

Grant was easily elected president in 1868 on the Republican ticket as a war hero, and was honest himself but had many dishonest people in his corrupt administration. In 1872, a faction of the party fed up with corruption, opposed to tariffs, anti-patronage, and backing an end to Reconstruction in the South called themselves the Liberal Republicans.

Seeing they could not prevent Grant's re-nomination, the Liberal Republicans held their own convention and nominated Greely for president. The beleaguered Democratic Party, with no viable choices, also nominated Greely. Greely had been a leading figure in the abolitionist movement and hawkish against the rebels, but now was very dovish on Reconstruction.

Republican newspapers portrayed Greely as a nut, which is

questionable. He was a vegetarian, once employed Karl Marx as a foreign correspondent for his newspaper and had odd habits. Still, Greely and the "Liberals," putting their name aside, advocated a platform demanding competency and ethics from government officials, free trade, lower taxes, and sound money about five decades before the mainstream Republican Party adopted these planks as conservative principles.

Robert Waters, a professor of history at Ohio Northern University, said:

> The Liberal Republicans were in some ways more like libertarians. They believed appropriating more power to the government would just create more graft. [123]

Grant crushed Greely on Election Day, but the campaign showed deep divisions in the Republican Party that could be exploited if Democrats could finally mount a post-war comeback after 16 years out of power.

Two years can make a big difference. Similar to how George W. Bush's re-election victory in 2004 and Barack Obama's 2012 re-election were followed by a mid-term shellacking, so was Grant's second term victory.

Democrats riding a wave of anger over Grant administration corruption, regained control of the House of Representatives with a 60-seat majority, a watershed victory after Republicans held a 110-seat majority. Democrats won seats in once-safe Republican states strongly associated with the Union, such as Wisconsin, Massachusetts, and Michigan, all of which also elected Democratic governors that year.

Without the Democratic victory in 1874, the presidential race two years later would almost certainly have been a far more expedited affair, as a party line vote would have been enough to recognize any decision by the state election boards. Instead, the GOP faced a raucous Democratic majority in the House.

Reform Candidates

Grant wanted a third term, which mortified the Republican Party leaders, who persuaded him against the move based on the two-term precedent that had yet to be broken. The old general surrendered on this front. [124]

The Republican National Convention was held June 14-16 in Cincinnati. Grant's preference for a successor was Radical Republican leader Roscoe Conkling. [125] But Conkling didn't have the party structure behind him, and at the time, the president's backing didn't exactly go a long way.

The presumptive nominee was Maine Sen. James G. Blaine, a popular and ambitious politician known as the "Magnetic Statesman." However, Blaine hit a wall when questions arose ahead of the convention about his involvement with the Little Rock and Fort Smith railroad scandal that made him almost as much an embarrassment as Grant. As has always happened when people run for president, past skeletons emerge.

In 1869, while Blaine was the Speaker of the House, he killed legislation that would have stopped a federal land grant from going to an Arkansas railroad. Shortly after, he received a commission from Boston railroad broker William Fisher. The Union Pacific Railroad further helped Blaine with his personal financial problems. The Democratic House majority eagerly started an investigation into the Republican frontrunner. The last thing the Republicans wanted was another scandal-plagued standard bearer. [126]

The party needed to start fresh with someone outside of Washington who could distance himself from Grant. Republican leaders—seeing Democrats as a potential threat for the first time in a while—feared the ethical quandary would make Blaine unelectable.

Blaine was a leader of the "Half Breeds," a somewhat reformist group in the Republican Party, though less so than the

Tainted by Suspicion

Liberal Republicans. "Half Breeds" strongly opposed the renomination of Grant. Conkling of New York was a leader of the "Stalwarts," more closely associated with the Radical Republicans, that were open for a third term for Grant. [127]

Republicans went through seven ballots, and nominated Ohio Gov. Rutherford B. Hayes, who was acceptable to the Liberal Republicans, most of whom returned to the party by 1876, for his moderate reform agenda in Ohio. To keep the divided party together, they nominated New York Rep. William Wheeler, a Radical Republican, to be the vice president. Hayes understood he was a compromise candidate, and his letter accepting the nomination indicated he would serve just one term if elected. [128]

The Republicans adopted a platform against patronage and the spoils system, and called for strong accountability for public officials, a demonstration of how toxic Grant was. It further demonstrated that despite splintering off four years earlier, the Liberal Republicans had significant influence in the party. [129]

The Democratic National Convention was held a few days later, June 27-29 in St. Louis and nominated New York Gov. Samuel Tilden and Indiana Gov. Thomas Hendricks, both men from Republican states. Democrats wanted to run an anti-corruption campaign, and said "a reform campaign without Tilden would be like the play Hamlet with Hamlet left out." [130]

The Democratic platform, as it had before, called for an end to the Reconstruction in the South. But it was similar to the Republicans in demanding civil service reform and "honest men" in government. [131]

Most evidence seems to show both men had integrity in public life, and had little room for corruption. Hayes, though a few years younger, actually had far more executive experience than Tilden, a first-term governor. And that's how their campaigns touted them. The Hayes slogan was, "Hurrah! For Hayes and Honest Ways," and for the Democrat, "Tilden for

133

Reform."[132]

Born in 1822, Hayes was educated in Kenton College and Harvard Law School. He was a successful Whig attorney in Cincinnati. One aspect that made him an attractive selection for the Republicans was his record of fighting for the Union in the Civil War, where he was wounded in action on several occasions and later became a major general. Based on his heroic record, the Ohio Republican party nominated him to run for the U.S. House of Representatives while he was still serving in the Army. He didn't campaign for the job, saying, "An officer fit for duty who at this crisis would abandon his post to electioneer … ought to be scalped."

Hayes easily won the election joining the Republican majority in December of 1865, expressing concern about the "Rebel influences … ruling the White House." He was referring to President Andrew Johnson, who would eventually be impeached by the House, but acquitted in the Senate.[133]

Hayes was elected governor of Ohio in 1867, defeating Rep. Allen G. Thurman in a close race with a 3,000 vote lead. He was elected twice more as the state's chief executive. In 1869, he campaigned for re-election on a platform of equal rights for all. He defeated anti-Fifteenth Amendment Democrat George Hunt Pendleton—the 1864 Democratic vice presidential nominee—with a 7,000 vote victory. After a second two-year term, he retired—so he thought—to private life. But, in 1875 Republican operatives in the state urged him to run for governor again fearing that only he could win. Hayes knew that a victory in 1875 would mean he would at least be mentioned for the presidency in 1876, so he stepped up.[134]

Though admired for integrity, he was known as a dull campaigner, in stark contrast to the livelier Tilden who was very popular on the stump and a member of the more radical and progressive wing of the New York Democratic party known as the "Barnburners."[135]

Tainted by Suspicion

Tilden, born in 1814, studied law at New York University and was admitted to the New York bar in 1841 with a successful career representing mostly corporate clients. He was a strong advocate for his political mentor, former President Martin Van Buren. The affection for Van Buren—a leading champion of the spoils system—seems unusual for Tilden the great reformer.

Tilden attained the position of corporation counsel for New York City in 1843 and became the attorney representing the legal interests of the nation's largest city. For a time, he even dabbled in the newspaper business, co-owning the New York Morning Daily News, a Democratic newspaper, but he sold his half to his business partner John O'Sullivan.

Tilden was a Free Soil Democrat, but he never broke away to join the new Republican Party as other anti-slavery Democrats did. While there is no reason to question his opposition to the expansion of slavery in to new territories, his affiliation with the Free Soil party might well have had more to do with a desire to back Van Buren, the Free Soil candidate for president in 1848. He remained loyal to the party he grew up with, and advised Franklin Pierce's successful Democratic presidential campaign in 1852. [136] Further, he disapproved of the Civil War that he never fought in. Republicans didn't let the public forget about Tilden's lack of combat experience.

Tilden frequently was sick for real, but supposedly also frequently just thought he was sick, visiting a doctor every day for a whole month at one point. One of the attacks on him during the 1876 campaign was that he was a hypochondriac. But he didn't let health issue interfere with a fast rising political career. [137]

After the war had wrapped up, and a decade before running for president, Tilden became chairman of the New York State Democratic Party. Tilden became a star battling the corrupt Tammany Hall when serving as the party chairman. Tilden opposed the machine less on moral grounds than thinking the graft William Marcy "Boss" Tweed was pushing in New York City was harming the Democratic Party. By 1871 Tilden openly called for Tammany Hall ring to be exposed and its members to be ousted from public office. That year, the Tilden-backed reform candidates defeated Tammany candidates in city elections. Tweed himself was charged with forgery and grand larceny in 1873 and Tilden testified against him at the trial, which ended in a hung jury. But Tweed was convicted in a second trial. It turned Tilden into a political hero in the state and garnered national attention. [138]

He was elected governor in 1874, a big Democratic year, defeating Republican John Dix, and became mentioned as a potential president. As governor, he went after the "Canal Ring," who used their political connections with individuals that made millions of dollars from contracts for the repair of the state's canals. Taking on yet another corrupt cabal solidified his national profile en route to the Democratic presidential nomination just two years after being elected governor. [139]

Though a good campaigner and orator, he was considered icy and aloof. Such contrast of excellent oratory versus the total lack of a personal touch is similar to Barack Obama. As former Chief Justice William Rehnquist wrote, Tilden "was by no means a gregarious backslapper, but a witty conversationalist much in demand for society dinner parties." [140]

The affability problem is what prompted the Tilden campaign to establish a Newspaper Popularity Bureau to build an image of Tilden for the public by constantly issuing press releases to newspaper across the United States. Separately, the campaign established a Literary Bureau for writers to crank out anti-Hayes propaganda, including a 750-page book about how the Ohio governor was no reformer and would just be another Grant Republican if elected. [141]

Conservatives and Liberals

On the conservative to liberal scale, that's yet again an open question. One of Tilden's slogans was "Retrenchment and Reform," meaning that he sought a fiscally responsible government that would spend tax dollars wisely. [142]

But Hayes was conservative in his commitment to the union as a soldier and member of Congress. That said, he was quite lenient toward the South for a Republican, and was, after all, the presidential candidate most acceptable to the "liberal" wing of his party. As Ohio governor, he held the line on spending, and fought to lower the state's legislature indebtedness. He was close to the Radical Republicans at least in making black voting rights a huge part of his tenure as governor. Both nominees opposed the spoils system, which would put them in opposition to government growth.

There was also another matter of personal life. Hayes was married with seven children, known to pray each morning with his family, thus a conservative lifestyle, compared to Tilden, the lifelong bachelor. Though "family values" was not yet part of the Republican strategy, operatives still spread rumors about Tilden's womanizing, including with some married women—even accusing him of contracting syphilis, none of which was ever proven.

The two candidates didn't joust much over Reconstruction, which had wound down in eight of the 11 former Confederate states, the exceptions being Florida, Louisiana and South Carolina. Hayes and Tilden further agreed on the other key national issues of civil service reform, reducing tariffs (a pro-free trade stance), and supporting hard money, which would have put them mostly on the conservative side of the spectrum.

Hayes was on record supporting women's suffrage, a movement that was underway at the time. Women were legally voting in some territories, but Hayes and the Republicans most certainly didn't make this a key issue to the campaign. Tilden remained silent on the matter.

Bloody Shirt and Accusations

Thus, the election was largely about personality and biography. It was still considered unseemly for the candidates to personally press the flesh for votes, but rather surrogates stormed the country giving speeches and openly partisan newspaper crusaded for their candidates. As had been the Republican tactic in 1868, they waved the "bloody shirt" to remind voters that Democrats were the party of the Confederacy. A Republican slogan was "Not every Democrat was a rebel but every rebel was a Democrat." As Colonel Robert Ingersoll, a Republican orator, put even more harshly on the campaign trail:

> *Every man that shot union soldiers was a Democrat. That man that assassinated Lincoln was a Democrat. Soldiers, every scar you have gotten on your body was given to you by a Democrat.* [143]

The theme was used particularly effectively by Republicans in 1868. By 1876, it was less effective. And eight years of Grant made even northern voters quite open to a corruption buster like Tilden. Still, Republicans saw the civil war as an issue since Hayes suffered several battle wounds (at the hands of Democrats you might say). Meanwhile, Tilden was just too busy to fight for his country because he was getting wealthy as a corporate lawyer, so the Republicans argued. Republicans further accused Tilden of involvement in fraudulent railroad deals. Republicans claimed "slippery Sammy" wanted to forgive Confederate debt, accused him of being a tax evader and of supporting the restoration of slavery.

Republican National Committee Chairman Zachary

Chandler committed what today would have been prosecutable in writing a letter to federal employees:

> We look to you as federal beneficiaries to help bear the burden. Two percent of your salary is ___. Please remit promptly. At the close of the campaign, we shall place a list of those who have not paid in the hands of the head of the department you are now in. [144]

What Chandler did to raise campaign contributions was nothing new at the time. If anything, it totally exhibited the need for civil service reform that both Hayes and Tilden strongly advocated.

Beloved American author Mark Twain gave one of the more notable stump speeches for Hayes in Hartford, Connecticut—chiefly because he thought the Republican nominee would be the only candidate who could reform the civil service system. Tilden, in Twain's view, was the standard bearer of the party of patronage.

> The system born of General [Andrew] Jackson and the Democrats is so idiotic, so contemptible, so grotesque that it would make the very savages of Dahomey jeer and the very gods of solemnity laugh. ... But when it comes to our civil service, we serenely fill great numbers of our minor public with ignoramuses ... Under a Treasury appointment we put oceans of money and accompanying statistics through the hand and brain of an ignorant villager who never before could wrestle with a two weeks wash bill without getting thrown. [145]

Twain's humor elicited immense laughter and—despite significant civil service reform since that time—the stump speech is hardly any different than the description you might hear Republicans make today of federal bureaucrats.

Democrats were no better in the category of mudslinging. Seeking to make Hayes strength of a war record his Achilles heel, they accused him of stealing money off dead soldiers when he was a general, said that he shot his own mother, and claimed he swindled Ohio out of millions of dollars while serving as governor.[146]

Suppressing the Black Vote

Though Tilden himself did not have a wretched history on race, much of his party's strategy for winning the presidential campaign relied on suppressing the African American vote in the formerly Confederate states.

Democrats typically did this through violence and intimidation. The Ku Klux Klan was still strong, and black voting would be key in the battle, in fact, it was the only way Republicans could win those states. Democrats used violence, lynching and riots to scare blacks away from voting, knowing it was possible for Republicans to carry some southern states. Republicans were intent that two could play at this game, and in some cases actually sought to persuade black to vote by shotgun.

The day before the election, U.S. Marshal J.H. Pierce of the Northern District of Mississippi telegraphed RNC Chairman Zach Chandler, asserting that "the election in the northern half of the state will be a farce."

The Pierce message said:

> *Colored and white Republicans will not be allowed to vote in many counties. The Tilden clubs are armed with Winchester rifles and shotguns and declare that they will carry the election at all hazards. In several counties of my district leading white and colored Republicans are now refugees asking for protection. ... A reign of terror of which I have never before witnessed in many*

> *large Republican counties to such an extent that Republicans are unable to cope with it.* [147]

The conventional wisdom has often been that Tilden was the rightful winner, but with so many irregularities, it's impossible to know. A majority of voters in East Feliciana, Louisiana, were black in 1876, but election results recorded one Republican vote in that parish.

The Red Shirts, a South Carolina paramilitary group, worked almost as hard as the Klan to stop blacks from voting. In Florida, Democrats handed out Tilden tickets decorated with Republican symbols among the illiterate former slaves. [148]

On Nov. 7, Tilden won the national popular vote 4,288,546 to 4,034,311 votes for Hayes, and 184 to 165 in the Electoral College. More than 80 percent of eligible voters actually turned out, some reportedly voting more than once, and others having their votes shredded if it was for the "wrong candidate." Not such a bad turnout for two dull candidates who didn't disagree on much.

Hayes was prepared to go to bed a loser. Election results in that day were coming in by telegraph and it seemed more than clear that Tilden had bested him in the presidential race. Hayes also knew that his loss would mark the first time a Democratic president was elected since 1856.

Tilden captured the swing states of Connecticut (the only New England state to vote Democrat), Indiana, New York and New Jersey. He had an obvious lock on the solid South for Democrats, so it seemed. Hayes carried his home state of Ohio by a much slimmer margin than Tilden carried his home state of New York. Hayes also carried Pennsylvania and Illinois.

So clearly it was competitive. Still, it appeared to be all but over with Tilden so close to the threshold needed for victory in the Electoral College.

Early editions of newspapers, such as the *New York Tribune*, were reporting that Tilden was the winner, which seemed a safe assumption since he had a secure 184 electoral votes by the wee hours of election night—just one short of the necessary 185 needed to claim victory.

The Republican newspaper, *Indianapolis Journal*, reported sadly:

> With the result before us at this time, we see no escape from the conclusion that Tilden and Hendricks are elected ... The announcement will carry pain to every loyal heart in the nation but the inevitable truth may as well be stated. [149]

Tilden likewise went to sleep that night in high spirits. There was plenty of reason to believe Tilden would be the first bachelor to ascend to the presidency since the last elected Democratic president, James Buchanan.

Election night telegraphs were coming in showing Tilden on what seemed a clear path to victory, when that obscure figure in history, Sickles, came into the Republican headquarters, then based in New York City. Not unlike today, western states came in much later. The states of California and Nevada went to Hayes, and it appeared that Oregon likely would.

Interestingly, the states with the most electoral votes at the time were New York's 35, Pennsylvania's 29, Ohio's 22 and the 21 votes from Illinois. Compared to the most electoral vote rich states today, in 1876 California had only six electoral votes, Texas had eight and Florida had four.

When he returned to Republican headquarters, Sickles wasn't caught off guard with the discouraging update from the clerk. He left for the theater earlier out of dismay.

But he crunched the numbers and saw a path to victory, particularly after the West was in and because Florida, Louisiana and South Carolina all had Reconstruction governments.

Tainted by Suspicion

Presuming Hayes held most northern states, and won these three southern states with sufficient black votes, the election was salvageable. [150]

CHAPTER EIGHT

Compromise of 1877

IT WAS AFTER midnight. Republican National Committee Chairman Zachary Chandler—like Hayes—had turned in for the night convinced of the party's loss. But using Chandler's signature from the RNC location, Daniel Sickles telegraphed the Republican governors of South Carolina, Florida and Louisiana to say, "With your state sure for Hayes, he is elected. Hold your state."

At 3 AM, South Carolina's Republican Gov. Daniel Chamberlain responded on a telegraph machine, "All right. South Carolina is for Hayes. Need more troops." [151]

It might not have been very scrupulous to send a telegraph in someone else's name, but Sickles was not someone particularly known for scruples. Sickles was elected to Congress as a Democrat in 1856. He was acquitted in 1859 of the shooting death of Phillip Barton Key, the son of Francis Scott Key. Sickles, reportedly a womanizer himself, believed Key was having an affair with his wife. His plea in court was temporary insanity, the first defendant to make such a plea and be acquitted. He went on to be a Union general in the Civil War. During the war, he lost his leg at the Battle of Gettysburg and was later awarded the Congressional Medal of Honor.

After the war he joined the Republican Party and would go on to serve as U.S. minister to Spain from 1869 to 1873. Some viewed him as a big part of the problem in the Grant administration's corruption and patronage. [152]

Hayes biographer Ari Hoogenboom referred to Sickles as having a...

> ...checkered past mixed politics and diplomacy with seduction and murder-personified for reformers what was wrong with the Grant administration and was an unlikely ally of Rutherford B. Hayes. [153]

It wasn't just Sickles leading the charge. While it's hard to imagine the *New York Times* ever backing a Republican today, in 1876 the *Times* was a very solidly Republican newspaper and wouldn't follow the media narrative that Hayes had lost. The Times staunch Republican Managing Editor John C. Reid got the Sickles-inspired news from the three southern states. Reid had reason to be a staunch Republican. When he was in the Union Army, he was captured and held as a prisoner of war in a Confederate prison, and adhered to the view that it was the party of rebellion. [154]

Moreover, New York State Democratic Party Chairman D.A. Magone inquired in a telegraph why the *New York Times* had not yet declared what other newspapers had. Reid inferred the inquiry was a sign of doubt by Democrats. A *New York Times* early addition on Nov. 8 read "The Results Still Uncertain." The second addition projected Hayes had 181 electoral votes, and Florida was too close to call. [155]

Reid was at the RNC headquarters at 6 AM Wednesday morning and showed RNC Chairman Chandler that the Associated Press—as objective as it could be in those days—was calling Florida and Oregon for Hayes and the Times believed the Ohio governor would be president. More messages were coming in from the states in question.

For a journalist to show up at a party headquarters would seem an astonishing affront today. Even commentators tend to keep a distance from being involved in a campaign. As we've seen in the other elections, journalists and newspaper were officially arms of the campaigns in those days. As we'll see, various newspapermen played huge roles in seeking to rally the party faithful and even in brokering an outcome.

The three southern states in question had 19 disputed electoral votes. One of the Oregon's three electoral votes was in dispute. South Carolina had seven votes, Florida had four votes and Louisiana had eight votes in the Electoral College. So, Tilden needed just one more vote to win. Hayes needed all 20.

As the frantic plotting and telegraphing continued by Republicans in New York. Hayes woke up in Ohio "contented and cheerful," blissfully unaware his campaign might be saved. He wrote a letter to his son in college at Cornell, saying the reaction of the other children ranged from "rejoiced because now we can remain in Columbus" to those that "don't altogether like it, but are cheerful and philosophical about it." Aside from being cheerful, Hayes wrote he regretted he wouldn't "establish Civil Service reform, and to do a good work for the South."

It wasn't long after writing the letter that Hayes learned in telegrams that the tide might have turned in a few Southern states. After rumors spread that Hayes actually won New York, a large crowd gathered outside his residence. He sought to calm the crowd and tamper expectations, asserting he didn't believe the rumor. He was of course correct. Tilden carried his own state. However, after talking to more Republicans and reading the morning newspapers about how Democrats used violence to block blacks from voting, Hayes asserted, "A fair election in the South would undoubtedly" have given him a clear electoral vote majority and "a decided preponderance of the popular vote." Still, Hayes told his friend, Missouri Sen. Carl Schurz, a Liberal Republican leader, it was important "that in the canvassing of results there should be no taint of dishonesty" from the Republicans. [156]

The Republicans were going to be aggressive in going for a win as Chandler stepped forward to tell the press, "Hayes has 185 electoral votes and is elected."

The New York Times backed him up with a joyous headline: "THE BATTLE WON.; A REPUBLICAN VICTORY IN THE NATION. GOV. HAYES ELECTED PRESIDENT AND WILLIAM A. WHEELER VICE PRESIDENT THE REPUBLICANS CARRY TWENTY-ONE STATES, CASTING 185 ELECTORAL VOTES A REPUBLICAN MAJORITY IN THE NEXT CONGRESS. MAJORITIES FOR GOV. HAYES. MAJORITIES FOR GOV. TILDEN." [157]

The Democrats were aggressive in their own right.

There was virtually no doubt that Hayes had carried Oregon, but Democratic National Committee Chairman Abram Hewitt encouraged Oregon's Democratic Gov. L.F. Grover to stir things up. A Republican elector, J.W. Watts, was declared ineligible because he was also a postmaster and the Constitution prohibits any federal office holder from being an elector.

A telegraph from Hewitt to Grover said the DNC's legal opinion is that:

> ...*votes cast for a federal office holder are void and that the person receiving the next highest known number of votes should receive the certificate of appointment. The canvassing office should act up on this, the governor's certificate of appointment be given to the elector accordingly. And the subsequent certificate of the votes of the electors be duly made specifying how they voted. This will force Congress to go behind the certificate and open the way to get into the merits of all cases, which is not only just, but which will relieve the embarrassment of the situation.* [158]

This happened even though Watts resigned as a postmaster. The governor sent two electors for Hayes and one elector for Tilden. Watts met with the two Republican electors and forwarded a separate count of three for Hayes to Washington.

Hewitt actually later admitted he thought Hayes won all three of Oregon's vote, but had to take action to "offset the fraud" by Republicans. [159]

Shenanigans and Rulings

President Grant sent more federal troops into the three southern states with the purpose of keeping the peace. It might have inflamed things a bit more, but was probably necessary. Nevertheless, it gave Democrats another political tool.

Three days after the election, Nov. 10, President Grant issued an order to General W.T. Sherman to instruct generals in Florida and Louisiana:

> ...to be vigilant with the forces at their command to preserve peace and good order and see that proper and legal Boards of Canvassers are unmolested in the performance of their duties. ... No man worthy of the office of President should be willing to hold it if it counted in or placed there by fraud. Either party can afford to be disappointed by the result, but the country cannot afford to have the result tainted by suspicion of illegal or false returns. [160]

A Republican delegation of "visiting statesmen" that included Ohio Senator-elect John Sherman notified Hayes of the "atrocious means" applied to prevent the black vote. Sherman further told the Ohio governor Republicans would win as long as the spirit and letter of the law are applied.

The cautious Hayes responded:

We are not to allow our friends to defeat one outrage and fraud by another. There must be nothing crooked on our part. [161]

Whether his wishes were honored might depend on how one defines "crooked" and just how flexible one is in rationalizing certain deeds for a perceived greater good. The Republican returning board in Louisiana threw out 13,000 Democratic ballots and about 2,500 Republican votes as well, but clearly politics was at work. This not only gave the state to Hayes by about 3,000 votes, but also the governorship to Republican Stephen Packard. In a move that would make some of Louisiana's most infamous political legends proud, the head of the state's returning board James Madison Wells attempted to sell the state's electoral votes for $200,000. To their credit, both parties rejected the offer. Wells sent an associate to Hewitt, with an offer to sell his vote for $1 million. Hewitt and Tilden both rejected the offer. While neither Democrat—particularly Hewitt—seemed beyond reproach, this was something a bit too flagrant, and one of those things that has the potential to be found out.

However, Tilden's nephew, Colonel William T. Pelton, did secretly negotiate with Wells. Pelton also reached out to Florida Republican electors about a bargaining price to get his uncle in the White House. Pelton apparently did this without Tilden's knowledge, even though he lived in his uncle's home. At any rate, the talks never produced a deal, but did produce a few telegrams that made Pelton look really bad and called Tilden's impeccable character into question after an 1878 House investigation. [162]

Just because Florida shared the stage with other states in 1876, doesn't mean it wasn't just as thorny as in 2000 when it had the stage to itself. Florida was the closest of all the states in 1876. The Republican boards determined Hayes won by 922 votes out of 47,000 cast. A Democratic count found Tilden won the state by 94 votes.[163]

On Dec. 14, the Florida Supreme Court sided with Democrats who argued that subsequent testimony proved Tilden won Florida and was robbed by a partisan governor and returning board. This marked the first time the Florida high court sided with a Democrat in a disputed presidential election.

The Republicans believed that Hayes won South Carolina by 600 to 1,000 votes. On Nov. 22, the Republican returning board invalidated all votes from Edgefield County and Laurens County, which meant the Republicans would carry the state, along with the governorship and the state legislature.

Hayes had become even more confident, telling Schurz, "I have no doubt that we are justly and legally entitled to the presidency."

Prevailing wisdom was beginning to shift in that direction, a massive change from Election Day. With the three states formally in the Republican column, the battle was now an uphill contest for Democrats.

Election Moves to D.C.

Members of Congress were mostly partisan when the decision moved to Washington, but some lawmakers started to jockey and see if they could score a concession from either side. Hayes and Tilden wisely avoided committing to or rejecting anyone.

Sen. Roscoe Conkling, the Radical Republican and head of the New York machine, wasn't eager for civil service reform, and a surrogate let Hayes know Conkling would stand with the Ohio governor as long as he repudiated reformers such as his friend Schurz. Southern Democrats of course much preferred Tilden, but wanted to keep their options open, particularly considering the returning boards. After being out of power for 16 years, what's another four if they could press him for "home rule," meaning the southern states could make their own rules without federal troops.

Col. William H. Roberts, publisher of the *New Orleans Times*, met with Hayes on Dec. 1, and got no more of a commitment than Conkling. Hayes publicly said he wanted to "deal fairly and justly by all elements of the party" and vowed "the southern people must obey the new amendments, and give the colored men all of their rights."[164]

The assertions weren't specific enough to please the hardcore elements on either side. While Hayes wasn't willing to wheel and deal, he didn't micromanage the desire for Republicans underlings that were perfectly willing to do so.

The Electoral College met in state capitols on Dec. 6 to cast ballots, and the results from each state was to go to Congress for certification. It was just a routine quadrennial matter for 34 capital cities, but not for Columbia, New Orleans, Salem and Tallahassee.

Congress got at least two sets of results from each of the four states in question. Louisiana, Oregon and South Carolina each ended up with two election results going to Washington, while Florida had three separate counts.

This was completely uncharted territory for the 100-year-old country: Multiple counts after well known mass voter suppression, or forced participation, all of which could lead to another civil war if handled wrong. There was no constitutional remedy.

The Constitution says the President of the Senate shall open and count the election certificates. In a regular outcome, that would be a formality. In this case, Senate President Pro Tempore Thomas Ferry, a Michigan Republican, could have considerable clout determining which results to certify. Ferry was acting in the role after the death of Vice President Henry Wilson in 1875, a vacancy not filled.

The Democratic House was not about to let the president of the Republican-controlled Senate certify the results in front of a joint session of Congress. The Republican Senate did not want to leave the matter to the Democratic House—the chamber that decided the previous disputed elections.

It was clear that Christmas and New Year's Day would pass before the public knew who the next president would be.

Henry Watterson, publisher of the Louisville *Courier-Journal* and a Democratic Congressman from Kentucky, on Jan. 8—which he called "St. Jackson's Day" because it marked the Battle of New Orleans—called for "the presence of at least 10,000 unarmed Kentuckians in the city" to march on Washington to ensure Tilden was elected. His friend Joseph Pulitzer, still building a vast newspaper empire, went further, calling for 100,000 people "fully armed and ready for business," to ensure that Tilden becomes president. [165]

Angry Democratic mobs across the country would chant, "Tilden or blood," and reportedly in a dozen states, club-wielding "Tilden Minute Men" had formed threatening to march into Washington to take the White House for their candidate. This came to Tilden's chagrin, who sought to calm the rowdiness, as he didn't want to be responsible for an insurrection, nor did he see it as a viable path to the presidency. Like most others, Tilden wanted the country to heal. [166]

Still, with all the bellicose verbiage from the newspapers and the masses, it was the Democrat hierarchy in the South that was ready to make a deal, though not the Northern Democrats.

Richard Smith of the Republican *Cincinnati Gazette* reached out to Southern powerbrokers. Hayes asserted to Smith in early January 1877: "I am not a believer in the trustworthiness of the forces you hope to rally." But, he told the newspaperman he did back internal improvements and education funding in the South believing it would "divide the whites" and help "obliterate the color line." [167]

Electoral Commission

On Jan. 25, the Senate voted 47-17 to set up an Electoral Commission with five senators, five House members and five Supreme Court justices. Under the proposal, a decision by the bipartisan committee would be final unless it was overridden by both houses of Congress. A day later, the House voted 191-86, and lame duck President Grant signed the bill on Jan. 29.

In a letter to Senate and House leaders asking for leave, the five House members and five senators said the makeup of the committee would be viewed as nearly incorruptible, both in fact and perception. The congressional members said in a joint letter to leaders:

> *It would be difficult, if not impossible, we think, to establish a tribunal that could be less the subject of party criticism than such a one. The principle of its constitution is so absolutely fair that we are unable to perceive how the most extreme partisan can assail it, unless he wishes to embark upon the stormy sea of unregulated procedure, hot disputes, and dangerous results that can neither be measured nor defined, rather than upon the fixed and regular course of law that insures peace and the order of society, whatever party may be disappointed in its hopes.*

The letter added:

> *In conclusion, we respectfully beg leave to impress upon Congress the necessity of a speedy determination upon this subject. It is impossible to estimate the material loss the country daily sustains from the existing state of uncertainty. It directly and powerfully tends to unsettle and paralyze business, to weaken public and private*

> credit, and to create apprehensions in the minds of the people that disturb the peaceful tenor of their ways and happiness. It does far more—it tends to bring republican institutions into discredit, and to create doubts of the success of our form of government and of the perpetuity of the republic. [168]

Supreme Court Justice Nathan Clifford, a Democrat, would serve as the chairman of the Electoral Commission.

Vermont Republican Senator George Edmunds, who had previously introduced a constitutional amendment to allow the Supreme Court to decide the election, also served. Interestingly, Delaware Democratic Senator Thomas Bayard, whose father, Representative James A. Bayard, as a Federalist, played such a large role in the 1800 disputed election, served on the commission.

Democratic Senator Allen Thurman lost a governor's race to Hayes, but was on the commission to determine his one-time opponent's future. Two other Republicans were Frederick T. Frelinghuysen of New Jersey and Oliver Morton of Indiana. From the House, it would be Democrats Josiah Gardner Abbott of Massachusetts, Eppa Hunton of Virginia and Henry B. Payne of Ohio. The two Republican House members were future president James Garfield of Ohio and George Frisbie Hoar of Massachusetts.

It's in the Supreme Court where things got complicated.

Besides Clifford, Democratic Justice Stephen Johnson Field, along with Republican Justices Joseph Brady and Samuel Miller were named. The fifth justice was initially supposed to be David Davis, a Republican but a very independent one.

For the most part, Republicans opposed the commission, according the Harper's Weekly, which reported on a breakdown of votes, when combining the House and Senate Republicans voted 84-57 against it, while Democrats were even more overwhelmingly favored it, 181-19. Some Republicans believed the Reconstruction governments in the states could assure a Hayes victory. Hayes said the commission would "surrender, at least in part, of our case." [169]

Radical Republicans argued intensely that the acting Senate president, Ferry, has the sole constitutional authority to certify the president and anything short of that would be a cave to the Democrats, though not every Radical Republican was so adamant. After failing to win the nomination, Roscoe Conkling and James Blaine, were thinking ahead four years, and weren't horrified by a Tilden term in office. Conkling even said he thought Tilden won Louisiana and Florida.

Democrats, for the most part, got what they wanted regarding process, with a joint session making the final call. Republicans were even more cranky when Democratic Speaker of the House Samuel J. Randall of Pennsylvania appointed moderate Republicans from the House to the commission. Hayes had plenty of concerns about Conkling and what compromise he might try to make on the commission. So many Republicans were happy when the cantankerous Conkling refused to serve on the commission, believing it "inconvenient if not distasteful." With his eyes on the presidency in four years, it was probably the best move. He seemed to want a Tilden victory, but couldn't swing it to the Democrat and expect to have any future with the Republican Party.

Still, plenty of hardcore Democrats also opposed the commission. Most Democrats accepted it was the best chance of victory after the returning boards. Tilden didn't like it but reluctantly accepted it. He believed an honest count would prove him the winner, and if Senate President Pro Tem Ferry attempted to certify the Republican results, the Democrats could challenge the count as illegal, meaning no majority. With no majority, he surmised, it would go to the Democratic House to decide. What Tilden didn't factor is that there were enough Democrats that feared Grant would use the military to ensure Hayes was inaugurated.

With 15 members, the Electoral Commission was to have seven Republicans, seven Democrats and one independent, Davis, who would likely be the tie breaker if things became too partisan. However, the Illinois state legislature's Democratic-Greenback coalition majority voted 101-99 to make Davis the new U.S. senator for the state. Davis accepted the position. Illinois Democrats thought it would be a means to sway his vote for Tilden on the commission. Tilden wasn't aware of the plan, but his nephew Pelton helped push it forward. Democrats weren't counting on Davis having integrity.

After the Illinois legislature's vote was finalized, Davis announced that with his resignation from the high court, he could not serve on the commission as the fifth justice. It was a spectacular backfire by Democrats and a defining moment in the election dispute.

The independent justice was replaced by Republican Justice Joseph Bradley, viewed as a moderate, but one who would side with Republicans on the commission. Put in the context of today, it might be like replacing swing-vote Justice Anthony Kennedy on a select board with Justice Samuel Alito, who would almost certainly vote with Republicans, or replacing Kennedy with Justice Ruth Bader Ginsberg, who would no doubt be a reliable vote for Democrats on a hypothetical bipartisan commission.

For its part, the House and Senate would meet in 15 joint sessions before a president was to be selected.

It was the first day of February when the Electoral Commission convened in the Supreme Court chamber. In what would sound familiar to those who lived through the 2000 debacle, the commission heard from Democratic and Republican lawyers arguing over who won Florida.

Same court chamber, but the first time, it was in front of the Electoral Commission. The Republican lead counsel was William Evarts, who argued for only allowing evidence before the commission that had previously been submitted to Congress. Evarts, though counsel for Republicans, had actually been the counsel for President Andrew Johnson during impeachment. Evarts argument was largely a practical one—that investigating the Florida vote by a county and local level would be endless, and not wrap up in time for inaugurating a new president in March. In short, he argued against the Democrat's goal to "go behind" the votes. "Go behind," mean to allow new evidence to investigate how all of the votes were cast in the four states.

His opponent in this case, Democratic counsel Charles O'Conor, argued for admitting additional evidence to make the case that Tilden carried the state.

Three days after the oral arguments, the commission was to cast its first decision. The commission was hearing arguments for each state of course. But if it ruled for Tilden on any single state, the Democrats would win the election.

John G. Stevens, a Democratic operative, visited with Bradley, the swing vote, the night before the Florida vote. Based on what Stevens immediately told Hewitt about the meeting, Bradley, the Republican justice, said he would vote with Tilden. Hewitt felt that would end the whole ordeal.

The next day, in a long line of 8-7 party-line votes, Bradley tipped the scale to block additional evidence Democrats sought. The next party line vote was a day later—giving Florida's four electoral votes to Hayes.

In this case, Bradley asserted that the Florida Supreme Court's decision only said the state's canvassing board acted mistakenly, but said neither the Florida courts nor the Florida state legislature can act retroactively to change the designation of electors after they had cast their vote and sent to the Senate. However, Justice Clifford, the Democratic president of the commission, contended that if the returns from Florida were fraudulent, then it's as if they had not accepted votes at all. [170]

Hewitt spread the word and the Democratic newspaper *New*

York Sun reported:

> *Judge Bradley's house in Washington was surrounded by carriages of visitors who came to see him, apparently about the decision of the Electoral Commission.*

The newspaper added:

> *These visitors included leading Republicans.*

Of course, the obvious question was if it was so wrong for Republican leaders to be there, what was so right about Stevens showing up?

"The whole thing is a falsehood," Bradley asserted, quick to defend his honor. "I had no private discussion whatever on the subject at issue with any persons on the Republican side and but very few words with any person."

However, reports later confirmed that Navy Secretary George M. Roberson and fellow commission member and New Jersey Republican Sen. Frederick Frelinghuysen visited to stress to him how frightening it would be if a Democrat was back in power.

It was a full-fledged controversy within the larger controversy that would stretch out. Democratic Missouri Sen. Lewis V. Borgy said:

> *The name of the man who changed his vote on that commission ... Justice Bradley will go down to after the ages covered with equal shame and disgrace. Never will [his name] be pronounced without the hiss from all good men in this country.* [171]

When the Florida vote went to Congress, the Republican Senate voted to affirm Florida for Hayes and the Democratic House voted to reject the Electoral Commission's findings.

Democrats, having mostly supported the commission, felt bound to it. But they believed they had a shot in Louisiana—the most disreputable count. If Conkling thought it belonged to Tilden, maybe Bradley or even one of the other Republicans on the panel might be convinced. The unofficial returns in Louisiana gave Democrats a big win, which warranted hearing more evidence. It was an all-Republican returning board. More ballots were tossed. It was the Democrats best cases. It was nevertheless as impractical to do a county-by-county canvassing in Louisiana as it would have been in Florida, if a president is to be named by early March. On mostly technical and practical grounds, the Commission cast another 8-7 party-line vote giving Louisiana to Hayes.

South Carolina by this time was almost a formality. Hayes began working on his inaugural address on Feb. 17. He had also decided to try to bring the United States together. He would appoint Confederate Gen. Joseph E. Johnston to his cabinet, but assured black leaders Frederick Douglass and James Poindexter he would continue to fight tirelessly for the Thirteenth, Fourteenth and Fifteenth Amendments. [172]

Democrats hoped that Conkling might block approval of the Louisiana vote in the Senate, or at least use his influence to try, but Conkling was absent from the Senate on Feb. 19. [173] After a two-hour debate that day, the Senate voted 41-28, along party lines, to accept the Commission's finding for Hayes, but the House voted 179-99, along party lines, to reject the commission's findings.

The only hope Democrats had was to delay the inevitable decision, and threaten chaos after March 4, with no president in office. Somewhat similar to how Federalists in the 1800 considered stretching the election beyond inauguration day, then trying to install one of their own.

Democratic House Speaker Randall came up with his own

plot. When House Democrats caucused, the speaker accused the southern Democrats of bargaining with Hayes—warning them not to trust the Republicans. He proposed delaying the counting, and forcing the Senate to confirm Secretary of State Hamilton Fish as the acting president, and establish a new election. The idea was far too over the top to gain any support from his own caucus. Thus, the nation was spared from even more turmoil of Randall's nutty scheme. A majority of Democrats didn't want to wreak havoc for fun, but they were ready to extract whatever further concessions they could reach. [174]

It was late February when the commission voted 8-7 to award Oregon's single disputed vote to Hayes. Again, the Republican Senate approved the commission's finding while the Democratic House rejected it.

In the midst of the proceedings, the Democratic House passed resolution declaring that Tilden was the "duly elected president." Along the way, Democrats made objections to various state returns beyond the four in dispute, but were overruled by both houses.

Wormley House

On Feb. 26, the Electoral Commission heard arguments from attorneys on South Carolina.

That night, four Southern Democrats, Reps. John Y. Brown and Henry Watterson of Kentucky, Senator J.B. Gordon of Georgia and Representative W. M. Levy of Louisiana met with Ohio Republicans James Garfield and Charles Foster, both House members and Ohio Sen. Stanley Matthews and Ohio Senator-elect John Sherman at the Wormley House hotel in Washington to see if a deal could be reached to prevent the House Democrats from blocking the results with a filibuster.

The men talked about details through the night, and by morning agreed to stop the House Democratic delay tactics that were blocking the certification of the Electoral Commission's findings, on the condition of ending Reconstruction, appointing a Southern Democrat to the cabinet and providing federal money for southern projects. These were things Hayes expected to do anyway.

The next day, the commission—in a ubiquitous 8-7 party line vote—awarded seven South Carolina electoral votes to Hayes, which the Senate affirmed and the House rejected one day later.

A letter from Matthews and Foster to the Democrats followed, saying Republicans wish:

> ...to give the people of South Carolina and Louisiana the right to control their own affairs in their own way, subject only to the Constitution of the United States and the laws made in pursuance thereof, and to say further that from an acquaintance with the knowledge of Governor Hayes and his views, we have the most complete confidence that such will be the policy of his administration. [175]

In a nutshell, no more federal occupation in the South, with the caveat, "subject only to the Constitution of the United States and the laws made in pursuance thereof," which meant there was a general expectation the rights of blacks would be protected.

This was the Compromise of 1877 that has remained a matter of debate even today. It diluted the Democratic Party's unity relating to a filibuster to stop the vote. Some historians contend that Reconstruction was about to go away anyway since there was no public support.

Further, since rejection of the Commission's determination required both houses of Congress, it was only a formality. Either way, the South did get much of what it asked for. Southern historian C. Vann Woodward said the American South had always been at odds with the federal government, and typically ended in compromises, beginning with the nullification crises and the Missouri Compromise. The Civil War marked a departure from a willingness to compromise, but the Compromise of 1877 represented a return, from Woodward's perspective.

DNC Chairman Hewitt, a New York House member, tried to keep the contest going by showing a second set of electoral returns from Vermont, but Ferry saw it for just a way to further muddle up the picture and led the Senate to reject it. The House Democrats made a big show of the Vermont dispute.

Tilden's clear advantage after Election Day had been erased. Hayes had all but won. But, Democrats could still block the Hayes victory, or make Republicans desperate to settle the matter before inauguration day, thus obtain greater concessions. It was of no real use though. The Democratic Party was no longer united, as the Southern Democrats had concessions they wanted. The South would have of course had a better deal under Tilden. But there was almost no hope of that happening at this point since, again, it would require both houses of Congress to overturn the decision by the Electoral Commission under the law duly passed by Congress and signed by President Grant creating the commission.

The last minute tricks the Democrats would use were little more than stalling tactics and political mischief. Southerners could either join in on the short-term fun of sticking it to the Republicans, or gain something valuable from the inevitable president. Southern Democrats agreed with Republicans to accept the Electoral Commission's report—breaking the filibuster, presuming that the Hayes administration would agree to end Reconstruction and provide federal money to the South for internal improvements that included aid for the Texas and Pacific Railroad, education and appoint at least one Southerner to his cabinet.

Congress came into session at 10 AM and went through the night on March 1. Democrats kept making motions to further delay with various parliamentary motions to reconsider, to call the roll, to recess—anything to push it a few more days and make Republicans sweat. Even Speaker Randall realized by this time it was pointless and refused to entertain any of the mundane motions. While the uproar was on, Louisiana's Democratic congressmen urged Grant to withdraw the troops immediately, and he approved the draft of a telegram. When the Vermont dispute was finally settled, the small New England state went to the Hayes/Wheeler ticket.

A faction of House Democrats led by Hewitt pushed one more filibusters, making another objection to Wisconsin—the birthplace of the Republican Party. The houses separated from their joint session and debated Wisconsin until 3:38 AM on March 2. The Democratic challenge died, a joint session finally came together to grant Wisconsin to the Republicans at 4:10 AM.

This cleared the final obstacle, and the joint session declared Hayes the president and Wheeler the vice president, with the bare minimum 185 electoral votes to the Democratic ticket's 184 electoral votes.

Sen. Ferry, before making the announcement, called for calm, and asked that:

> ...nothing shall transpire on this occasion to mar the dignity and moderation which have characterized these proceedings in the main so reputable to the American people and worthy of the respect of the world.

He went on to announce:

> Rutherford B. Hayes, having received the majority of the whole number of electoral votes, is duly elected president of the United States.

Nation Reacts

The *Brooklyn Daily Eagle* reported:

> The work finished in the House of Representatives at 4 o'clock this morning—fruitless efforts of delay—exciting scenes and strong language—the consummation of the presidential fraud compared to the crucifixion on Calvary—the Democratic Party makes its appeal to the American people.

The *Indianapolis Daily News* reported:

> The agony is over. The count is finished. And Hayes and Wheeler are elected by one vote. Washington never saw such a scene as that of yesterday.

Hayes actually got word while traveling to Washington on a train, as *The New York Times* described it:

> The news created quite a jubilee among the governor's friends on board the train, who congratulated him on his being able to enter the capital of the nation as the actual president-elect, with no further doubt resting upon his title to the office.

The Republican-leaning *Times* went on to say:

> Many Democrats seem to be really well satisfied at the peaceable declaration of the election of Mr. Hayes, and even more violent filibusters are not nearly so angry as they were last night. Indeed, some of them go so far as to say that no matter what may come, the country is well rid of the pretender Tilden. For that person no one

Tainted by Suspicion

has a good word. [176]

The Democratic press was predictably outraged. It was a newspaper in Hayes own state, the *Cincinnati Enquirer*, that raged one day after it became official:

> *It's done. And filthy in the dark. By the grace of Joe Bradley, R.B. Hayes is in the White House is 'Commissioned' as President, and the master of the fraud of the century is consummated.*

During the ordeal, someone fired a shot through the window of Hayes's home while his family was eating dinner. This came amid numerous death threats from angry Democrats. Because of the threats of violence, Hayes was secretly sworn in as president on March 3, a Saturday, in the Red Room at the White House. The formal inauguration event was held on Monday, March 5, with the crowds, the inaugural address and celebrations.

In the inaugural address, Hayes was clear he supported home rule for the southern state governments, but on the basis those southern government respected constitutional rights for all citizens:

> *The calamitous efforts of the tremendous revolution which has passed over the Southern States still remain. The immeasurable benefits which will surely follow, sooner or later, the hearty and generous acceptance of the legitimate results of that revolution have not yet been realized. Difficult and embarrassing questions meet us at the threshold of this subject. The people of those States are still impoverished, and the inestimable blessing of wise, honest, and peaceful local self-government is not fully enjoyed. Whatever difference of opinion may exist as to the cause of this condition of*

> things, the fact is clear that in the progress of events the time has come when such government is the imperative necessity required by all the varied interests, public and private, of those States. But it must not be forgotten that only a local government which recognizes and maintains inviolate the rights of all is a true self-government. With respect to the two distinct races whose peculiar relations to each other have brought upon us the deplorable complications and perplexities which exist in those States, it must be a government which guards the interests of both races carefully and equally. It must be a government which submits loyally and heartily to the Constitution and the laws of the nation and the laws of the States themselves—accepting and obeying faithfully the whole Constitution as it...Let me assure my countrymen of the Southern States that it is my earnest desire to regard and promote their truest interest-the interests of the white and of the colored people both and equally—and to put forth my best efforts in behalf of a civil policy which will forever wipe out in our political affairs the color line and the distinction between North and South, to the end that we may have not merely a united North or a united South, but a united country.

He at least seemed to have the best intentions. That spring, Hayes commenced removing all the remaining federal troops in the South from guarding statehouses and government buildings and ending the era of the Republican Party's protection of the civil rights of blacks. He also installed southern Democrats in his cabinet. He named Tennessee Democrat David M. Key as the Postmaster General, an exalted cabinet post at the time because it provided the most patronage opportunities, and appointed other Southern Democrats to various federal post at local levels.

Some Democrats even called him "the greatest Southerner of the day." [177]

After this, Democratic governments in the South eventually set up what became known as Jim Crow laws, with segregation not only in public places, but also mandating that private businesses segregate. There was never a smoking gun of a quid pro quo for 1876, just as there wasn't for either 1800 or 1824. But for all the tit-for-tat with the Electoral Commission and in the joint sessions of Congress, it's widely believed the matter was settled at the Wormley House.

Still, there is much reason to believe Wormley did little more than reinforce what had already been agreed to by Hayes, ending Reconstruction and a one term presidency. The sweeteners were pork spending and patronage for southerners. Even Democrats in the cabinet was something Hayes was open to as a gesture of uniting the country.

It's true that with the Liberal Republicans backing him, Hayes was inclined to have a respectable end to military occupation in the South. Maintaining federal troops was not politically tenable. But had he won clear cut, it almost certainly would not have happened so quickly. He might have been able to reduce federal troop presence, rather than a total withdrawal. Moreover, whatever his personal preference, he would still have to balance the concerns of his party to deal with the hawkish Radical Republicans that wanted to keep troops present until blacks were fully integrated. However, the election going the way it did, weakened the hand of all Republicans on the question of Reconstruction.

Of all disputed elections, this one damaged the country the most—almost irreparably. As noted, 1800 demonstrated that a young nation can survive a harsh political dispute without going to war, while 1824 just drew a more partisan and regional polarized lines in the country. The 1876 election set back civil rights progress for about a century.

Tainted by Suspicion

Some "carpetbagger" Republican governments in southern states had indeed become corrupt. Still, Reconstruction was the only means to prevent the southern states from retaliating against black Americans and imposing Jim Crow laws.

In all fairness, given the circumstance, Republicans may not have had a better option. A Democratic president, even a northern one, would have almost certainly brought a rapid end to Reconstruction. Keeping Hayes in office theoretically allowed Republicans to manage its downfall with a president and Justice Department of their party to enforce the Fourteenth and Fifteenth Amendments, as well as other federal laws.

Hayes and Republicans that found withdrawing troops acceptable and even desirable did so on the grounds of a compromise. The other end of the bargain was supposed to be that southern governments—once free of carpetbaggers—would protect the rights of blacks. Democrats didn't hold up their end of the deal.

E.L. Godkin, the Republican editor of *The Nation* magazine, greatly regretted these events and wrote:

> *The negro will disappear from the field of national politics. Henceforth the nation, as a nation, will have nothing more to do with him.* [178]

The Supreme Court struck down numerous civil rights laws in 1883, including voting protections in the South. Without blacks in the south, the Republican Party withered away in the region.

The compromise didn't help the perception that Hayes had been selected instead of elected.

Democratic politicians and newspapers continuously called Hayes "Rutherfaud," "His Fraudulency" or "Old 8 to 7," regarding the commission vote.[179] The 1880 Democratic Party platform actually included language asserting that the only reason the party accepted Hayes as president was to avert another civil war, not because he was legitimate. Interestingly enough, it accused Hayes of stealing the electoral votes in two states, without saying which two of the three. [180]

Though Tilden never conceded the race, he jokingly found the silver lining:

> *I can retire to private life with the consciousness that I shall receive from posterity the credit of having been elected to the highest position in the gift of the people, without any of the cares and responsibilities of the office.*[181]

But if only a few things had gone differently, he *would* have had the responsibilities of the office.

CHAPTER NINE

President Tilden

ON ELECTION NIGHT 1876, Daniel Sickles leaves the theater. He considers dropping by Republican headquarters, but let us suppose that maybe, instead of doing so, he assumes—much like the Republican candidate Rutherford Hayes and Republican National Committee Chairman Zachary Chandler—that it's over. Suppose he believes some of the early newspaper editions released that night. Or, maybe, Sickles just wants to go to sleep. If the theater show was pleasant enough, perhaps the he would not want to end his night on a bad note.

Or, maybe he does stop by the nearly abandoned headquarters and when the clerk tells him it's over, Democrats are victorious, he sighs, turns around and leaves.

It might have all been different.

But this hero on the battlefield during the Civil War, who killed a man for having an affair with his wife, had a fighting instinct. The shred of hope he saw turned a Tilden victory that most of the political class had expected into a month's long battle for the presidency and changed the course of history.

It's certainly possible someone else might have contacted Republican leaders in Florida, Louisiana and South Carolina, or that those states might have figured it out on their own, if they could hold, it would put Hayes over the top. It's plausible that Wednesday morning, Hayes or Chandler or someone else in the Republican hierarchy would have crunched the numbers and considered the voter suppression in the Southern states. None of this happened though. Sickles was the only guy who saw the potential, except perhaps *New York Times* Managing Editor John Reid.

So what if Reid—who played nearly as big a role—just went along with the conventional media wisdom? He might well have begrudgingly done so if not contacted by the state Democratic Party, a message he perceived as doubt.

Or, everything happens just the same up to the Electoral Commission. But Illinois Democrats don't make the fatal political miscalculation of naming Justice David Davis as a senator. Davis on the Electoral Commission is no guarantee for Tilden, but it might have made his victory somewhat more likely.

The gracious Hayes concedes either the next day or in February. The fact that he expected to lose and the fact that the family was divided on moving to Washington probably makes it a little easier for the old warrior who clearly knows how to take a licking and keep going.

Republican newspapers editors might well figure weeks later what Sickles figured out on election night, and perhaps even run a few banner headlines across the country, "ELECTION STOLEN." But to no avail.

Tilden is sworn into office in March and most of the country is glad to see President Grant go. Would Tilden have a more aggressive governing agenda than the conciliatory Hayes who pledged to serve a single term? Possibly. On the other hand, Hayes believed presidents should be able to serve uninhibited by the concerns of a second term.

Beyond who might have a more aggressive style, there is a real question about who would have been more substantive. Both

Hayes and Tilden favored ending Reconstruction. Both Hayes and Tilden were anti-corruption and wanted to ditch the spoils systems. Both Hayes and Tilden were pro-hard money. Both were fiscal conservatives.

'Negro Supremacy' Alarmism

But style, priorities and implementation would have made an immense difference, historians said—especially on Reconstruction and race. Robert Waters, a history professor at Ohio Northern University and author of *Historical Dictionary of U.S.-Africa Relations*, said:

> As president, Hayes vetoed Democratic attempts to pass laws that would have gutted the Fifteenth Amendment, thus ending all possibility of the U.S. government in the future enforcing voting rights. [182]

He continued:

> African-Americans would have been worse off under Tilden. At least under Hayes, Southern governors always had to worry that if they went too far, the president might do something, but if Tilden were president, they would have known that they could do anything that they wanted to the Freedmen.

After Democrats won control of the Senate in 1878, for the first time since before the Civil War, the fully Democratic Congress attached riders to appropriations bills that would have repealed laws to enforce the Fourteenth and Fifteenth Amendment. Hayes vetoed the legislation, and the usually amiable president took the fight to Democrats, accusing them of seeking more voter fraud and intimidation. Most of the public rallied to his side and the divided Republican Party united behind its leader. [183]

A President Tilden almost certainly would not have been so bold against his own party. Then again, it's less likely Democrats would have won the Senate had Tilden been president.

Tilden opposed slavery, but like other northern Democrats who opposed slavery, he thought equality to be somewhat dangerous. Ahead of the Civil War, he favored a conciliatory approach with the South to prevent going to war.

In a letter written on Oct. 26, 1860 to his political rival William Kent—before Abraham Lincoln was elected president, the rising star Tilden serving in the New York state Assembly, opposed the Republican Party's anti-slavery stance as a means to prevent southern succession. The letter said:

> 1. That the southern states will not by any possibility accept the avowed creed of the Republican Party as the permanent policy of the federative government as to slavery either in the states or territories.
> 2. That upon this creed the Republican Party will not establish any affiliations with considerable minorities in the southern states...
> 3. A condition of parties in which the federative government shall be carried on by a party having no affiliation in the southern states is impossible to continue...
> 4. Nothing short of the recession of the Republican Party to the point of total and absolute non-action on the subject of slavery in the states and territories could enable it to reconcile to itself the people of the South. Even then, it would have great and fixed antipathies to overcome and men and parties act chiefly from habit. [184]

Tilden supported the union when the war started, but expressed typical partisan criticism of what he considered executive overreach by President Lincoln. When the war was over, Tilden favored a very lenient policy for the South, opposing the Radical Republicans. That said, Lincoln also supported a more lenient policy than the Radicals of his party.

After the war, when serving as the New York State Democratic party chairman, Tilden delivered a severe warning about the threat southern blacks posed to northern whites on March 11, 1868 at the Democratic state convention in Albany. His warnings of "negro supremacy" sounded similar to southern Democrats in the mid-20th century.

Tilden argued:

> *When the Republican Party resolved to establish negro supremacy in the 10 states in order to gain itself the representation of those states in Congress, it had to begin by governing the people of those states by the sword. The 4 millions and a half of white composed electoral bodies. If they were to be put under the supremacy of the 3 millions of negroes, and 20 senators and 50 representatives were to be obtained through three millions of negroes, it was necessary to obliterate every vestige of local authority, whether it had existed before the rebellion, or been instituted since by Mr. Lincoln or by the people. A bayonet had to be set to supervise and control every local organization. The military dictatorship had to be extended to the remotest ramifications of human society. That was the first necessity.*

In 1868, he went on to lay out the math for the New York convention goers, and what it would cost for even northern whites:

> *If those 3 millions of negroes elect 20 senators and fifty*

representatives, they will have 10 times as much power in the Senate of the United States as four millions of whites in the state of New York. On every question which concerns the commercial metropolis—every question of trade, of finance, of currency, of revenue, and of taxation—these three millions of liberated African slaves will count 10 times as much in the Senate as four millions of New Yorkers. One Freedman will counterbalance 13 white citizens of the Empire State. These 3 millions of blacks will count 10 times as much as three millions of white people in Pennsylvania; 10 times as much as two and a half million in Ohio; ten times as much as two and a quarter or two and a half million in Illinois; 10 times as much as 1 million and half in Indiana. These three millions of blacks will have twice the representation in the Senate as which will be possessed by five great commonwealths—New York, Pennsylvania, Ohio, Indiana and Illinois—embracing 13 and a half million of our people. [185]

It's quite likely that in this 1868 address, Tilden was expressing more partisan concerns than racial concerns—since black enfranchisement was the only way Republicans could have parity in the South. Tilden was also seeking to convince northerners—not so sympathetic to the rebels—why they should care about federal occupation in the South. Still, the 1868 speech Tilden delivered in some ways articulated an "us vs. them" philosophy that drove his party since the days of Jackson, be it race or economics. Tilden, as president, would have been worse than apathetic to black suffrage. He would have in fact been hostile to it, believing it to be a threat.

Tilden ran in 1876 as a different kind of Democrat of sorts, playing down much of the race demagoguery that had characterized his party. But there was no sign of a public epiphany

having occurred after his 1868 "negro supremacy" speech.
Waters said of the comments:

> *Tilden said that so called negro governments dominated the South and were helping to impose their corruption onto the whole nation. Tilden delivered speeches, warning that so called negro governments would not just affect the South, but the entire country because it would put blacks in these 10 states in position of electing members of Congress and the president. Tilden opposed the Civil War. He didn't fight because he thought it was the 'negro war.' He would say the South knows how to handle their affairs. The Democratic Party was the anti-black party.*

It would definitely be wrong to cast Tilden in the same light as some of truly horribly Democratic politicians that promoted terrorizing blacks, most, but not all of whom were in the South. Experts agreed that Tilden was in the middle, if not on the more enlightened side of his party for his day. He was part of the "Barnburners" faction of the Democrats that opposed the expansion of slavery, and joined the Free Soil party to support the 1848 presidential candidacy of former President Martin Van Buren, his political mentor. He was part of the "soft faction" of the Free Soil Democrats that resisted joining the Republican Party and made amends with the Democratic Party.

Nevertheless, it's highly doubtful Tilden would have had any interest in truly taking on the worst elements of what would become Jim Crow. What's more, the southern governors would have felt virtually unrestrained with a Democrat in charge of the federal government.

Protection for the freed slaves and lifting the military boot off the throats of fellow countrymen both seemed to be moral imperatives, but they were moral imperatives that obviously

Tainted by Suspicion

conflicted. As president, Hayes pledged protection of the newly freed blacks, even as he withdrew some of that protection. Hayes and other contemporaries believed that Reconstruction was ineffective. Hayes did promote "wise, honest, and peaceful local self-government" for the South. He believed and hoped both were possible.

Hayes was an economic conservative and pro-business, and some southern businessmen were fond of Republican policies. Hayes believed conciliatory policies might bridge the divide and build a "new Republican party" in the South with the support of white conservative businessmen—along with the freed slaves. Still, joining the party of the Yankees was not politically feasible for leaders, and business supported what was a safe bet. Hayes's successors could not compete in the Solid South.

Waters said:

> *Hayes was a strong supporter of civil rights, had defended runaway slaves before the Civil War, supported abolition during the Civil War and worried that if Tilden were elected, he would see to it that the Thirteenth, Fourteenth, and Fifteenth amendments were obliterated in the South. Tilden wouldn't have been able to get the amendments repealed. But he could stop legislation, or work to repeal legislation. Constitutional amendments are not self executing. You have got to put in place legislation and enforce it. The 1866 Civil Rights Act would not have been enforced under Tilden and might have been repealed.*

The last Democrat to sit in the Oval Office—Andrew Johnson—vetoed the 1866 Civil Rights Act that granted equal rights "without distinction of race or color, or previous condition of slavery or involuntary servitude." The Republican supermajority in Congress had enough votes to override the veto and enact the law, and did so. Still, with a Democratic House, Tilden would obviously have a stronger deck to play against the Republican Senate.

Adam Arenson, a professor of history at Manhattan College, with a concentration on slavery, the Civil War and Reconstruction, said:

> Race was not Tilden's motivation. He was an anti-corruption candidate from the North. But as president he would have to build on the commonalities in the West and South where there were neo-Confederates. That's what coalition building looks like. We saw that with Franklin Roosevelt's coalition that allowed Jim Crow laws to continue to get New Deal legislation passed. [186]

No what-if is a certainty. It is worth entertaining that Tilden might have risen to the occasion in a way only a Democrat could. In the 20th Century, it took southern Democratic President Lyndon Johnson to push the Civil Rights Act through Congress, and a Republican President Richard Nixon, with a proven anti-communism record, to open trade to China. In the 19th Century it might have taken a Democratic president to stand up to southern Democrats.

This seems less likely but not entirely implausible.

Tilden, the champion of reform, never afraid to topple government corruption, might well have viewed Reconstruction carpetbagger governments as the target for reform. If he was truly consistent, it's possible Tilden would have also considered the corruption of the racist Democratic governments to be just as detestable. Of course he would have needed his coalition, but Tilden rose to prominence in New York by tackling his party establishment. Far from destroying his career, it made him the Democratic nominee for president—and in this counterfactual, president. He would have made enemies among southern Democrats and more than a few northern Democrats. But he might have shown enough leadership to force needed change in the party. Moreover, he might have gained some Republican allies in Congress.

Certainly, he would have known that black voter suppression in the South helped put him in the White House. That would have created a tightrope. But taking on Tammany Hall created a tight rope. That political experience might have given him a certain confidence.

The aforementioned views about "negro supremacy" are disturbing to say the least. But, it's perhaps worth granting the benefit of the doubt for the context of the time. His larger point seemed to be his own perception of what is just and fair—first in terms of his problems with a military dictatorship in the South even after the war had ended.

Plus, Tilden would have the clout of being the leader of his party, the man who dragged it out of the wilderness, which would have given him considerable cache. Having inspired the public in New York, he might have been able to rally enough northern Democrats to confront the party's southern wing. The "Nixon in China" moment might well have taken a Democrat to responsibly end Reconstruction.

Waters argued that Reconstruction was doomed regardless of who won the election. It largely depended on the style for exiting:

> *Most white Americans in the North were tired of Reconstruction and believed that black Americans had to make it on their own after 10 years. This was not fair to African-Americans, who had much to overcome and often faced violence and intimidation throughout the South even while troops were in the South, but it was a common trope.*

Waters made a more contemporary analogy:

> There was the same sense that 'enough is enough' after 10 years as Americans felt about Iraq and Afghanistan, not a perfect analogy since soldiers were not being killed during Reconstruction. The problem is that people just lost faith. In the last couple of years in Iraq, there were very few casualties. But there were so many people still frustrated it was taking so long and said let's end this now. Even if Hayes thought it would work to keep the U.S. Army in the South to protect African-Americans and Republican governments, he could not have done it for long because the House was Democratic, and they had voted to cut off funding to keep the Army in the South.

One scenario, from the 2000 book, *Almost America* by Steve Tally, which includes several historic what-ifs, argues that if Tilden had won, his vice president would have been the real threat. Thomas Hendricks, had previously been at attorney for the racist group Knights of the Golden Circle. Hendricks—portrayed in the what-if as the worst villain, pushes for the end of the Fourteenth and Fifteenth Amendments, which are repealed by 1879. [187]

That would indeed be the worst case scenario of a Tilden presidency. However, it could be quite a leap. Hendricks became vice president under Grover Cleveland, serving less than a year before he died in office. The Democrats then didn't attempt to repeal the amendments. True, in 1877 things were more fragile. But, assuming the worst of Tilden, it's not clear he would have a super majority in Congress to amend the Constitution—or to rally a Convention of the States—and open up the wounds of the war. Tilden didn't want Democrats to take up arms to install him in the White House. Reversing the amendments could have caused another civil war. While Tilden might have been hostile to the plight of blacks, he was a New Yorker, not a neo-Confederate crusader. As for Hendricks, vice presidents weren't all that powerful. Grant's vice president died in office and the vacancy wasn't filled. After Hendricks was elected with Cleveland, and died in 1885, Cleveland didn't fill the vacancy. Hendricks might have turned some public sentiment against the amendments by saying Reconstruction can't end without their repeal. But repealing the young amendments would be a mighty undertaking.

The best that can be said of the end of Reconstruction is that it might have been worse.

Hayes salvaged what could be salvaged out of withdrawing the final troops from the South, and leveraged promises that the rights of freed blacks would be protected. After Democrats regained power, they broke those promises.

If Tilden had been willing to show force—granted a big if—might some of the southern Democrats have been more compliant?

Civil Service Reform

Frequently, the most overlooked aspect of many presidential legacies are appointments—primarily to the judiciary—but also to the cabinet and other high federal offices. Arenson said:

> Had Democrats gained power at the federal level, it would have been more explicit. Just as there is a claim today that there is no difference between the Democrats and Republicans, there is a difference on the presidential level in terms of cabinet appointments, in terms of federal judges. That's where you could have seen a pronounced difference.

Upon coming into office in the Gilded Age, that power was even more pronounced. Arenson said:

> It was a total spoils government. It was not a civil service system. A lot has been written about how Woodrow Wilson segregated African Americans in the federal government. Had Tilden won that likely would have happened much sooner. You probably would have seen Tilden removing African-Americans from public office.

Tilden would have most certainly sought some civil service reform. It was central to his presidential campaign. But to keep the Democratic coalition together, such reform would have certainly been more race based, Arenson suspected.

The good-government reforms would not likely have been any more sweeping than some of the incremental changes that occurred under Hayes. The political class on both sides wanted to stand in the way of reforming the spoils system as long as possible. Arenson explained:

> You had politicians emerge with a different style from the North and the Midwest. With Tilden and later Teddy Roosevelt, we saw leaders with a prominent voice rise out of a large media market. Midwestern leaders were reformers with a more moderate tone. Hayes had a more moderate Midwestern way.

Tilden would have had greater difficulty than Hayes pushing any meaningful reforms, said Brooks Simpson, an Arizona State University history professor and author of *The Reconstruction Presidents*. He said:

> Hayes had to battle leaders in his own party. He would have had to battle the same Republican Senate that probably wouldn't let him get many appointments confirmed. [188]

Hayes had considerable problems with Sen. Roscoe Conkling, the Stalwart Republican that wanted to maintain patronage, and Conkling likely would have been rougher on a Democrat, Simpson said.

But perception in politics plays a tremendous role. Hayes had the same commitment to civil service reform, but doubtfully had the same moral authority in the public's mind as the man known for rounding up crooks in one of the biggest political swamps of all, New York. If Tilden had won an election outright—albeit a close one—he would still have the strong mandate to clean up the federal government. It was fundamental to his persona, to nearly all of his support. A Democratic House would have backed him up, as would a significant number of Republicans—particularly those that backed Horace Greely in 1872.

Tildenomics

There were of course other matters facing the country that Hayes had a mixed record in dealing with. Tilden would have had to deal with the same economic problems.

In July 1877, the Great Strike broke out with the Baltimore & Ohio railroad. Railroad workers, responding to repeated wage cuts, led the most severe strike in U.S. history to that day. Other unemployed Americans joined the strikers in their cause, engaging in violence.

The railroad interests wanted Hayes to use the military to break the strike, but the president refused. Instead Hayes waited for state and local officials to go through the proper channels before he sent the military to keep the order. The military did not kill anyone and the strikers eventually gave up. [189]

Tilden, on the other hand, had a great affinity for the railroad chieftains. That's how he made his fortune. It raises the question whether he would have taken swift action to break up the strike, if not to help his buddies out, then out of a sincere belief on his part in the railroad industry.

Simpson, of Arizona State University, doesn't think so, given party politics:

> *Tilden would not have used federal troops against American workers. That was the constituency of the Democrats. Democrats were not viewed as the party of capitalists interests. He would have been no more eager to use force than Hayes, who was in the party of business. The Republicans wanted labor to know its place.*

Farmers wanted currency inflation for increasing commodity prices and paying their debts. Both parties were split among hard money advocates backing the gold standard and supporters of non-gold backed paper currency.

In February 1878, more than enough Republicans and Democrats came together to pass the Bland-Allison bill to allow limited silver coinage. Hayes vetoed the bill, but Congress mustered up a two-thirds majority to override the veto. Though a stinging defeat, Hayes managed to return to the gold standard in 1879 by redeeming greenbacks in gold. [190]

Tilden was in line with Hayes on hard money. So monetary policy would have remained the same regardless of which candidate won. Tilden would have almost certainly taken the same stance as Hayes against paper currency and maybe even against coining silver. Hayes thought inflation was an enemy of economic growth, and Tilden—having been in the business world—had similar concerns.

One fairly minor point that got significant attention at the time was the no-booze policy in the White House under the Hayes administration. That went over about as well in official Washington then as it would today. But it made the Woman's

Christian Temperance Union very happy. First lady Lucy Webb Hayes made sure all wines and liquors were kept out off the White House complex. While Tilden wanted to change most things significantly from President Grant—who was quite well known to be fond of drinking—Tilden would likely have kept liquor flowing had he won the Electoral College vote.

Political Consequences

The Senate Republican majority would have likely gone out of their way to obstruct President Tilden's agenda and would likely consider him an illegitimate president over voter suppression in the South. "Til-legimate" might have replaced "Rutherfraud" as the means to denigrate a president.

This is what happened in real life in 1878 when the bitter House Democrats began an investigation that didn't turn out as they anticipated, resulting in denting Tilden's seemingly bulletproof armor of a corruption fighter more than it harmed Hayes.

The special House investigative panel known as the Potter Committee was formed in hopes of embarrassing Hayes and maybe even driving him from office. This would only embolden the Tilden fans who felt their man was robbed. But instead of toppling Hayes, the bombshell from the Potter Committee was wrongdoing by Tilden supporters, chiefly his nephew.

The *New York Tribune* published coded telegrams which it had deciphered between Tilden's nephew, Colonel William T. Pelton and other Democrats, including Manton Marble, editor of the *New York World*, a Democratic newspaper. The telegrams showed there were attempts to bribe election officials. The *Tribune*, a Republican paper, printed selective portions of the cipher telegrams in August. For maximum impact, the *Tribune* published the telegrams little by little and in October printed telegrams showing Marble and another Democratic operative

C.W. Wooley making a bribery offer to election officials. Republicans on the Potter Committee pushed the committee to investigate the very opposite of what the House majority wanted to probe—corruption by the Tilden campaign.

Before the congressional panel, Pelton and Smith Weed of South Carolina both confessed to their part in the bribery scandal. Pelton said his uncle was furious about the bribery attempt in November 1876. This would mean Tilden didn't approve, but apparently knew. Marble didn't admit guilt and said his telegrams were "danger signals" to war against Republican corruption. Tilden denied knowledge of the matter and voluntarily testified to the congressional committee insisting he played no role in the matter. History has never turned up counter evidence to dispute this, so it's likely Tilden was innocent but his overzealous supporters were not.[191]

He was cleared of wrongdoing, but the matter was damaging for someone who built his career as a reformer. Had Tilden been president, and the press came upon these telegrams, it seems likely the Republican Senate would have relentlessly badgered the Democratic president in hearings and it might well have been devastating to his presidency even if no one could prove he knew of the skullduggery. A Democratic House would have never impeached Tilden, but the hearsay might have caused him to limp to the end of his first term and not seek a second.

Also in 1878, Democrats regained their majority in the Senate—something that very likely would not have occurred under a Democratic president. And with a President Tilden, Republicans might have been able to win back the House. That would put House Republican leader James Garfield of Ohio in as Speaker. That could have meant Garfield would be content with his leadership role and decline a run for president, or it would have propelled him to frontrunner status, possibly foregoing the 35 ballots before his nomination in 1880.

Though damaged from the hearings, many Democrats still

wanted Tilden to mount a comeback similar to Old Hickory's return in 1828. That became less likely after Republicans won the New York governor's race in 1879 against the Tilden-backed candidate. The former governor didn't seem quite as strong, maybe not a sure lock to win his own state.

The Cipher Telegrams made some Democrats a little cautious about the 1876 nominee, while Tilden was demonstrating a cautious attitude himself about 1880, not fully saying if he planned to stand for the office again. He wrote a letter to a friend expressing concerns that his health would force him to decline the nomination. Thus, it's likely, given the fatigue of being president; he almost certainly would not have run for a second term.

Regardless of his ability to run for a second term, a strong Democratic Party apparatus would have been in place. Given that General Winfield Scott Hancock was nominated by the second ballot at the 1880 Democratic National Convention to be president, it's plausible that he would have been the nominee if Tilden were a one-term president. It's perhaps more likely that Tilden would have handpicked his successor. His 1876 running mate, Thomas Hendricks, sought the nomination in 1880. Had Hendricks been a loyal and valuable vice president during a Tilden administration, the president might have supported his number two for the job. Other Democratic contenders at the convention were House Speaker Samuel Randall and Sen. Thomas Bayard of Delaware. Had Tilden won the presidency through the Electoral Commission vote, he would have had some obligation to Randall and Bayard.

Tilden's presidency would have significant influence on what Republicans would have done. If the party believed Hayes was robbed, they might urge him to run again. But Hayes's heart might not have been into going through the ordeal again. He might well have guided his support to fellow Ohioan James Garfield. James Blaine might have reemerged in 1880 as he did in

1884.

What hasn't changed about the Republican Party is its habit of breaking up into factions and nearly devouring itself. Even though it was the party in power in 1880, with Hayes stepping aside, the party was split between the Stalwarts (many former Radical Republicans), that wanted to maintain patronage and the Half Breeds who, like Hayes, backed civil service reform and an end to patronage, many of them former Liberal Republicans. Blaine was backed by the moderate Half Breeds while Grant was the favorite of the Stalwarts. Garfield was nominated on the thirty fourth ballot as the compromise candidate.

This new split came during the term of Hayes. Success typically allows room for some disagreement, while the opposition party sticks together. If Tilden were president, the Republicans might have presented a more united front.

It is difficult to know if a Tilden presidency would have any decisive role in the 1880 race. As the party in power, Democrats would have a stronger machine than if not. On the flip side, the race would have been a referendum on Tilden's presidency. If northern apathy were not shaken by the impact of a more severe Jim Crow, it's quite likely the public would have supported his strong civil service reforms.

***

Even if Garfield or Blaine or another Republican managed to win back the White House in 1880, the new Republican president would have significant troubles in reversing the damage done of four years of southern governments run amok, the most likely scenario under a Tilden administration.

Of course, Tilden did not become president. He died in 1886, a decade after the controversial election and what would have been two years after what could have been the end of a second term. A lifelong bachelor with no children, Tilden left $7 million for the establishment of a free public library in New York

City. In 1895 it was formally called the New York Public Library. It's a noble legacy from a man that most evidence would indicate had a flawed but a mostly noble character. Given that the more likely scenario is he would bend to the party's will on the South, his personal legacy might well have been protected by not being president.

PART IV

Non-Disputed Controversies

Tainted by Suspicion

CHAPTER TEN

Cleveland Uninterrupted

IT WAS ONLY 12 years and four presidents after the 1876 boondoggle. Even fewer votes separated President Grover Cleveland and his Republican challenger Benjamin Harrison—than separated Hayes and Tilden. The contest was not close however in the Electoral College and did not end up being challenged as 1824 and 1876 had been (and 2000 would be).

Another similarity to both 1824 and 2000: the winner was part of a presidential dynasty. The most forgettable of the four elections where the electoral and popular vote went into the opposite direction—1888 might have had more far reaching consequences than known at the time. A different result might have propelled the populist movement further ahead, said one scholar.

President Cleveland, born in 1837, won a razor thin victory in the election of 1884 against former House Speaker and Secretary of State James Blaine. Similar to Samuel Tilden, Cleveland was a reform-minded Democratic governor of New York who took on Tammany Hall. He managed to overcome a scandal about an illegitimate child in that election to defeat Blaine.

Just as Cleveland didn't mind making enemies with the

New York Democratic establishment, he also didn't mind shaking things up as president. Cleveland vetoed more bills—414—than all of his predecessors combined. That was once the case with Jackson, who had fewer predecessors.

"What is the use of being elected or re-elected unless you stand for something," Cleveland told his political advisors. [192]

Cleveland's Challenging First Term

Cleveland was a fiscal conservative and sought to force Congress to hold the line on spending. Though much of that spending was for popular causes such as pensions for union soldiers. However, one of the bills he vetoed allowed people whose pensions were rejected as fraudulent by the Pensions Bureau to get a federal pension nonetheless. He vetoed another bill that expanded pensions to veterans whose injury wasn't traceable to the Civil War. Republicans established a veterans group called the Grand Army of the Republic to oppose Cleveland's policies.

Cleveland, the first Democratic president elected since James Buchanan, sought an act of national unity. He issued an executive order to return Confederate battle flags and other relics captured from the Civil War to the southern states from which they were retrieved. Republicans had been sort of missing the "bloody shirt" as a campaign tactic since many voters were ready to move on. But this presented a golden opportunity to remind the country again: not all Democrats were rebels but all rebels were Democrats. Republicans could point to the northern Democratic president who vetoed expanding pensions for union soldiers but seemed to have a soft spot for the old Confederacy. It became so toxic that the president rescinded the executive order after two weeks. [193]

The federal pension system had gotten out of control, and Cleveland wasn't going to let a goodwill gesture to the South derail his efforts to rein in spending.

Cleveland also clashed with congressional Republicans over civil service reform, which he wanted to expand even beyond the Pendleton Act signed under Republican President Chester Arthur. Some of these Cleveland reforms would require replacing Republican political appointees in the federal bureaucracy with merit employees.

Congressional Republicans threatened to expand the Tenure of Office Act—the obvious implication being this was the law that led to President Andrew Johnson's impeachment. But Cleveland managed to get public support behind him and the Tenure of Office Act—that required Senate approval before removing presidential appointees—was repealed. [194]

Trouble with Trade

The defining issue going into the re-election battle would be tariffs.

Tariffs had been a massive issue in American politics since the country's beginning, and clearly are playing a major role in politics today.

By 1888, the tariff issue was somewhat less straightforward than what Henry Clay advocated in the early 1800. Clay wanted tariffs to cover the cost of infrastructure improvements. By the late 1800s, tariffs were primarily about protecting certain industries and certain jobs.

Though the Liberal Republican faction of the party had won internal party struggles a decade earlier on ending Reconstruction and managed to chisel away at the spoils system, they had clearly lost out against tariffs. Free trade was a dirty phrase in those days, but Cleveland heeded the call of southern farmers who complained the tariffs made consumer prices too high. Republicans, meanwhile, positioned themselves solidly in favor of tariffs with an economic nationalist message. The Democrats as a whole were divided on the issue.

Immigration was also blamed for the plight of American workers. Rep. William Scott, a Pennsylvania Democrat, got bipartisan backing for a law that permanently banned the immigration or the return of Chinese laborers. The result is that 20,000 Chinese who thought they were leaving the United States temporarily were refused reentry. The move was framed as protection American jobs, but Scott also backed tariff reform.

The most pro-tariff Democrat was Pennsylvania Rep. Samuel Randall. Cleveland's operatives worked to undermine Randall's influence in the party, fearing the former Speaker of the House might back someone else for the 1888 Democratic nomination. Cleveland's people ensured that Scott—a proponent of tariff reform—took control of the Pennsylvania delegation.

Cleveland was re-nominated unanimously on the second day of the Democratic National Convention held from June 5-7 in St. Louis.

To combat attacks from Republicans that he was "free trade," Cleveland called for language in the Democratic platform to reject free trade, while supporting compromise language on tariffs. Protectionist Maryland Sen. Arthur Pue Gorman introduced the plank, which was meant to allay concerns among Democrats, but also voters throughout the country.

The compromise plan called for tariffs to continue, but ones that would only raise money to cover the cost of federal expenditures, not for the purpose of protecting a specific industry from foreign competition. Further, reducing the tariffs would reduce the cost of living for consumers, Democrats argued. The plank was couched in harmless compromise language, however, Henry Watterson, a trade reformer and editor of the *Louisville Courier-Journal*, was named as chairman of the Resolutions Committee at the Democratic convention. This sparked concerns among the anti-free trade crowd.

Cleveland's vice president Thomas Hendricks had died in office. Like Grant, Cleveland didn't fill the vacancy for the remainder of his first term. At the convention in St. Louis, Democrats settled on the rather seasoned former Ohio Sen. Allen Thurman.

Harrison's Road to the Nomination

Republicans gathered in Chicago just two weeks later to nominate a candidate at the national convention, and the outcome was a surprise.

The first frontrunner was Blaine. After running such a close race in 1884, the party presumed he was their best chance at retaking the White House. However, the chief reason for his loss four years earlier had been the revolt of the Mugwumps—yet another faction of the Republican Party.

In the 1870s, the divide between the Radical and the Liberal Republicans gave way to a divide between the Stalwarts and the Half Breeds. The Mugwumps emerged in the 1880s, and were the newest incarnation of the liberal/half breed wing of the party— the more reform minded group opposed to the spoils system and corruption. That said, there was no precise overlap on these factions. For examples, the Liberal Republicans and Mugwumps didn't take the same stance on trade and tariffs. But generally— there was a repetitive cycle of new blood arising to challenge the old guard—even though the Republican Party was just more than 30 years old at the time. By 1888, the party was referring to itself as the Grand Old Party, or GOP.

Though Blaine had once been a Half Breed, some of the suspected financial corruption in his past prompted the Mugwumps to endorse Cleveland in 1884. It was widely believed that had the Republicans been united, Blaine would have sailed to victory. Some Mugwumps stayed with the Democratic Party. One prominent Mugwump who didn't abandon his party or Blaine's candidacy was Indiana Sen. Benjamin Harrison.

In 1887, Harrison lost his Senate seat when Democrats took

over the Indiana state legislature and named a Democrat to the seat. Since he didn't lose by the vote of the people, he was still in a reasonably good position to run for president.

As for Blaine, by 1888, his health was failing and he opted against another run. Ohio Senator John Sherman emerged as the new Republican frontrunner, but Blaine's absence still created a vacuum, welcoming seven candidates to compete for the nomination at the Republican National Convention in Chicago. Former Union General Walter Q. Gresham, who served as a federal judge, was also seen as a viable contender. However, Pennsylvania Senator Matthew Quay, the chairman of the Republican National Committee, couldn't accept the general's desire for civil service reform.

The only other candidate with a national following was Harrison, born in 1833. Indiana was among the most important swing states going into the election, so he had geography on his side. Moreover, he was the grandson of the ninth president, William Henry Harrison, adding political pedigree to a heroic military record as a colonel in the Civil War—not a bad way to rally the veterans already angry at Cleveland to turnout on Election Day. Democrats derided him as "Little Ben" for his 5'6" stature.

Harrison had a smart and energetic group of surrogates getting campaign literature out across the country and placing favorable newspaper articles about their candidate. Harrison also delivered two speeches ahead of the convention that garnered much press attention, but didn't go deep into controversial policy, such as his opposition to banning Chinese workers. His slate of delegates won at the Indiana convention in April over his fellow Hoosier, Gresham. His campaign slogan was "Rejuvenated Republicanism."[195]

At the Chicago convention, his supporters sought out the backers of the other candidates seeking to make Harrison the second choice of delegates committed to someone else on the first

Tainted by Suspicion

ballot. That's very similar to how Abraham Lincoln won the Republican nomination at the Chicago convention in 1860 against a field of more experienced rivals—become the prevailing second choice.

The Republican platform included supporting protective tariffs, endorsing Chinese exclusion, and backing statehood for western territories. The platform also blamed the Cleveland administration for "inefficiency and cowardice." A day after the platform was adopted, the nominating began.

Early on, it looked to be Sherman's to lose, as he got 229 votes on the first ballot, more than twice as many votes as his nearest runner up, Gresham at 107. New York Central Railroad president Chauncey Depew got 99 votes. Harrison came in fourth place with 85 votes. Sherman lacked a majority, but it wasn't looking good for Harrison. However, after Depew dropped out, most of his supporters went to Harrison, as the former colonel surged to second place in the fourth and fifth ballots.

Stephen Elkins, a party leader who had promoted the Harrison campaign, telegraphed Blaine who was in Scotland during the convention. Blaine, remembering Harrison was a rare Mugwump supporter, sent a telegram back endorsing Harrison for the nomination. This was enough to put Harrison over the top for the nomination on the eighth ballot with 544 delegates.

Blaine wanted a ticket of Harrison and William Walter Phelps, a longtime ally of Blaine. But the delegates chose New York banker Levi P. Morton as the vice presidential nominee.

Harrison hoped to fire up his supporters with some lively speechifying:

> We have joined now a contest of great principles and ... the armies which are to fight out of this great contest before the American people will encamp upon the high plains of principle and not in the low swamps of personal defamation or detraction. [196]

Harrison told the managers of his campaign:

> Remember, no bargains, no alliances, no trades. I may like to be president, but if I am to go to the White House, I don't propose to go shackled.

But the campaign would be plenty negative from both sides.

Conservatives and Liberals

Though a Democrat, Cleveland is widely remembered as a small government conservative. By today's standards, he would for the most part still be a conservative. Presidential historian Craig Shirley, a Ronald Reagan biographer who worked on Reagan's campaigns before starting an influential political public relations firm, said:

> Cleveland was definitely a conservative. He was a very good president on taxes, on trade, on regulation, and economically he was definitely a conservative. [197]

However, it's not clear Harrison would be on the left. His protectionist views would still fit in with some anti-free trade Republicans. But with the anti-free trade stance, Harrison clearly favored a bigger government than Cleveland. Shirley said:

> Harrison was a protectionist, but protectionism has gone back and forth between the right and left for many years. It used to be assumed Republicans were for free trade. Now we see Republican protectionists and Democrats for free trade.

The Campaign

One major consequence of the 1876 election deal, ending Reconstruction in the South, was to give Democrats a big advantage in the Electoral College. Ending Reconstruction established the Solid South, where there was little effort at the federal level to assist the voting rights of blacks or any Republicans in the region, and the South included 156 electoral votes out of 201 required for victory.[198]

Democratic National Committee Chairman William Barnum ran most of the Cleveland campaign, while the president did no stumping for himself, believing it unseemly for a president, and leaving that to party surrogates.

Both campaigns were targeting New York and Indiana—not only the respective home states of the two nominees but also two Republican-leaning swing states that Cleveland won in 1884. Connecticut and New Jersey were also key battlegrounds that would go either way. So the election was primarily in the north, as the Solid South was behind Cleveland (thanks in part to the 1877 compromise) and the Midwest and West was backing Harrison.

The American Free Trade League stumped hard for Democrats, while the party apparatus covered Connecticut, New Jersey and New York with tariff reform and Cleveland-Thurman literature. In the absence of the president, the 74-year-old vice presidential nominee Thurman hit the trail with stump speeches in the Midwest, the Northeast, and the South explaining why tariffs were bad for the working man.

Thurman collapsed twice during his speaking tour, once at Madison Square Garden in New York another time in Newark, New Jersey, which created big press headlines about his health. Barnum complained, "We might just as well nominate a corpse," when referring to Thurman.

Further, despite the natural advantages that typically come

with incumbency, Cleveland's campaign burned through most of its money and lacked the strong organization that Republicans had.

But Democrats managed to target the Republican standard bearer as a religious bigot, as anti-labor, and a supporter of letting Chinese laborers back into the United States to lower American wages.

Republicans certainly didn't go easy on Cleveland.

RNC chairman Quay managed Harrison's political strategy, and while Democrats had only the American Free Trade League, the Harrison campaign had the American Iron and Steel Association, the American Protective Tariff League and various local Republican clubs across the country working to get out the vote.

Republicans were also prolific in raking in money, raising $3 million for the Harrison-Morton ticket, an unheard of amount for a campaign in that era. Further, both Blaine and Sherman hit the trail stumping for the Republican ticket—demonstrating party unity. That's juxtaposed to Democrats, where Cleveland and his successor as New York governor, David Hill, did not like one another over issues of Tammany Hall, reform and trade. Hill didn't try to block the Cleveland re-nomination, as the president had once feared. But Hill didn't bother showing up for the Democratic National Convention. Cleveland never endorsed Hill's campaign for governor that year. Ultimately though, Hill did stump for the Democratic ticket in the critical state of New York.

Tammany Hall threw their resources behind re-electing Hill as governor and very little into ensuring victory for the president in the state where he was once their headache. Meanwhile, New York was rich with Civil War veterans perturbed with Cleveland's vetoes of the pension bills. Even those getting their pensions were reading news stories and hearing Republican speeches about how the rebel party's administration is slashing pensions for Union veterans and it resurrected old hostilities among those who put their lives on the line to keep the country together.

While Cleveland rarely left the White House, Harrison didn't tour the country either. He did, however, carry out a vigorous front porch campaign—in which crowds of supporters and reporters would gather in front of his Indianapolis home. The charismatic Republican delivered 94 well-attended speeches that *Harper's Weekly* described as having a "clear, logical and emphatic manner." Harrison denounced the Democratic free trade agenda, which he warned would lead to lower wages and fewer American jobs. [199]

Republicans problem came from the third party movement, the Prohibition Party, which drew away their voting bloc among more religious voters. The Democratic Party was a few decades away from becoming dominated by secularism, but conservative Protestants tended to view Republicans as the morals party even in those days. Temperance was actually emerging as a mainstream issue but was still a few decades away from having a majority, and it was something Republicans had to handle carefully. The party managed to support high licensing fees on alcohol sellers without supporting an outright ban.

Scandals and Scurrilous Charges

Republicans claimed that Cleveland was the "Beast of Buffalo" who beat his wife in a drunken rage. The first lady denied the allegation and issued a statement saying the allegation was:

> ...*a foolish campaign story without a shadow of foundation.*

She said she could wish:

Tainted by Suspicion

> *...the women of our country no greater blessing than their homes and lives may be as happy and their husbands may be as kind, considerate and affectionate as mine.* [200]

After both conventions had ended, the House passed the Mills Tariff Reform bill, named for House Ways and Means Committee Chairman Roger Mills, a Texas Democrat. A substitute bill by Republican Sen. William Allison of Iowa lowered some tariff rates for raw sugar and did away with taxes on domestic tobacco and medicinal alcohol. Ultimately the Republicans put forth a $70 million tax and tariff reduction bill that made the Democratic plan —a $55 million tariff cut—a tougher sell. The difference was that Republicans kept a stronger tariff structure in place.

The Cleveland administration struck a treaty to resolve a dispute between U.S. and Canadian fishermen, but the Republican-controlled Senate rejected the treaty. Republicans, chasing the Irish vote, said the treaty was too pro-British. They further linked Democratic tariff policy to free trade with Britain. Cleveland bluffed Republicans when he asked Congress to pass a bill banning all trade of goods from British-linked Canada. He knew Republicans wouldn't do it. This put Republicans in a precarious spot, as they couldn't continue to jawbone the issue, while it made Cleveland look tough on Britain. It was actually one of the few clever campaign moves that year on the part of the president.

In the backdrop of the debate over trade and Britain came the most comical chicanery of the race known as the Murchison Letter scandal.

A Republican operative George Osgoodby wrote a letter posing as British-born businessman living in the United States named "Charles F. Murchison." The letter was sent to Sir Lionel Sackville-West, the British minister to the United States, inquiring which party would be friendliest to British interests. It said he was inclined to vote for Cleveland because of a free trade and anti-Irish stand, and opposed Harrison for being, "a believer in the American side of all questions" and "an enemy of British interests." He said the Cleveland's position on the Canadian fisheries made him uncertain.

Sackville-West's naively wrote back that the Cleveland administration was "still desirable to maintaining friendly relations with Great Britain" and that the president would, "manifest a spirit of conciliation in dealing with the questions involved in the message." Republican newspapers across the country published the letter to the British diplomat's great embarrassment. [201]

Despite his successful front porch campaign, Indiana was going to be a struggle for Harrison. Democrats pointed to the railroad strike in 1877 to argue Republicans were hostile to labor, which played well in a state full of working class voters.

Then came an October surprise when Democrats obtained a letter from Republican National Committee Treasurer Colonel W.W. Dudley explaining to Indiana party leaders how to be absolutely certain that voters they buy off, known as "floaters," actually cast their vote for Republicans. Dudley's suggestion was to:

> Divide the voters into blocks of five and put a trusted man with necessary funds in charge of those five and make him responsible that none get away and that all vote our ticket.

Dudley said his signature was a forgery and sued for libel, but he dropped the libel suit after the election was over. [202]

Election Results

Some good news for President Cleveland came on election night, Nov. 6. Despite the Republican effort to badger him over Britain, he carried the Irish vote in New York and Boston by a higher margin than in 1884. More good news, it was close, but he won the national popular vote by fewer than 100,000 votes nationwide, 5,540,329 to 5,439,853, or 49 percent to 48 percent.

The bad news for Cleveland, of course, was that he didn't win the election.

Harrison managed to win Cleveland's home state of New York and its 36 electoral votes, by just 13,000 votes statewide. Harrison barely won his own home state of Indiana's 15 electoral votes, by fewer than 2,500 votes statewide. He lost his hometown of Indianapolis—demonstrating that the vote-buying allegations stung, and that chicanery might have made the difference for the GOP. Cleveland captured Connecticut by just 336 votes and New Jersey by more than 7,000.

But in the Electoral College it wasn't at all close. Harrison won 233 electoral votes to 168 electoral votes for Cleveland.

With the lopsided Electoral College result, there was little basis for a challenge. Cleveland might have been justified in asking for at least a re-canvassing in New York or Indiana. Harrison would have been just as justified in seeking another count in New Jersey and certainly in Connecticut. The election ended without the controversy of 1824 or 1876—with no handwringing and claims that the will of the people had been thwarted.

Harrison, though he insisted on no political bargains, his supporters didn't listen. The new president-elect said, "Providence has given us this victory."

RNC Chairman Quay said it was quite to the contrary, once declaring, "He ought to know that Providence hadn't a damn thing to do with it" and added that the president didn't know, "how close a number of men were compelled to approach the gates of the penitentiary to make him president." [203]

A short-term consequence was to frustrate President Harrison, who found all-too quickly his warning against deals was ignored and he was indeed shackled.

"I could not name my own cabinet," President Harrison said. "They had sold every place to pay the election expense."

Cleveland, meanwhile, could sleep better at night, in his decision against challenging the results. He said:

> It is better to be defeated battling for an honest principle than to win by cowardly subterfuge. [204]

Had Cleveland risked looking like a sore loser in 1888, he might not have been able to take advantage of voter remorse in 1892. The popular vote helped encourage Cleveland to mount a comeback four years later to become the first and only president to serve two non-consecutive terms, defeating Harrison in a three-way matchup that included Populist Party candidate James Weaver. Cleveland won 46 percent of the popular vote and 277 electoral votes while Harrison won 43 percent of the popular vote and 145 electoral votes. Weaver won five states and 8 percent of the vote to capture 22 electoral votes, remarkably successful for a third party candidate.

Shortly after taking office for his second term, the Panic of 1893 hit, driving unemployment higher than 20 percent in several states as thousands of businesses went under. Cleveland took the voters wrath when Republicans scored big gains in the 1894 midterm elections. The Democrats merged with the Populist Party but lost the presidency to Republican William McKinley in 1896, as the Republicans ran on restoring prosperity.

Cleveland's Earlier Second Term

Had Cleveland served the more traditional back-to-back term and carried the Electoral College in 1888, it likely would have been his successor that dealt with the serious depression. Republicans took a beating for the Panic of 1873. In the midst of a populist uprising in the 1890s, it might have shifted things. Brooks Simpson, a presidential historian at Arizona State University, said:

> *Cleveland thought what government needs to do during a recession is get out. When Republicans were in office and a depression came, they tried to use the government and it didn't help. So both parties would have been seen as failures.* [205]

Simpson thinks Cleveland would have been succeeded by another Democrat in 1893, who might have tried a half measure to revive the economy, which he believes would have failed as much as the more aggressive Republican measures of the 1873 recession had.

This would have given voters the view that both parties were unable to address problems, which would have likely strengthened the hand of populists, such as William Jennings Bryan, the outsider who surprisingly captured the Democratic nomination in 1896 after his "Cross of Gold" speech, and went on to win the nomination twice more. Simpson said:

> *So, instead of McKinley eventually running as the party of prosperity in 1896, you might have seen more people rally behind the populist movement to elect a president—Bryan or someone more critical of the entire system might have emerged.*

Moreover, no William McKinley might well have meant no Teddy Roosevelt as president. Even without TR, the progressive movement of the early 20th Century—greatly influenced by the Populists—would have surely developed. A Bryan presidency would have likely been disastrous.

In real life, even though Bryan never became president after three tries, he did win the war against Cleveland supporters in shifting the Democratic Party leftward on economic issues. It's possible that Bryan, a devout Christian who would be considered a social conservative, had more influence over history as an almost president than he would have had as a failed president.

So, perhaps much was riding on the most forgettable of all the controversial elections.

CHAPTER ELEVEN

Kennedy, Nixon and the Minimal Challenge

SHORTLY AFTER JOHN F. Kennedy was inaugurated president, Senate Republican Leader Everett Dirksen—certain that election fraud in his home state of Illinois cost Richard Nixon the election, called FBI Assistant Director Cartha DeLoach to ask why there wasn't an FBI investigation into the chicanery and voter fraud emanating from Chicago's Daley machine.

"I told him that the Department of Justice was investigating this," DeLoach recalled to the Washington Post. "I referred him to the attorney general."

The exasperated Dirksen sarcastically asked, "Who's the attorney general?"

DeLoach answered, "Bobby Kennedy."

Dirksen slammed the phone. [206]

Thus was the aftermath of the election in which Kennedy, the 43-year-old Massachusetts senator, defeated Nixon, the 47-year-old vice president. Well before the legend of Camelot and the scandal of Watergate, Dirksen was not alone in a separate frame of reference, viewing the Kennedy clan as akin to a political mafia of sorts, a privileged family taking what it wants and insulating itself from the accountability, in contrast to Nixon, who epitomized an up from the bootstraps American success story.

Whatever one thinks about the two candidates and whether their legacies are deserved, two myths persist as almost certainties about the presidential election and its aftermath from that year.

One is that separate and apart from fraud suspicions, Kennedy undisputedly carried the popular vote against Nixon. The other myth is that—unlike 40 years later with Bush v. Gore—there was no prolonged legal challenge to the results. Because of a complicated ballot in Alabama, it's not clear that Kennedy really emerged with the popular vote win. Also, while Nixon didn't file any legal challenges, his surrogates did.

It can surely be said that 1960 does not belong in the same category as 1800, 1824, 1876 and 2000 in the sense that the country wasn't left wondering for an extended period of time after Election Day who actually won, nor was it ultimately decided by another branch of government. But there were indeed legal challenges and even recounts—albeit not to the extent of demanding hand counts and bickering over standards.

Caution on Race

The election was notable for being the first presidential contest where both candidates were born in the 20th Century. Though only four years apart in age, Nixon's eight years as vice president to the popular President Dwight Eisenhower certainly gave him a leg up on the experience issue.

Both Nixon and Kennedy came into the contest supporting civil rights. Nixon in fact had an arguably stronger record, but made a critical mistake in the course of the campaign that might well have shaped politics and the black vote for a generation.

The vice president gave a strong civil rights speech in Harlem during the 1956 presidential campaign, a year when he ran on a party platform that endorsed the Brown vs. Board of Education Supreme Court ruling. Democratic Congressman Adam Clayton Powell endorsed the Eisenhower-Nixon ticket for re-election that year. The majority of the black vote that had once been reliably Republican shifted to the Democrats starting with Franklin Roosevelt and the New Deal. The Republicans believed they could win back this voting block in 1956, and managed to increase the party's share from 24 percent in 1952 to 39 percent in 1956. Republicans could only dream of having that much of the black vote today.

Kennedy unsuccessfully sought the Democratic vice presidential nomination in 1956, but much of his support actually came from southern delegates. He was clearly a bona fide star going into 1960, so he treaded carefully on civil rights. He voted against bringing the 1957 civil rights bill up for a vote in the Senate, and then voted for amendments to weaken it. After that, he voted for the watered-down version. Kennedy even criticized President Eisenhower for taking action against Arkansas Democratic Gov. Orval Faubus, who sought to fight the desegregation order. In contrast to Nixon, Kennedy spent most of his career straddling the fence on civil rights. Going into 1960, Kennedy got the endorsement of Alabama Gov. John Patterson, a strong segregationist. [207]

Road to the Nomination

Kennedy's main rival in the Democratic primaries was Minnesota Sen. Hubert Humphrey, a champion of civil rights and future vice president. Just 13 states selected delegates through primaries that year. Humphrey planned to strike a blow in Wisconsin as a regional favorite son. But Kennedy had a better political operation and won the state. The next big contest was in West Virginia, where both candidates tried to outspend the other, normally a hopeless fight against a Kennedy. But West Virginia was also a

Tainted by Suspicion

southern state with a sizable number of low-income Protestants who weren't entirely sold on a Catholic New Englander born into wealth. Nevertheless, Kennedy's financial advantages were too insurmountable for Humphrey, who dropped out after losing West Virginia.

The nomination fight wasn't over, as the very powerful Senate Majority Leader Lyndon B. Johnson of Texas mounted a challenge at the Democratic National Convention in Los Angeles. Kennedy won on the first ballot, but tapped Johnson to be his running mate as a means to pull in southern voters. Kennedy delivered an awe-inspiring acceptance speech about how the nation stood...

> ...on the edge of a New Frontier—of the 1960s—a frontier of unknown opportunities and perils-a frontier of unfilled hopes and threats.

In 1860, the Republican National Convention was held in Chicago to nominate "Honest Abe" for president. A century later, the party would gather again in Chicago to nominate "Tricky Dick" for president. Nixon hoped to repeat the success of Abraham Lincoln, the first Republican to win a presidential election.

The vice president faced little opposition for the nomination. New York Gov. Nelson Rockefeller considered mounting a challenge but declined. Arizona Sen. Barry Goldwater got the votes of 10 delegates at the convention, but did not make a strong push that year. Nixon chose U.S. delegate to the United Nations Henry Cabot Lodge, a former Massachusetts senator, to be his vice presidential candidate, believing it would deprive Kennedy of winning his home state.

A Gallup poll in late August showed Nixon and Kennedy tied at 47 percent, with 6 percent undecided. So despite peace and prosperity under Eisenhower, voters found Kennedy a little more likable than Nixon, they just weren't certain about turning over the keys to him during the Cold War.[208]

Conservatives and Liberals

Knowing the popularity of Eisenhower, Nixon argued for continuity. Kennedy argued for turning the page for a new generation, and that the country was in a "conservative rut" under the Republicans—positioning himself as another Roosevelt.

Regardless of how JFK tried to position himself, on the issues, one might have a tough time today with the conservative and liberal labels—chiefly with Kennedy, who would at least be a moderate Republican by modern standards and almost certainly would be too far right for the Democratic party.

Kennedy believed in supply side economics before it was called supply side economics, campaigning on across-the-board tax cuts to rev up the economy. Further, he was a defense hawk and a staunch anti-communist. That said, if Kennedy had lived, he might not have gone as far as Johnson did with the Great Society programs, but there is no evidence he found such growth in government to be repugnant.

As for Nixon, it might be a bit much to call him a liberal, particularly in 1960. Eisenhower actually put him on the ticket in 1952 to attract conservatives after Nixon's impressive handling of the Alger Hiss case. Nixon had strong anti-communist credentials and was strong on defense issues. Like Eisenhower, he supported fiscal prudence, but was not eager from a political standpoint to dismantle the New Deal, only prevent its further expansion.

When Nixon finally became president in 1969, he was by no means a conservative, growing the government, establishing the Environmental Protection Agency and supporting price and wage controls. He also took America off the gold standard. Who is to say he would have taken this approach in the early 1960s? What's clear is that Nixon didn't think government was the problem.

Religion and Debates

One critical moment in the campaign came when Kennedy sought to address questions about his Catholicism. The religion questions for Kennedy came up in a similar way in 1960 that such questions came up for Mitt Romney in 2012 about his Mormon faith, with muttering about who he would be loyal to.

Kennedy spoke to a group of Protestant pastors in Houston and did a question and answer forum where he talked about his belief in the separation of church and state to allay any fears his White House would be taking orders from the Vatican.

To tackle the questions about whether he had the same gravitas as Nixon, he sought to debate the vice president, an event that would revolutionize presidential campaigns for decades.

Nixon had debated Nikita Khrushchev in the famous "Kitchen Debate." He and supporters thought there was little reason for him to worry about debating Kennedy. Kennedy had done well with mastering TV, which he knew would be key. The four debates were carried live on network television—the only channels available in those days and on radio stations.

Nixon was expected to win and did win—for those listening on the radio at least—regarding thoughtful answers and well articulated points. However, Kennedy owned the debates on TV, which was far more valuable. The first debate, with 70 million viewers, occurred after Nixon had gotten out of the hospital because of an infection caused by a severe cut. Nixon seemed uncomfortable while Kennedy seemed confident in the TV images.

The debates were a watershed event for Kennedy in putting him on an even footing with Nixon and casting him as presidential. He managed to get a three-point lead afterwards, but the polls returned to a dead heat just before Election Day.

Jackie Robinson and Harry Bellefonte

Civil rights also loomed large. Kennedy's support for it—even if tepid—was enough to upset some southern states where the state Democratic parties opted against listing him on the ballot as the nominee, or at least as the only nominee.

During the campaign, baseball great Jackie Robinson, who broke the color barrier in his sport, endorsed Nixon for president, and said, "Senator Kennedy is not fit to be president of the United States."

A concerned Kennedy sought advice from popular black singer Harry Bellefonte. Bellefonte told the senator to get Martin Luther King Jr. on his side. Kennedy responded: "Why do you see him as so important? What can he do?" [209]

But a critical point—not only in the 1960 campaign, but also in American political realignment—came when Kennedy made a call to King's wife Coretta after the civil rights leader was jailed for a peaceful demonstration in Atlanta on Oct. 19. Nixon's advisors told him to at least make a public statement calling for King's release. But Nixon feared it would look as though he is criticizing Eisenhower's lack of action.

Kennedy worked with Georgia state Democratic officials to get King released, and made sure the public knew. The black vote for Republicans dropped 7 points from 1956, likely because this pivotal event made Kennedy look like a man of action. Had Nixon maintained the same 39 percent of black voters in 1960 that he and Eisenhower received in 1956, he likely would have at least carried the popular vote or won outright the 1960 election.

Bruce Bartlett, in his book *Wrong on Race: The Democratic Party's Buried Past* projected that had Nixon carried the same portion of black votes in 1960 as Eisenhower-Nixon got in 1956, he would have carried the two key states of Illinois and Texas, but also New Jersey and Michigan. [210]

Alabama 'Absurdity'

The Solid South was far less solid for Democrats than in the past. The region's movement toward Republicans marginally began in 1928 but was interrupted by the New Deal. Then in 1952, Eisenhower broke the Democratic stronghold by winning Tennessee, Virginia and Texas. In 1956, Eisenhower carried these states, and added Kentucky and Louisiana.

The Rutherford B. Hayes view about the South had Republican values—with the exception of race—was at long last showing signs of becoming true. This was extremely worrisome to Democrats and prompted them to crank up racial politics in their own borders, even though the national Democrat realized it was no longer a winning strategy.

Several southern states—instead of listing candidates on the ballots—listed the actual names of the slate of electors that were pledged to a candidate. That is, of course, what people in every state are voting for in a presidential election, a slate of electors pledged to a candidate, rather than the candidate.

Since the national Democrats were nominating a civil rights supporter for president, the southern states took action to allow their voters to support the Democratic ticket but not the national Democratic nominee—a means to avoid backing a Republican.

It was a convoluted mess and particularly in Alabama, where it was nearly impossible to know precisely who won the popular vote in 1960, even if it was an entirely fair election. Let's presume every Kennedy vote from Illinois, Texas or other states in question was an honest vote. The results coming out of Alabama still cast a large shadow over whether the recorded popular vote for 1960 is accurate.

The Alabama of 1960 had so few Republicans that winning a Democratic primary for any office was essentially equivalent to winning the election. If Alabama Democrats didn't support the national nominee, they could override the choice on a state ballot. This tradition began in 1948 when Alabama and other southern states made South Carolina Gov. Strom Thurmond the Democratic nominee, not placing President Harry Truman on the ballot. In the 1956 presidential election, Democrats in Alabama, Louisiana, Mississippi and South Carolina had "unpledged" electors who could vote for whomever they wished. [211] The unpledged delegates would continue into 1960. In 1964, Alabama would list its slate of electors pledged to its own Gov. George Wallace as the Democratic presidential nominee instead of President Johnson (Goldwater won the state's electoral votes that year). It was a truly odd system based almost entirely around racial politics. [212]

Mississippi and Louisiana had unpledged Democratic delegates as well. Kennedy Democrats won in Louisiana and lost in Mississippi.

In 1960, Alabama actually held a Democratic primary regarding its 11 electoral votes, where 35 Democratic electors ran individually. The primary contest included 24 unpledged electors—meaning they were not bound to vote for the national Democratic nominee—and 11 "loyalists," meaning they would support the party nominee. Theoretically, having 11 electors gave the "loyalists" an advantage against the splintered unpledged. It's likely the anti-Kennedy electors could have won had they been united behind a single candidate, but they were split, some backing Virginia Sen. Harry Byrd and others backing Thurmond. Democratic primary voters backed six anti-Kennedy or unpledged electors and five pro-Kennedy "loyalist" electors to be the Democratic slate on the November ballot. Thus, an Alabama vote for Democrats in the general election was a 6-5 split slate.

Alabama voters overwhelmingly voted straight ticket in elections, but as far as casting a vote for presidential electors it would be a 45.4 percent vote for Kennedy and a 54.6 percent vote for another Democrat.

The certainty is that a slate of Democratic electors defeated a slate of Republican electors in Alabama. Those six unpledged electors cast their vote for Byrd, who ultimately got 15 votes in the Electoral College. Had Byrd been listed as the sole Democratic nominee in Alabama, as in other southern states, he would have likely won all 11 electoral votes, bringing his tally to 20 and reducing Kennedy's to 298. So, this would not have been a game changer in the Electoral College result, but it likely would have changed the popular vote outcome.

The strange circumstances prompted some in the state to wonder if their vote in the presidential race actually mattered. The night before the election, Alabama Gov. John Patterson—who backed Kennedy—delivered a televised address urging state residents to vote Democrat in order to ensure they send a strong message for segregation.

After Election Day, some national publications, including the *New York Times*, noted that Kennedy may not have won the popular vote.[213] Congressional Quarterly estimated Nixon won the national popular vote by 60,000, based largely on Alabama.[214]

The CQ assessment might be the most accurate assessment, according to Sean Trende, a co-author of the *2014 Almanac of American Politics*, who wrote in Real Clear Politics:

> In the end, there are three ways to count the popular vote in Alabama: Allocate all Democratic votes to Kennedy, allocate all Democratic votes to Byrd, or allocate the Democratic votes proportionally between the two candidates. Two of those three methods result in a Nixon victory in the national popular votes. Historians choose the one that results in a Kennedy win. I don't think this is because of any conspiracy, nor is it due to bias. At the same time, though, I don't think it's because awarding Kennedy all of those votes is the best

> method either. Rather I think it's just due to a lazy counting of votes for Kennedy electors, combined with inertia. It's probably time for electoral historians to revisit that. [215]

Many counts—quite inaccurately—credit Kennedy for having carried the popular vote in Alabama even though his electors lost the state's Democratic primary, thus, lost the general. How much Kennedy electors lost the general is the question that the late George Mason University economist Gordon Tullock raised writing in the New York Review of Books in November 1988:

> The ultimate outcome was 324,000 votes for all eleven Democratic electors. The anti-Kennedy electors received eight thousand more votes than the pro-Kennedy electors. The popular vote is very difficult to disentangle.

He continued suggesting his own methods to make a determination:

> I personally would suggest that we simply discard all these votes in the popular total on the grounds that we can't tell what these voters thought. Another possibility would be to divide the popular vote cast for these eleven electors in the same ratio as the popular vote in the earlier primary. Either of these corrections would lead to Nixon having more popular votes nationally than Kennedy.

Francis Russell, an author and presidential historian, wrote in response:

> Given the Byzantine intricacies of Alabama politics, it

Tainted by Suspicion

> is indeed possible that Nixon's popular vote may have slightly exceeded Kennedy's in that close election.

Russell continued:

> There must have been considerable vote-splitting in 1960, for an anti-Kennedy elector topped the list with 324,050 votes, trailed by a pro-Kennedy with 318,303 votes. The 'Others' then, with some six thousand votes, take six electors whereas the Republicans with thirty times that total get no electors at all. This, as Professor Tullock points out, is an absurdity.

Russell presented his own model:

> There is no tabulating the vote exactly, but for a reasonable approximation one can divide 318,303 by eleven, multiply it by five for the pro-Kennedys and by six for the anti-Kennedys. The Kennedy Alabama total would then be 144,685 instead of the [Congressional] Quarterly's given 318,303. If we then deduct the 179,838 anti-Kennedy Alabama votes from the national total, then Nixon did have a final 64,165 vote plurality in the 68,828,960 votes cast.

Importantly, this would not have changed the result or the Electoral College, but allocating so many "other" votes to Kennedy cast obvious doubt on his supposed popular vote victory, as Russell added in the New York Review of Books:

> But if the Electoral College votes had been as close in 1960 as in 1876, the six anti-Kennedy electors from Alabama would have decided the election. Would they

219

> then have chosen Kennedy or Nixon? No one knows. [216]

Tullock did a further analysis for the January 2004 edition of *PS: Political Science and Politics*. University of Illinois at Urbana-Champaign professor Brian Gaines also did a similar study challenging the popular vote outcome in the March 2001 edition of the same journal. Gaines suggested adding up ballots cast for the 11 Democratic electors, then provide six-elevenths of the total to Byrd and five-elevenths of the total to Kennedy. That would have given Nixon a national popular vote victory of about 60,000 votes. [217]

'Down to the Wire'

The Electoral College totals didn't come down to Alabama. After a long night, Kennedy had 303 electoral votes to Nixon's 219, and Byrd's 15. What can be said with certainty is that 113,000 votes separated the Democrats and Republicans. Less certain is whether or how many of those Democratic votes in Alabama were for Kennedy.

However, the path to that result was complicated. Very similar to 2000, the networks would make mistakes early on election night.

Nixon and his team were in Los Angeles at 5 PM local time when CBS News on Eastern Time—8 PM called the election for Kennedy with just 8 percent of all totals in and West Coast polls still open. CBS News reporter Eric Sevareid said, "All of the computing machines are now saying Kennedy." Nixon campaign manager Leonard Hall approached awaiting reporters to let them know that wasn't the case in Nixon land, saying:

> We should put all those electronic computers in the junk pile. This one is going down to the wire. [218]

NBC also predicted Kennedy, but then reversed its prediction when the race was tighter that night. NBC called Ohio for Kennedy then called the state for Nixon.

The *New York Times* even went to press with a headline, "KENNEDY ELECTED PRESIDENT" before midnight. As the counting tightened up, the newspaper's managing editor Turner Catledge—worried about embarrassment—later confessed, he started to hope that "a certain Midwestern mayor would steal enough votes to pull Kennedy through." [219]

It was a reference of course to Chicago Mayor Richard Daley, known even before the 1960 race for doing whatever it takes to swing elections for his candidates in a city where stuffing ballot boxes was just business.

Nixon actually appeared to have a significant lead in Illinois—on track to win that state's 27 electoral votes. That greatly upset Sargent Shriver, the Illinois campaign manager for his brother-in-law Jack Kennedy, who couldn't believe what he was seeing while watching from the Kennedy compound in Hyannis Port, Massachusetts that night. The man who would go on to become the 1972 Democratic nominee for vice president recalled to the Washington Post:

> I was devastated. I thought that the fact that I had lost my state, Illinois, would mean that Kennedy would lose the presidency. ... I went back to my bedroom and almost cried myself to death.

At midnight Pacific Time, Nixon came to the Los Angeles ballroom to tell his supporters, "If the present trend continues, Senator Kennedy will be the next president of the United States."

When Kennedy aides at the compound on election night bemoaned the half-concession, JFK reportedly said, "Why should he concede? I wouldn't."

By the next morning, Illinois, Minnesota and Nixon's home

state of California were too close to call. When Nixon woke up he learned Kennedy and Johnson won Texas by 46,000 votes and Illinois by 9,000 votes—after a suspiciously overwhelming tide in Cook County turned out for Kennedy.

Eisenhower told Nixon he heard rumors of fraud in those two states, and thought Nixon should check it out, possibly even take it to court. Eisenhower however, reportedly thought better of that view, and advised Nixon against challenging the result. [220]

In the case of California, it was called for Kennedy, but its 32 electoral votes went to Nixon after the absentee ballots were counted. Meanwhile, Hawaii's three electoral votes went from Nixon back to Kennedy after a recount.

So while Republicans led court challenges, this race does not count as being disputed in the same sense as 1800, 1824, 1876 and 2000. That's because Nixon conceded the contest the next day in a congratulatory telegram to Kennedy that his press secretary Herb Klein read publicly. Nixon felt his earlier half-concession sufficed for a speech. Also, unlike 1800, 1824, 1876 and 2000, another branch of government didn't make the ultimate decision on the executive branch.

In a meeting, campaign manager Hall and Kentucky Senator Thruston Morton, the chairman of the Republican National Committee, asked Nixon to demand recounts. And there was some speculation he would. But three days after the election, press spokesman Klein read another statement to reporters, "The vice president ran the race and he accepts the decision of the voters. The decision made on Tuesday stands."

'Gross and Palpable Fraud'

Though Nixon kept his distance, the battle for votes did not end with his concession. He wanted to be a gracious loser and keep his political options open, but his closest aides and the RNC were not taking the same approach.

Tainted by Suspicion

In his book *Six Crises* published in 1962, Nixon wrote he didn't challenge the result because he didn't want to send the wrong message to the world that in the United States, "the presidency itself could be stolen by thievery at the ballot box." In his memoir "RN," written after he resigned, Nixon wrote he also worried a challenge would mean, "Charges of 'sore loser' would follow me through history and remove any possibility of a further political career."

Just three days after the election on Nov. 11, Morton called for recounts in 11 states. Beside Illinois and Texas, also Delaware, Michigan, Minnesota, Missouri, New Jersey, New Mexico, Nevada, Pennsylvania and South Carolina. Days later, top Nixon campaign aides Hall and Robert Finch sent political operatives to eight of the 11 states to conduct "field checks." [221]

Sen. Dirksen was among the first Republicans in Washington to blame the Daley machine. This was followed by Goldwater, who said, Chicago had "the rottenest election machinery in the United States." [222]

Washington state Democratic Sen. Henry "Scoop" Jackson attacked the recount demands as a "fishing expedition." But even the *New York Times* editorial board, which endorsed Kennedy for president, said in a Nov. 26 editorial, "It is now imperative that the results in each state be definitively settled by the time the Electoral College meets." [223]

GOP operatives conducted field tests elsewhere but ultimately only found evidence of wrongdoing in Illinois and Texas.

In Texas, with 24 electoral votes, Fannin County—which Kennedy won overwhelmingly—4,895 were registered to vote but 6,138 votes were cast. In a single precinct in Angelica County, Texas, just 86 people voted, but the tally somehow broke down to 147 votes for Kennedy and 24 votes for Nixon. These were anecdotal, but enough for Republicans to call for a statewide recount. However, the Texas Election Board, controlled entirely by Democrats, rejected the call and certified Kennedy as the winner. [224] When the GOP filed suit, a federal judge claimed the party had no jurisdiction to challenge the results. [225]

RNC chairman Morton went to Chicago to establish the National Recount and Fair Elections Committee. RNC Treasurer Meade Alcorn as late as Nov. 23 insisted Nixon won the state.

Further, the Cook County state's attorney, Benjamin Adamowski—a Republican who himself lost his election by 25,000 votes—led the investigation in the early stages. A recount of 863 precincts found that Nixon's vote was undercounted by 943 votes. That didn't come close to cutting that 9,000 vote statewide lead.[226] But it doesn't answer the questions about where so many of Kennedy's votes actually came from—real or imagined people, living or dead. These are fraudulent practices that wouldn't be detected in a recount.

What some may have seen as cheating, Mayor Daley simply saw as politics, pointing to what others did. Daley was quoted as saying in the 2000 book *American Pharaoh: Mayor Richard J. Daley—His Battle for Chicago and the Nation* by Adam Cohen and Elizabeth Taylor:

> You look at some of those downstate counties, and it's just as fantastic as some of those precincts they're pointing at in Chicago. [227]

A Republican National Committee member in Chicago filed suit to challenge the results in Illinois, but Circuit Court Judge Thomas Kluczynski, a loyalist to the Daley machine, dismissed the lawsuit. Meanwhile, the Illinois State Board of Elections—which unlike the Texas board included Republicans—rejected the claims of the Republican National Committee.

Nixon won most counties in Illinois but lost Chicago by more than 450,000 votes. Local press began reporting that dead people were on the voter rolls and the *Chicago Tribune* concluded:

> ...*the election of November 8 was characterized by such gross and palpable fraud as to justify the conclusion that [Nixon] was deprived of victory.*

Earl Mazo, a Washington reporter for the *New York Herald Tribune*, began his investigation after he said Chicago reporters were "chastising" him and other national reporters for missing the real story.

He traveled to Chicago, obtained a list of voters in the suspicious precincts and began matching names with addresses. Mazo told *The Washington Post*:

> *There was a cemetery where the names on the tombstones were registered and voted. I remember a house. It was completely gutted. There was nobody there. But there were 56 votes for Kennedy in that house.* [228]

Mazo also found that Daley's charge that other counties were doing the same thing in favor of Republicans proved to be true—but nothing on the scale of what happened in Chicago.

In Texas, Mazo found similar circumstances.

The *New York Herald Tribune* planned a 12-part series on the election fraud. Four of the stories had been published and were republished in newspapers across the country in mid-December.

At Nixon's request, Mazo met him at the vice president's Senate office, where Nixon told him to back off. Nixon told him, "our country cannot afford the agony of a constitutional crisis" in the midst of the Cold War. [229] Mazo recalls:

> *I thought he was kidding but he was serious. I looked at him and thought, 'He's a goddamn fool.'*

Mazo didn't back off and Nixon called his editors. The newspaper did not run the rest of the series. "I know I was terribly disappointed. I envisioned the Pulitzer Prize." [230]

But elsewhere, Republicans didn't find as much chicanery. In New Jersey—a state known for corruption as much as Illinois—Republicans got court orders for recounts in five counties, but turned up no evidence of foul play and on Dec. 1 conceded the recount found no major discrepancies. Kennedy won the state with 22,091 votes. [231]

The RNC dropped its case after the Electoral College certified Kennedy as president on Dec. 19, and despite his campaign operatives and the RNC's involvement, Nixon had no fingerprints on any of the legal challenges—presumably how he wanted it.

It's possible had he taken the hands-on approach that Al Gore would take four decades later, things could have turned out differently. But Nixon likely thought he would lose and might have been right.

Though he sought to remain above the fray, Nixon told guests at a Christmas party in 1960 that "We won but they stole it from us." Pat Nixon was even angrier and honed in on the head of the Chicago Election Board:

> *If it weren't for an evil, cigar-smoking man in Chicago, Sidney T. Holzman, my husband would have been president of the United States.* [232]

The entire matter wasn't void of accountability.

Illinois state special prosecutor Morris Wexler, named to investigate charges of election fraud in Chicago, indicted 677 election officials, but couldn't nail down convictions with state Judge John M. Karns, another Daley loyalist. [233] It wasn't until 1962 when an election worker confessed to witness tampering in Chicago's 28th ward that three precinct workers pleaded guilty and served jail sentences.

Pulitzer-winning journalist Seymour Hersh reported hearing tapes of FBI wiretaps about potential election fraud. Hersh—whose books indicate he is a fan of neither Kennedy nor Nixon—believed Nixon was the rightful winner. Moreover, Hersh wrote that Hoover believed Nixon was the winner, but opted against pressing the case to the new attorney general. [234]

It would take a herculean level of partisan denial to believe there was no voter fraud in 1960 and that it was greatly advantageous to Kennedy. It's not even arguable that there was an attempt to steal the election for Democrats. The only debatable point: was the election stolen?

Analysis suggests that Kennedy would have at least won in the Electoral College without the fraud.

Edmund Kallina Jr., a professor of history at the University of Central Florida did an extensive study of the 1960 race that was part of his 1988 book, *Courthouse Over the White House*, that concluded there was massive fraud in Chicago and elsewhere in Illinois, but it did not determine the outcome. [235]

He further determined that most of the fraud benefited down ticket candidates. By that, he notes the special prosecutor was able to determine that Republican state's attorney Adamowski was cheated out of an estimated 10,000 votes, but Kallina does not believe that means Nixon was cheated out of that number of votes. Ultimately, Kallina determined it is still unknowable, writing:

> It appeared that in Chicago, Nixon was cheated out of several thousand votes, at a minimum, but the estimate was not so overwhelming that one can assert with confidence that Nixon was swindled out of Illinois's electoral votes. ... The fact is that no one can say with certainty who really carried Illinois in 1960. The available evidence is too fragmentary and inconclusive

to permit a final judgment.[236]

President Nixon, Eight Years Early

So, without the fraud, it's quite plausible Nixon would have been elected president in 1960, which might have dramatically changed history.

The Madman Theory is an alternative history novel by Harvey Simon written in 2013 that reimagines the Cuban missile crisis with Nixon as president, and asserts that Nixon would have brought the country to nuclear war with the Soviet Union if he were president.

But historians have their doubts about this view. University of Dayton history professor Larry Schweikart, who co-authored *A Patriot's History of the United States of America*, said:

> The Cuban missile crisis wouldn't have happened. Nikita Khrushchev respected Nixon after the 'Kitchen Debate'[237]

Schweikart added:

> Khrushchev thought Kennedy would be a pushover. Also, the Cuban Missile Crisis was precipitated by the Bay of Pigs. I don't think Nixon would have tried to assassinate Castro.

Conceding that the planned Bay of Pigs invasion was hatched when Eisenhower was in office, and further conceding the point that the later Nixon was prone to dirty tricks, Schweikart said he didn't think the Nixon of 1961 would be the type to launch an assassination attempt of a foreign leader, no matter how undesirable the leader.

Craig Shirley, a presidential historian, believes Nixon would have taken a more hawkish stance during the standoff over the Cuban missiles. Shirley said:

> Nixon would have conducted airstrikes to take out the missiles rather than a quarantine. [238]

He doesn't believe this would have led to nuclear war, but thinks it might have prompted the Soviets, "to move against West Germany or Turkey."

Civil rights laws might not have advanced as far had the election gone different, said Bruce Bartlett, a former domestic policy adviser for President Ronald Reagan and Treasury Department official for George H.W. Bush, who wrote the book *Wrong on Race*.

He explained that it isn't because of Kennedy, who was dragged into proposing a civil rights bill only after the TV images swayed public opinion with the brutality carried out against demonstrators in Birmingham, Alabama.

Bartlett said:

> I think Nixon would have been stronger on civil rights than Kennedy, but that is saying very little. However, I doubt he would have been as strong as LBJ. [239]

Johnson, in part because he was a southerner, was able to push a tougher civil rights bill than Kennedy had proposed. Further, the mourning of a slain president and lack of a strong Republican opponent in the 1964 election allowed Johnson to push a bolder legislative agenda with an eye on his legacy. Johnson signed both the Civil Rights Act and the Voting Rights Act.

Shirley said:

> JFK was slow on civil rights and Nixon was more progressive on that issue and would have pushed harder.

> *But it might not have gone through. With LBJ it took all Republicans and some Democrats to pass civil rights. It was a Democratic majority. It's questionable whether Nixon could have gotten that many Democrats. It's possible he would have since civil rights time had come.*

Schweikart is uncertain whether Nixon would have supported the Vietnam War. Although a hawk, he had a strong grasp of foreign policy. But Schweikart believes if Nixon had won in 1960, he would have fought the Vietnam War more effectively. Noting that President Johnson didn't follow the advice of military advisors to do around-the-clock bombing, Schweikart said:

> *Just as Nixon bombed Cambodia, Nixon would have ended it early.*

Vietnam under Nixon is also an uncertainty for Brooks Simpson, a presidential historian with Arizona State University. But Simpson thinks Nixon would have handled the matter more decisively than Kennedy or Johnson:

> *Nixon viewed himself as a foreign policy expert for good or ill. He would not have surrounded himself with people giving him direction from both sides. Under Nixon, we would not have seen the gradual descent into Vietnam. He would have made a decision.* [240]

Brooks is largely of the same view as Schweikart on the Cuban Missile crisis as well, believing it would not have happened:

> *Khrushchev would have been less willing to test Nixon's leadership. It's far less likely that Khrushchev would put missiles in Cuba if Nixon were president. Khrushchev didn't respect Kennedy.*

Tainted by Suspicion

Bigger questions arise regarding 1964.

Many credit Barry Goldwater with losing a landslide, but building a movement that paved the way for Ronald Reagan's political realignment election in 1980. Thus a Nixon victory might have prevented the rise of the conservative movement, or at least the rise of Reagan, whose presidency was so critical.

It was during the Goldwater campaign that Reagan really launched his political career with his "A Time for Choosing" speech. Two years later he was elected governor of California. Had the 1960 election gone the other way, that would have changed. Shirley, who authored three books on Reagan, most recently, *Last Act: The Final Years and Emerging Legacy of Ronald Reagan*, said:

> Reagan probably never would have given the speech because Nixon would have been re-nominated. He might still have run for governor of California but in 1970 instead of 1966 and by then, he would have really been a has-been and not a future conservative star. Or 1962 but both '62 and '70 were strong Democratic years, so it's possible Reagan would have lost to Pat Brown or to Jesse Unruh.

Shirley continued:

> Without Nixon losing in 1960, there is no Goldwater in 1964 and without Goldwater in '64, there is no Reagan speech. It was that speech which really, truly propelled him into national politics. So no national radio commentaries, no columns, no hundreds of speeches on the lecture circuit. Reagan would have faded into oblivion, like so many other actors who, while good, were not great.

By any measure, Reagan was a far better president than Nixon, so, if that's the case, the country might well have benefited from a dishonest 1960 election. This doesn't automatically mean the conservative movement would not have emerged, but it would have been delayed, said Adam Carrington, a professor of politics at Hillsdale College:

> With National Review already in existence and the number of conservatives growing, I think they still would have arisen and taken over the party. But doing so would have been more gradual and it isn't clear that Reagan would have gotten off the ground or at least as easily, since there would have been no context for his 'Time for Choosing' speech. [241]

Nixon likely would have faced either Johnson or Humphrey in 1964. In Johnson, he would have faced a similar problem with voter fraud from the LBJ machine in Texas. Whatever missteps Nixon might have made in his four to eight years as president in the early 1960s, he likely wouldn't have gone into history as a disgrace. The paranoia that drove him to the Watergate scandal was at least in part prompted by the view that he had to closely watch political opponents and play dirtier tricks than the Democrats. Simpson said:

> He would have been less haunted by the demons of the 1960 election. He believed the 1960 election was stolen and he believed that Kennedy and Johnson got away with doing the things he did. Had Nixon been elected in 1960, it would have been a more secure Nixon. He wouldn't be haunted by the Kennedy ghost.

PART V

George W. Bush vs. Al Gore

CHAPTER TWELVE

Clash of Dynasties

JUST AS PAST disputed elections involved rematches—John Adams vs. Thomas Jefferson, John Quincy Adams vs. Andrew Jackson—the 20th Century would end with a quasi-rematch of sorts.

The 2000 election would mark the Bush dynasty's opportunity to get revenge against the Clinton-Gore machine. It was the Bill Clinton-Al Gore ticket that trounced the George H.W. Bush-Dan Quayle ticket in 1992.

As *Time* magazine characterized the race:

> America has always loved rematches, fierce rivalries full of emotion and tangled history: Yankees and Dodgers, Frazier and Ali, 49ers and Cowboys. And now Bush-Cheney-Bush against Clinton-Gore-Clinton. Let the rematch begin. [242]

As president, Clinton presented two faces, one being a highly corrupt administration with endless federal investigations not only of the president and first lady Hillary Clinton, but also of administration officials. The other was of great prosperity. Bush's campaign architect Karl Rove even said that if the election had been about the economy and not Clinton's scandals, "We would have gotten our brains beat out."

The nation was already polarized going into the 2000 presidential race, resulting from the 1998 impeachment of President Clinton for perjury and obstruction of justice in connection with the Monica Lewinsky affair – which might have been the most minor but also most provable of all the Clinton scandals. Conservatives were outraged that a president would remain in office after committing felonies. Democrats insisted his crimes were of a personal nature and "don't rise to the level" of impeachment. The House impeached Clinton in December of 1998, but the Senate acquitted him in February with neither charge getting a majority vote—much less the two-thirds required for removal.

The public, in most opinion polls, sided with Democrats—expressing disappointment in Clinton but thinking it didn't quite warrant ousting him from office. The strong economy that helped Clinton win a resounding re-election victory in 1996 also made much of the public cautious about roiling the status quo. However, Clinton's personal approval ratings were much lower than his job approval ratings. Voters did not want to oust an elected president from office, but they weren't quite ready to reward him by electing his successor, Vice President Al Gore.

Even before Clinton was impeached, the big donors were coalescing around Texas Gov. George W. Bush, the son of the last Republican president.

Like 1824 and 1828, the battle in 2000 would be between the son of a former president and a Tennessee politician. Gore was nothing like Andrew Jackson and Bush—who had a cowboy shtick—was not very much like the aristocratic John Quincy Adams. While Jackson was a populist outsider running against the Washington machine, Gore was part of a Tennessee political dynasty embedded in the Washington establishment. The younger

Bush, though he grew up in politics, did not live a life in government as younger Adams had.

The younger Bush's White House biography even says:

> While John Adams had groomed his son to be president, George Bush, the 41st president, insisted he was surprised when the eldest of his six children became interested in politics, became governor of Texas, and then went on to the White House. [243]

Also, the 2000 election had astonishing similarities with 1876 in that Florida played a key role in both election aftermaths. In 2000, Florida played the only role.

What made it seem even more awkward is that the Republican candidate's brother, Jeb Bush, was the governor of Florida. The litigation that ensued also introduced a young attorney named Ted Cruz into the national political scene, who played a significant role behind the scenes.

The aftermath was assuredly different from 1876, 1824 and 1800. Congress played no role in the outcome. Though it seemed to most Americans at the time like it would never end, it only lasted 36 days—a mere five weeks. While 1800 and 1876 decision bumped up to the March inauguration day, in 2000, a winner had been selected well in advance of the January inauguration day.

Politics of Personality

Texas Gov. Bush pledged to be "a uniter not a divider" when running for president in 2000, and it seemed an attractive enough campaign pledge from someone having established a record as a pragmatic governor that reached across the aisle in Austin. The nation was reeling from crass scandals and divisive partisanship in Washington, and, as so often is the case, a governor from outside of Washington can provide the best solution politically. Bush frequently talked about how he would "change the tone in Washington."

What Vice President Gore had going for him was that he was viewed as very different from Clinton in terms of honesty and character despite being part of a corrupt administration, and despite his rather curious role in the campaign finance scandal from the 1996 election. Gore also had the Clinton record to run on, the strong economy, balanced budget and relative peace that kept public behind Clinton through the turmoil. But Gore was wrapped up in the untenable position of distancing himself from Clinton corruption while seeking to take some ownership of the governing record.

Another thing that helped Bill Clinton be such a survivor was his personal charisma and a near-Reaganesque ability to connect with Americans. Gore was nearly crippled on this front, never at ease before a crowd. When he would deliver a fiery speech it would just come across as if he was trying too hard to have personality. He was actually far better on the stump after he was out of politics, when referring to himself as a "recovering politician."

Ironically, Gore's personality traits were far more similar to George H.W. Bush than to that of Clinton. Meanwhile, George W. Bush's regular-guy persona was far more similar to Clinton than his own father, whose political problem was that he came across as out of touch. The younger Bush didn't quite have the political skills of Clinton. But he came across as affable, with no major skeletons even out of an admittedly wild youth. The proverbial candidate you'd rather have a beer with finally favored the Republicans—except Bush had stopped drinking.

The younger Bush was born in New Haven, Connecticut while his future president father was attending Yale University after serving in World War II. George H.W. and Barbara Bush moved to Midland, Texas. He would return to New Haven where he also graduated from Yale and later Harvard School of Business.

After returning to Midland, he married Laura Welch. Much of his early life was a string of unsuccessful business ventures. His first campaign came in 1978, for the 19th Congressional District in Texas. He beat two opponents in the Republican primary, but lost rather convincingly to Democrat Ray Hollis in November. This race was two years before his father first ran for president and ended up getting elected vice president.

In the 1980s, while his father was vice president, Bush became an evangelical Christian and stopped drinking. He worked on his father's 1988 presidential campaign, and attained controlling interest in the Texas Rangers baseball team. In 1994, the year Republicans swept control of both houses of Congress, Bush upset the popular Texas Governor Ann Richards, winning a close but decisive race over the incumbent. In 1998, Bush won a landslide re-election, with 68 percent of the vote, carrying much of the Hispanic vote.

Gore was also from a political dynasty, as the son of Sen. Albert Gore, Sr., who lost re-election in 1970 in part for his opposition to the Vietnam War. Al Gore Jr. joined the Army and served in Vietnam as an Army journalist. Two years before Bush launched his losing campaign for a Texas House seat, Gore was elected to his first of four terms in the U.S. House of Representatives in 1976. In a huge Republican year—1984— Gore managed to win a landslide victory in his state for a U.S. Senate seat. He took up environmental causes in the Senate, building liberal bona fides, while still having a mostly moderate record to endear him to the Democratic Leadership Council, a coalition of centrist Democrats, many who pushed him for president in 1988.

Gore earned a reputation for going for the jugular in the 1988 Democratic primary, trotting out the Willie Horton narrative to attack frontrunner Michael Dukakis, accusing the Massachusetts governor of being soft on crime. That didn't help Gore, who dropped out and eventually endorsed Dukakis for president. But it did help the elder Bush when Republican supporters used Horton in one of the most effective TV ads in the history of presidential campaigns. Gore easily won a second Senate term in 1990, and Clinton tapped him for the Democratic ticket in 1992.

Primary Problems

Unlike the previous years covered, by 2000, the presidential nominations were almost entirely decided by primary voters, while the party conventions were mere coronations and pep rallies.

In the early stages of 1999, it appeared that Bush had his party's nomination locked up certainly in terms of big Republican donors. His "compassionate conservative" message was sort of the GOP version of Clinton running as a "New Democrat," a variation of moving the party to the center.

Gore, on the other hand, looked to have a challenge ahead in former professional basketball player Bill Bradley, who served as a New Jersey senator. Bradley seemed to have impeccable character, was popular, and began as a prolific fundraiser. At one point, he was tied with Gore in New Hampshire. Bradley was a viable candidate, and the only one to challenge Gore. Notable Democrats such as Democratic House Minority Leader Richard Gephardt of Missouri and Sen. Bob Kerrey of Nebraska opted to sit out the election. This also seemed to be to Bradley's advantage, as there would be no one else to split the anti-Gore vote.

But on the stump, Bradley sometimes came across as a waxing college professor who actually made the notoriously drab Gore seem pretty darn energetic. Bradley fizzled without winning a single primary. To fend off the challenge, Gore was particularly ugly—calling out Bradley for having supported the Reagan economic plan in the 1980s and challenging his liberal bona fides. During a debate in front of a predominantly African American audience in Harlem, Gore said of his opponent, "Racial profiling practically began in New Jersey, Senator Bradley." [244]

The surprise was on the Republican side where Arizona Sen. John McCain thrashed Bush in the New Hampshire primary, sending shockwaves not only with a victory but also for the 20-point margin. Other Republican presidential candidates, such as billionaire magazine publisher Steve Forbes, activist Gary Bauer, Utah Sen. Orrin Hatch, and former ambassador Alan Keyes, all fell by the wayside as it became a two-man contest between Bush and McCain for the nomination. McCain, widely admired for having been a prisoner of war for five years during the Vietnam War, was a moderate Republican able to draw Democratic votes in open primary states.

It was a somewhat rare instance actually when both the establishment and the insurgent were moderates. Though up to this point, Bush's entire campaign was predicated on being a different kind of centrist Republican, the early success of McCain prompted Bush to move to the right to shore up the conservative vote. It was in South Carolina—where rumors emerged that McCain had fathered a black child, a reference to his adopted daughter from Bangladesh—that Bush capitalized. Team McCain was sure that Bush's campaign architect Karl Rove was behind the rumors, but there wasn't proof that tied it directly to the Bush campaign.

To combat the barrage of innuendo, McCain cut an ad in which he said that Bush was "twisting the truth like Clinton." The ad backfired on McCain far more than any of the negativity aimed at him. There were things acceptable for Republicans to say about one another in the heat of a primary. Comparing their opponent Bill Clinton wasn't among them. Though polls initially showed South Carolina was too close to call, Bush defeated McCain in the state by 12 points. McCain's campaign collapsed, as he managed to win only six more states before dropping out and endorsing Bush.

Clinton Fatigue

Oddly, Bush and Gore were much softer on one another than they were their primary opponents. The shots they took at one another weren't out of the ordinary. Republicans were obviously going to take advantage of Gore's awkward Clinton problem. Gore's team sought to play up Bush's occasional mispronunciations to cast him as not bright enough to be president.

Shortly before the Republican National Convention was held in Philadelphia. Bush—who had been seeking to stand on his own record—tapped his father's Defense secretary, Dick Cheney, to be vice president. Cheney had been a congressman from Wyoming and also President Gerald Ford's White House chief of staff—thus setting up a media narrative that Bush sought "gravitas" for the ticket.

Speaker after speaker at the Philadelphia convention referred to the "Clinton-Gore administration" and Cheney gave a memorable acceptance speech:

> *Mr. Gore will try to separate himself from his leader's shadow, but somehow we will never see one without thinking of the other.*

During his speech accepting his party's nomination, Bush acknowledged the good economy, but told the convention, "Instead of seizing this moment, the Clinton-Gore administration has squandered it." He then called for "prosperity with a purpose."

Gore had not yet chosen a running mate, but *Time* wrote, "Bush made the decision for him. He picked Bill Clinton." [245]

Bush got a 17-point bounce from the convention. Gore's team had to address the Clinton fatigue matter and did so with its choice of moderate Connecticut Sen. Joe Lieberman to serve as vice president. Lieberman was the first Democrat in 1998 to speak out against Clinton on the Senate floor.

Lieberman said in the 1998 speech in the midst of the Lewinsky scandal:

> Such behavior is not just inappropriate, it is immoral and it is harmful, for it sends a message of what is acceptable behavior to the larger American family, particularly to our children.

Lieberman was known even before that as the conscience of the Senate. But this 1998 speech assured his place on the Democratic ticket two years later. The pick was also historic, in that Lieberman was the first Jewish candidate on any major party ticket.

The *Wall Street Journal* said:

> So once again Democrats are calling in the symbolic moral cavalry to save them from Bill Clinton's legacy. By making Connecticut Senator Joseph Lieberman his running mate, Al Gore has picked someone as far away from his president as he could go and still stay within his own party. ... Now, with his Lieberman selection, Mr. Gore is all but admitting that his boss could cost him the election. This is the price of putting your ethics in a blind Clinton trust. [246]

However, as Gore refused to let President Clinton campaign for him, Bush made a perplexing mistake. At each of his campaign rallies, he talked about restoring honor to the White House after the Clinton scandals. Though saying, "There is no question the president embarrassed the nation," when asked if Gore could restore honor to the White House, Bush answered, "I think he can ... I don't think Clinton is an issue as we go forward." [247]

Third Party Spoilers

Clinton was not Gore's only problem.

Consumer advocate Ralph Nader was the Green Party nominee for president and was polling as high as 8 percent. The far left Nader railed against the Clinton-Gore administration nearly as much as Republicans, but for different reasons. Clinton had sold out progressives, Nader would say:

> *The two parties have morphed together into one corporate party with two heads wearing different makeup. Every time I hear Al Gore say, 'I'm going to fight for you against big corporations, big insurance and big oil,' I say, where were you the last eight years?*

Nader traveled the country ripping Gore for supporting free trade and defense spending, and said, "These frightened progressives say I'm undermining my own legacy of reform. What they don't know is that the Democratic Party has already done it."

Nader drew big crowds, and if he captured 5 percent of the popular vote, the Green Party would be eligible for federal matching funds in the next presidential election—potentially building a new national political party

So Lieberman helped with the Clinton problem of winning over swing voters, but Nader created a Democratic base problem.

When the Democrats held their convention in Los Angeles, Gore delivered a speech that might have made Tennessee icon Andrew Jackson proud. He departed from his moderate record to start an "us vs. them" campaign reminiscent of Jacksonian Tennessee Democratic tradition, announcing:

> *And that's the difference in this election. They're for the powerful, and we're for the people. ... I know one thing about the job of the president. It is the only job in*

> *the Constitution that is charged with the responsibility of fighting for all the people. Not just the people of one state, or one district; not just the wealthy or the powerful—all the people. Especially those who need a voice; those who need a champion; those who need to be lifted up, so they are never left behind.*

In an obvious slur at Clinton, Gore said, "I stand here tonight as my own man, and I want you to know me for who I truly am." Gore would spend much of the campaign repeating, "I am my own man."

After wrapping up the speech, Gore famously gave his then-wife Tipper Gore a big kiss on stage—an unusual move for nominee after an acceptance speech—that was perceived as another means of telling America he isn't Clinton, because Al Gore loves his wife. Almost no one would have suspected at the time that the Clinton marriage would outlast the Gore marriage.

Nader wasn't the only third party candidate. Former Nixon and Reagan White House official Pat Buchanan was the Reform Party nominee, and there was plenty of reason to be concerned about a candidate who had significant Republican support four years earlier and had federal matching funds to be competitive. Buchanan won the New Hampshire Republican primary in 1996, and was courted by third parties that year, but endorsed eventual Republican nominee Bob Dole. Had he run third party in 1996, he might have done well, similar to Ross Perot in 1992.

The Reform Party, founded by Perot, was eligible for federal matching funds, but the conservative Buchanan split much of Perot's centrist coalition, thus had little party infrastructure behind him. Though initially he was a major concern to Republicans, Buchanan barely ever broke 1 percent in the polls. In 2000, with the Supreme Court on the line and the chance to rebuff Clinton, voters on the Right were far less inclined than voters on the Left to make a statement in their votes. They wanted to win. Purists could have their say another year. Interestingly, Nader would be the Reform Party nominee in 2004.

Rats and Chains and 30-Second Spots

Among the harshest campaign commercials was one by the NAACP Voter Fund, which attacked Bush for not signing a hate crimes bill in Texas. The ad dealt with the brutal murder of James Byrd who was tied to a vehicle and dragged to death. The commercial showed a chain being pulled behind a pickup truck, with an eerie metallic clanking as a female voice said:

> I'm Renee Mullins, James Byrd's daughter. On June 7, 1998 in Texas my father was killed. He was beaten, chained, and then dragged three miles to his death, all because he was black.
>
> So when Governor George W. Bush refused to support hate-crime legislation, it was like my father was killed all over again. Call Governor George W. Bush and tell him to support hate-crime legislation. We won't be dragged away from our future. [248]

The Republican ad that garnered the most attention was a message that supposedly used subliminal messages. An ad attacking Gore's prescription drug plan had the words move across the screen saying, "BUREAUCRATS DECIDE." However, at one point, only the letters "RATS" were seen scrolling across the screen. [249]

It went almost unnoticed until a Gore campaign volunteer reported to the campaign officials who managed to make hay out of it, getting the *New York Times* to cover the matter. It was on the screen for one-thirtieth of a second, but the *New York Times* asserted it was the largest image on the commercial. The *Times* coverage later prompted all the networks newscasts to cover the matter.

The distraction of the "RATS" ad obscures the fact that both candidates had a lot in common, in that they both supported a Medicare prescription drug plan. Bush pushed for a tax cut, hoping not to get burned the way his father did on a "no new taxes" pledge, which Gore opposed. But aside from his populist rhetoric, Gore wasn't proposing any new sweeping federal programs that Bush wasn't supporting. It's one reason Nader said the contest was between Bore and Gush, or twiddle dumb and twiddle dumber. The highest import dividing the candidates was Supreme Court nominees, where it was believed as many as four vacancies could open.

Another uproar came when a week before the election, Fox News reported that in 1976, Bush's wild youth included an arrest for drunken driving in Maine. The impact of the late report on the election is questionable.

Electoral College Expectations

During the three presidential debates Gore smirked, rolled his eyes and sighed—all of which were off-putting. Nevertheless, Bush had hardly sealed the deal. The race was tight. Gore seemed to have made the case that he was not Clinton to a sizable number of voters and possibly a majority. Bush, meanwhile, sometimes fell short of seeming ready to be leader of the free world, at least to enough voters.

Speculation abounded ahead of the election that Bush would win the popular vote, but Gore would win the Electoral College. There were numbers to demonstrate this. Days before the election Bush was leading Gore by four points in the Gallup poll, by three points in the Zogby poll and by one point in the CBS News/New York Times poll. However, Gore was running well in battleground states. Columbia University political science professors even released a paper ahead of the election projecting that Gore would win the Electoral College so long as he lost the popular vote to Bush by no more than 2.2 points.

The Columbia paper's co-author Robert Erikson told the *Los Angeles Times*:

> Gore would be the favorite as long as he doesn't lose by more than that amount. The reason is that most of the battleground states are a little bit more pro-Gore than the nation overall.

Pollster John Zogby told the *L.A. Times*:

> Where Bush leads he leads big, where Gore leads he leads small. [250]

That meant Bush could have a popular vote lead, but Gore could win enough important states to take the election.

Both camps were prepared for this. Gore's team was prepared to argue fidelity to the Constitution while Republicans hoped to make a public case to electors to honor the will of the people.

CHAPTER THIRTEEN

36 Days

ULTIMATELY, THERE JUST wasn't a lot of enthusiasm for either candidate. Just 51 percent of eligible voters showed up on Election Day. Some pre-election polls showed Bush with a comfortable lead of up to five points.

The first Tuesday of November in 2000 came the same day as the Election Day 1876—on the seventh. Half the country may have had better things to do than follow the Bore and Gush contest before election, but a decisive majority of Americans were glued after Election Day.

One who did reportedly take notice was Justice Sandra Day O'Connor, the slightly conservative-leaning swing vote on the Supreme Court at the time. She attended a gathering on election night with friends. When Florida was called for Gore early, O'Connor was said to have looked visibly shaken, leaving the room, saying, "This is terrible." Her husband reportedly told others, "She's very disappointed because she was hoping to retire." [251] The reported exchange fed into future conspiracy theories about the court's involvement.

The networks were relying on exit polls from Voter News Service. VNS called Florida early Tuesday night before polls had closed in the heavily Republican panhandle region in the north. But later the networks changed their projection to Bush having won the state. Then the networks were uncertain. As various swing states swung to one candidate, Florida remained a mystery.

Bush would almost certainly have had significantly more votes had the networks not called Florida before polls closed in the heavily-Republican Panhandle, which is in the Central time zone. Gore campaign strategist Bob Beckel said that Bush lost at least 8,000 votes in the Panhandle alone because of the incorrect reporting.

Meanwhile, Republican polling firm McLaughlin and Associates estimated that Bush lost 11,500 votes because the networks reported the polls were closed in the Panhandle. Economist John Lott estimated between 7,500 and 10,000 voters in Republican counties were dissuaded from showing up. [252]

Gore lost Tennessee, the state he previously represented in the U.S. Senate, and carried twice on a ticket with Clinton. In this case, he likely lost the state and other southern states because of President Clinton. To be fair, Bush lost his birth state of Connecticut, a state his grandfather Prescott Bush represented in the U.S. Senate, but that was widely expected to go to the Democrats, particularly with Lieberman on the ticket.

By around 2 AM, it appeared Bush had won Florida's 25 electoral votes with 97 percent of the votes in, by just 950 votes—close by any standard. But it was going to get much closer. Gore made a call to Bush, conceding the race. However, just before delivering his concession speech in Nashville, he was stopped as staff got further word it was too close to call in Florida. Florida Attorney General Bob Butterworth called the Gore team in Tallahassee after getting word of the concession.

"What's he doing? He can't concede," Butterworth said, explaining a race this close triggers an automatic recount in Florida.[253]

In one of the most dramatic moments in the history of

presidential election nights, Gore called to un-concede.

"Circumstances have changed dramatically. The state of Florida is too close to call," Gore told Bush at about 2:30 AM on Nov. 8.

"Are you saying what I think you're saying? Let me make sure I understand. You are calling to retract that concession?"

"Don't get snippy about it," Gore said, in what was likely the most memorable line of the entire election even though it was never broadcast. Gore told Bush if Florida was called for the governor, he would concede, but now, it's too early.

Bush responded, "My little brother says it's over."

Gore said, "I don't think this is something your little brother gets to decide."

What else could Bush say?

"Do what you have to do," Bush responded.

The War for Florida

Gore's legal team, led by former Clinton Secretary of State Warren Christopher, requested a hand recount of ballots in Palm Beach, Dade, Broward and Volusia counties—all Democratic strongholds. Of course, the campaign would hunt for votes where they were most likely to find them. But there was a practical basis. Hand counts in all 67 Florida counties would be nearly impossible, and would have met with public resistance. Local governments in Democratic-run counties were happy to pitch in to produce a Gore presidency.

In the popular vote, Gore beat Bush nationally with 50,996,582 to 50,456,062. That's a half million votes. Not insignificant, roughly what Richard Nixon beat Hubert Humphrey by in 1968. Neither candidate had 270 votes in the Electoral College. Gore had 266 votes. Bush had 246. The 20-electral vote spread was not that different from Hayes-Tilden.

Contrasting the know-it-all Gore to the frat boy Bush, a

Tainted by Suspicion

common joke was: Who knew that Gore would be the popular one while Bush would do well in college? Doing well in college was of course contingent on winning Florida.

Newly-elected New York Sen. Hillary Clinton said:

> *I do believe that in a democracy we should respect the will of the people. And to me, that means it's time to do away with the Electoral College and move to the popular election of our president.*

Albert Gore, Sr. is said to have raised his son to be president in contrast to "Dubya" who surprised his family. Some Democrats pondered whether Gore—still young enough—should simply run again in four or eight years, similar to Nixon, and avoid looking like a sore loser. But he was too close to the presidency to step away. Gore reportedly told aides:

> *I'm not like George Bush. If he wins or loses, life goes on. I will do anything to win.* [254]

Other Democrats would insist the popular vote should be followed, while Republicans said the Constitution should be upheld. That's a slight shift in the argument each camp was preparing to make before the election.

On Thursday Nov. 9, the tally was completed showing Bush leading by 1,784 votes out of nearly 6 million votes cast in Florida, narrow enough to trigger an automatic machine recount under Florida law in all 67 counties. The machine recount was completed and Bush's lead was slashed to just 327 votes over Gore. Bush could still say the 6 million votes were counted and recounted and he won twice.

Finding more votes for Gore would next require hand counting ballots. This whole ordeal presented a new glossary of terminology such as butterfly ballots, chads (hanging, dimpled pregnant and various other varieties).

Rage over Butterflies

The butterfly ballots looked like an open book, with different candidates down each side.

Bill Daley, former Clinton chief of staff and son of the infamous Chicago Mayor Richard Daley who played such a big role in swinging the 1960 election to John F. Kennedy, was a key member of the Gore legal team. He was considerably more aggressive than Warren Christopher. Daley didn't waste time with academic arguments over the Electoral College. He instead insisted Gore won Florida. He called the butterfly ballots "deliberately confusing." He said:

> I am announcing we will be working with voters from Florida in support of legal actions to demand some redress for the disenfranchisement of more than 20,000 voters in Palm Beach County.

Daley argued that since Gore received 63 percent of the valid votes in Palm Beach County, he should receive 63 percent of the disputed 19,000 votes as well for the overvotes. As it turned out, the Gore legal team did not sue for overvotes, but only for undervotes.[255]

Reform Party candidate Pat Buchanan—whose name appeared close to Gore's name on the butterfly ballot—got 3,000 votes in Palm Beach County, prompting Democrats to say it's impossible such an ultra-conservative politician could get such a high number of votes from a large Jewish population.

Some voters appeared to have voted for both Gore and Buchanan, or overvotes. A ballot marked for two candidates would typically be a spoiled ballot, or disqualified. The design was odd, but if it confused anyone, it couldn't be blamed on a

Tainted by Suspicion

Republican conspiracy. The ballots were designed by a Democrat, Theresa LaPore, Palm Beach County election supervisor, and approved by both parties for use. Democrats estimated there were 61,000 undervotes. [256]

Still, even before polls closed in Palm Beach County, Democrats sought to exploit this. The Gore campaign contacted a Texas marketing firm, TeleQuest. Provided with a list of Democratic voters, the firm contacted 5,000 Florida voters and informed them:

> *Some voters have encountered a problem today with the punch card ballots in Palm Beach County. These voters say they have said that they believe that they accidentally punched the wrong hole for the incorrect candidate ... If you have already voted and you think you may have punched the wrong hole for the incorrect candidate, you should return to the polls and request that the election officials write down your name so that this problem can be fixed.* [257]

The marketing firm was able to collect 2,400 names of voters. The Gore campaign did not use these names on Election Day since it was not yet apparent they would need to.

When a paper ballot was partially punched, the hanging piece of paper was called a chad. This was an undervote, if it caused the ballot not to be counted. "Dimpled" and "pregnant" chads were essentially the same thing, a ballot with a hole pushed forward but still completely there. Based on overvotes and undervotes, the Gore legal team wanted the state to discern voter intent. Hanging chads were pieces of paper hanging from one corner. Swing door chads were chads connected to the ballot at two corners. Tri-Chads were attached at three corners. The almost ridiculous images beamed to TVs across the country showing Florida election officials holding punch card ballots up to the light to determine if someone had tried to punch a hole. During the process, these election workers had Democratic and Republican operatives keeping a close eye on them. In some cases, election boards began altering their own rules because existing rules were unworkable in ascertaining voter intent.

As for Buchanan votes, the 3,000 votes he got as an active third party candidate in Palm Beach County in 2000 is fewer than half as many votes as he received in Palm Beach County during the 1996 Republican primary. Buchanan got those 8,000 votes after he had suspended his 1996 campaign. A Buchanan cousin was also running a strong grassroots campaign for him during 2000 in the county. [258] So, even though Buchanan publicly said he believed most of his votes were for Gore, it seems rather unlikely given the support he received as an inactive candidate four years earlier.

The Rev. Jesse Jackson, an activist who ran twice for the Democratic presidential nomination in the 1980s, led demonstrations outside the Palm Beach County government building, chanting "We want justice." Jackson told the crowd, "Every vote must count and to this point, we do not know who won the election because all the votes have not been counted." [259]

Technically the votes had been counted twice by this point, but not hand counted or fully researched for voter intent.

On Nov. 11, Palm Beach County officials voted to manually recount all 462,657 votes cast in the Democratic-leaning county. The Bush campaign, with former George H.W. Bush Secretary of State James Baker heading the legal team, sued in U.S. District Court to block the hand counts.

The next day, Volusia County began to do a hand recount. On Nov. 14, the day that Florida election officials were set to certify results, the Volusia County's hand recount was completed. It cut Bush's lead to 300 votes.

Disenfranchising Soldiers

Democratic lawyers also began targeting the overseas absentee ballots from the military—which seemed to be more likely Republican voters. The attorneys threatened to sue Seminole County, where election officials corrected errors on thousands of applications for absentee ballots—many for military personnel. Democrats also targeted Duval County, which had one of the heaviest military populations in the United States. This prompted Republicans to say Democrats wanted to disenfranchise military voters.

Before this, Democrats had been able to control much of the message of demanding that every vote be counted. But when a memo surfaced from Democratic attorney Mark Herron that laid out a legal strategy for disqualifying military votes, Democrats found themselves on the defense. Despite a public relations problem, Democrats managed to disqualify 1,420 military ballots over various legal technicalities by Nov. 17.

Retired Army General Norman Schwarzkopf, hero of the Gulf War and Bush supporter, issued a strong statement, asserting:

> It's a very sad day in our country when the men and women of our country are serving abroad and facing danger on a daily basis in places like Bosnia, Kosovo or on ships like the USS George Washington, yet because of some technicality out of their control, they are denied the right to vote for the president of the United States, who will be their commander-in-chief.

The general added:

> Other ballots that have already been counted twice are being counted a third time. For the sake of fairness

> *alone, these armed forces ballots should be tallied.* [260]

Democrats began to backtrack. Joe Lieberman actually said on NBC's *Meet the Press* that military ballots should get "the benefit of the doubt." Florida's Attorney General Bob Butterworth, who ran Gore's campaign in the state, sent a letter telling election officials:

> No man or woman in military service to this nation should have his or her vote rejected solely due to the absence of a postmark. [261]

By this time, though the damage had been done, both for military members and for the Democrats public relations.

Some good news came for the Bush campaign on Nov. 18 when his lead grew to almost 1,000 over Gore because of absentee ballots that were counted.

State Courts

Florida's top election official, Secretary of State Katherine Harris, gave counties until 2 PM on Nov. 15 to provide reasons why they would need to conduct another recount. Democrats expressed concern that Harris, the honorary chairwoman of Bush's Florida campaign, was the chief election official presiding over the matter. On Nov. 15, Harris turned down requests from both Broward and Palm Beach counties to conduct hand counts. With the backing of the Gore campaign, the counties took their case to the Florida Supreme Court with seven justices, all Democratic appointees. The state's high court sided with the counties and permitted the manual recounts in both Palm Beach and Broward to go forward. The Gore campaign hoped to scrounge enough votes to pull their candidate to victory.

In words Baker might well have regretted, he angrily said after the Florida Supreme Court's ruling that, "It's a sad day for

America and the Constitution when a court decides the outcome of an election." [262]

That said, the Bush campaign didn't set out to bring the matter before the highest court in the nation, but once the Florida high court had ruled, there was only one response—appeal.

With the state Supreme Court intervening in a positive way for Gore, Miami-Dade County, which had been waiting, announced it will conduct a hand recount.

'Trying to Kidnap Electors'

The Gore campaign talked a lot about overvotes, but did not make that part of the legal challenge. Gore campaign operative Bob Beckel said there isn't a legal case to be made for counting overvotes, but there is a moral case based on his belief that most of those votes were intended for Gore.

Beckel intended to make that moral case to Florida's electors—and perhaps electors in other states —who could be convinced to follow the will of the people. Gore did not need all of the state's electors, just four. For that matter, he didn't think it had to be limited to Florida. He thought demonstrating statistics to prove Gore's win could sway enough of the Bush electors to switch their votes since they were not legally bound.

The *Wall Street Journal* first reported that Gore's team:

> ...has been checking into the background of Republican electors with an eye toward persuading a handful of them to vote for Mr. Gore.

Beckel insisted afterwards he never had plans to try to blackmail electors to collect Gore votes, which he thought the article implied. But in an interview on Fox News on Nov. 17, Beckel said:

I'm trying to kidnap electors. Whatever it takes.

Beckel later explained what the Founders wanted:

The idea was that electors, early on, were to be lobbied.

Pro-Gore websites even started popping up listing the names and contact information of Republican electors across the country, asking the public to barrage them with demands to vote for Gore and follow the will of the people. Republican National Committee Chairman Jim Nichols sent an email to supporters asking them to "Help Stop Democratic Electoral Tampering." Responding to the chairman, Beckel said:

The Constitution gives me the right to send a piece of mail to an elector.

It never made a difference. No electors shifted, but it did serve as another twist as the 2000 election story unfolded—and another PR fumble for Democrats. [263]

'Stick with the Appeal'

The Florida Supreme Court ruled unanimously on Nov. 21 that the hand counts must be added to the statewide total if they could be counted by 5 PM on Nov. 26. Miami-Dade bowed out at this point, saying it could not meet the Nov. 26 deadline. The state Supreme Court actually rejected the attempt by the Gore team to force Miami-Dade to count their votes. Some canvassing boards in the state reinstated some of the absentee ballots, giving Bush another 176 votes.

Bush's appeals team was led by Theodore Olson, a senior partner at the prestigious firm of Gibson, Dunn & Crutcher. Among the stable of young attorneys working under Olson for the

Tainted by Suspicion

Bush campaign was Ted Cruz, who had clerked for Chief Justice William Rehnquist. The young up and coming Cuban-American attorney from Texas had worked on the Bush campaign as well. Olson would go on to become the solicitor general of the United States. Cruz became the solicitor general of Texas, then U.S. senator, then a presidential candidate. [264]

After the defeat by the Florida Supreme Court, the Bush legal team plowed through the pros and cons of appealing to the U.S. Supreme Court.

Another option was drop the appeal while he was in the lead, which would put political pressure on Gore to end the litigation. Further, this line of thinking went, continuing the process all the way to the U.S. Supreme Court would only give Gore's team more time to find votes.

Moreover, some were concerned Bush would lose if conservative justices were purists on states' rights issues. If the Bush team had taken this course, they could continue a legal fight, but it would be in the hands of the Democratic Florida Supreme Court to decide his fate. As Bush campaign policy director Josh Bolton recalled to the *Washington Post*, Bush told the team, "We're going to stick with the appeal because it's the right thing to do," and that he wanted it ratified by the Supreme Court so the public would believe it was legitimate. [265]

It was not lost on either side that Democrats, who have a strong preference for federal control, wanted to keep the matter in state courts, where they had a friendly state Supreme Court. Meanwhile, pro-states rights Republicans, skeptical of judicial supremacy, had pushed the matter into federal courts. Why? Simple answer. Plaintiffs typically look for the friendliest court they can find in any case. When the presidency is on the line, principles rarely matter.

A day after the Florida court's unanimous ruling, Bush's attorneys appealed to the U.S. Supreme Court, saying the state's court rewrote the state's election law, usurping the authority of the state legislature to determine presidential electors. That's because the Constitution granted only state legislatures the right to select electors. The Bush team also argued that counting selective Democratic counties was a violation of the one-man-one-vote principle of the Fourteenth Amendment because the votes in Miami-Dade, Broward, Palm Beach and Volusia counties would value the votes of those counties over the missing votes of 63 other Florida counties. The justices agreed to hear Bush's appeal of the Florida court's ruling.

On Nov. 26, the deadline day, Harris declared Bush to be the winner by 537 votes more than Gore. Democrats pointed out this did not include the Palm Beach County tally that was completed after the deadline on the same day. Gore's team sued Harris to contest the tally, but Leon County Circuit Court Judge N. Sanders Saul's rejected Gore's petition for an immediate hand recount of disputed ballots from Miami-Dade and Palm Beach counties, saying a hearing must first occur.

Before the entire case went to the highest court in the land, it was Ted Cruz, along with another attorney on the case Tim Flanigan, who determined a way out for the U.S. justices that for the most part would prefer not to enter a political dispute. The two attorneys cited case law that would allow the court to vacate the Florida court's decision and remand it back for reconsideration. They contacted Olson, who added it to the brief. Flanigan called it a "backdoor" for the court. [266]

December began with the Bush team arguing before the U.S. Supreme Court that the Florida Supreme Court acted improperly.

The U.S. Supreme Court seized on the Cruz-Flanigan idea in the brief. On Dec. 4, U.S. justices ordered the Florida Supreme Court to clarify its ruling on expanding the certification date. In a 5-4 ruling it halted that hand recount pending a hearing. For the majority, Justice Antonin Scalia wrote:

Tainted by Suspicion

> *Count first and rule upon legality afterwards is not a recipe for producing election results that have the public acceptance democratic stability requires.*

But in the dissent, Justice John Paul Stevens wrote:

> *Preventing a recount from being completed will inevitably cast a cloud on the legitimacy of the election.*

He added:

> *The Florida court's ruling reflects the basic principles, inherent in our Constitution and our democracy, that every legal vote should be counted.* [267]

The Florida state legislature voted mostly along party lines to call a special session to appoint electors on Dec. 12, six days before the Electoral College was set to meet. While the legislature picking electors before the court decided might seem controversial by modern standards, it might well have been the most constitutional step taken in the process. It also would have been a far preferable precedent for the state legislature to make the call than for the U.S. Supreme Court. It is, after all, the job of state legislatures to make such decisions.

On Dec. 6, Gore appealed his case calling for immediate hand recounts in Miami-Dade and Palm Beach counties to the Florida Supreme Court.

On Dec. 8, the Florida Supreme Court voted 4-3 to order immediate hand recounts of all undervotes, ballots in the state with no presidential vote recorded. The court in fact gave Gore more than he asked for in a decision that provided him with what would probably be 215 votes in Palm Beach County (even though the canvassing board found 174 votes) and another 168 votes in Miami-Dade County. Further, 9,000 votes could be recounted.

The majority opinion made no reference to the U.S. Supreme Court vacating the earlier ruling. This concerned Gore campaign aide Ron Klain, fearing the U.S. justices would see it as an insult. Klain, handling the political side of things, helped rally union supporter and Democratic attorneys from all over the country to come to Florida. [268]

Bolton recalled painting a gloomy picture for his boss in a phone call. Bolton recalled to the Washington Post:

> *I told him that the counting was bad for us from a PR standpoint because it posed the risk at some point Bush should fall into a deficit and then we'd have serious public relations problems.*[269]

In the parallel legal fights in the lower courts, Leon County Judge Terry P. Lewis, a Democratic appointee, ordered local boards to determine on their own the "intent of the voter." It was a gift to the Bush team because it meant the counting standard was arbitrary by locality, which potentially solidified the campaign's Fourteenth Amendment argument.

Bush campaign attorney George Terwilliger and Ben Ginsberg left the Leon County court room thrilled over their loss. Terwilliger bumped into Gore attorney David Boies, and said, "You know what David, we just won the case." Ginsberg said, "This is so bad, it's good." They recalled that Boies looked at them as if they were crazy. [270]

Supreme Court Decides

Expedited, the cases of Bush vs. Palm Beach County Canvassing Board and the case of Gore vs. Harris, both having reached the court, became the case of Bush v. Gore. Attorneys filed briefs on Dec. 10 and made oral arguments on Dec. 11.

This is where history has arguably been quite distorted,

intentionally or not. Most books and news story passively reference the "5-4" ruling by the court, which fits nicely with the narrative that a partisan Supreme Court set out to get their guy—Bush—installed in the White House.

The court waited until 10 PM on Dec. 12, two hours before the deadline in which the legislature had certified.

The conservative justices joined by liberals David Souter and Stephen Breyer ruled 7-2 in the decision siding with Bush that counting only selected areas of the state violated the equal protection clause of the Fourteenth Amendment. The decision reads:

> *Seven Justices of the Court agree that there are constitutional problems with the recount ordered by the Florida Supreme Court that demand a remedy. The only disagreement is as to the remedy ... None are more conscious of the vital limits on judicial authority than are the Members of this Court, and none stand more in admiration of the Constitution's design to leave the selection of the President to the people, through their legislatures, and to the political sphere. When contending parties invoke the process of the courts, however, it becomes our unsought responsibility to resolve the federal and constitutional issues the judicial system has been forced to confront.*

The decision goes on to describe the equal protection issues.

The opinion adds:

> *The State Supreme Court ratified this uneven treatment. It mandated that the recount totals from two counties, Miami-Dade and Palm Beach, be included in the certified total...Yet each of the counties used varying standards to determine what was a legal vote.*

Though seven justices sided with Bush on the equal protection argument, four of the liberals on the court insisted Florida should be given more time to count the votes—thus it's where the often repeated 5-4 ruling comes from.

This is not to dismiss the secondary ruling. Equal protection was the core of the argument, but it was a 5-4 vote that stopped the recount.

The majority opinion was unsigned, being "per curium" or from the court. But it's widely believed that Justice Anthony Kennedy wrote it. David Kaplan's book, *The Accidental Presidency*, describes Kennedy as "the justice who picked the president."

In the dissent, Justice Souter argued the matter should have been remanded to the Florida court with instructions to require a uniform standard. Souter further argued, "political tension could have worked itself out in Congress." If that's the case, the month of litigation certainly seemed a waste if Souter thought Congress should simply decide.

Behind the scenes, Souter worked to convince Kennedy to side with the liberals to give the state more time to tally votes under a uniform standard. If the votes couldn't be counted in time, then the Florida legislature and ultimately U.S. Congress could decide. Souter spoke to a group of prep school students a month after the decision about his frustration in Bush v. Gore, saying if only he had "one more day—one more day" he thought he could have convinced Kennedy to be on the other side of the 5-4 split. Souter told the students from Choate:

> It should be the political branch that issues political decisions. [271]

In another dissenting opinion, liberal Justice John Paul Stevens wrote:

> Although we may never know with complete certainty

> the identity of the winner of this year's presidential election, the identity of the loser is perfectly clear. It is the nation's confidence in the judge as an impartial guardian of the rule of law.

When the decision came forward late that night, CBS News anchor Dan Rather, perhaps representing wishful thinking, went on the air to say:

> What it does not do, in effect is deliver the presidency to George W. Bush ... It keeps alive—keeps alive—at least the possibility of Al Gore trying to continue the contest.

After more clarity, Rather referred to the ruling as "bitterly divided." [272]

Even before the court ruled, the Florida House of Representatives voted to give Florida's 25 Electoral votes to Bush. However, that would have been subject to the dispute if the court ruled the other way.

Bush won the presidency with 271 electoral votes to Gore's 266 votes.

Victory and Defeat

On Dec. 13, both candidates delivered their long awaited concession and victory speeches. Gore issued his conciliatory concession speech with a joking tone:

> Just moments ago, I spoke with George W. Bush and congratulated him on becoming the 43rd president of the United States, and I promised him that I wouldn't call him back this time.

He added:

> Now the U.S. Supreme Court has spoken. Let there be no doubt, while I strongly disagree with the court's decision, I accept it. I accept the finality of this outcome which will be ratified next Monday in the Electoral College. And tonight, for the sake of our unity of the people and the strength of our democracy, I offer my concession.

For the first time, he used a title:

> President-elect Bush inherits a nation whose citizens will be ready to assist him in the conduct of his large responsibilities. ... And now, my friends, in a phrase I once addressed to others, it's time for me to go.

Gore spoke for seven minutes.

Bush's speech lasted for about 10 minutes before a cheering audience of the Texas state capital, where he said he and Gore felt similar emotions and he understands what Gore and his family must be going through. He also praised Gore's "distinguished record" of public service, and talked about the need to "heal the country," after the divided contest. He said:

> Tonight I chose to speak from the chamber of the Texas House of Representatives because it has been a home to bipartisan cooperation. Here in a place where Democrats have the majority, Republicans and Democrats have worked together to do what is right for the people we represent. We've had spirited disagreements and in the end, we found constructive consensus. It is an experience I will always carry with me, an example I will always follow ... I am optimistic

that we can change the tone in Washington, D.C.

Bush spoke to audience applause in the House chamber of the Texas legislature, and promised to reach common ground.

Despite a victory, many conservatives concluded the presidency should not have been decided by the Supreme Court, a fairly consistent view of federalism.

Craig Shirley, whose firm Shirley and Banister Public Relations, worked to book pro-Bush surrogates on cable news and talk radio, said seeing Republicans take the matter to the Supreme Court was a disappointment. Shirley said:

> *Bringing this to the Supreme Court violated Republican philosophy and offended a lot of conservatives at the time. Florida should have been decided by Florida.* [273]

Still, what struck some conservatives is how many on the left were outraged at the court making the choice, as *Washington Post* columnist Charles Krauthammer wrote:

> *Within hours of election night, the Gore campaign parachuted dozens, ultimately hundreds, of lawyers in to Florida with one objective: to find judges to undo their loss... Where did they expect all this lawyering to wind up if not the U.S. Supreme Court? After five weeks of testing every legal mechanism to overturn the results, they are now shocked—shocked—that the Supreme Court has, by its final verdict, determined the identity of the next president. Live by the courts, die by the courts.* [274]

Allowing the judiciary to pick a president is not desirable in principle, but might well reflect the litigious society of 2000 as compared to 1800, 1824 or 1876. While 1960 involved litigation in Illinois, it never matched this scale. While five Justices served on the 1876 Electoral Commission, it was not the sole domain of the judiciary to decide. An electoral commission to decide the 2000 Florida vote seemed farfetched, but would have been preferable to leaving it up to one branch.

Because this was not simply a matter of no candidate winning a majority of electoral votes, it could not simply be decided by the House. But, if it did, Republicans controlled the state delegations of 28 of the 50 states. So, Bush would have been elected president. The most constitutionally preferable outcome would have been the Florida state legislature simply certifying electors. It would have happened on a party line vote, but it would be perfectly legal.

None of these would have been fully satisfactory, but if the nation was facing a convoluted mess, it would have been better for the elected branch than the unelected branch to settle it. Large portions of the public would have perceived any solution as thwarting the will of the public. But the Supreme Court's intervention didn't satisfy anyone either, and keeping the high court out might have prevented it from being blamed for partisan politics.

The *New York Times* protested:

> *No one expects the justices to shed their political instincts entirely when they join the court. But when five conservative justices, however reluctantly they entered the case, swing the election to the conservative candidate—increasing the odds that the next nominees for the Supreme Court will share that political outlook—the court risks appearing blatantly partisan.*[275]

The *Times* approved of Bush's conciliatory words on Dec. 13 as a "promising start," but stressed the Texas governor's "absence of a numerical mandate." The newspaper further added that given the way he came into office, he must not move toward the conservative agenda of Senate Majority Leader Trent Lott and House Majority Leader Tom Delay. The *Times* said:

> ...they want Mr. Bush to push right away for tax cuts for the wealthy and a repeal of abortion rights. Mr. Bush should ignore such talk and start by forging alliances with Democrats and Republicans on practical legislation for which there is already a national consensus. Two issues that come to mind are education, for which Mr. Bush has a natural affinity, and campaign finance reform, where he can draw strength from a public conversion. There is also a promising, if somewhat awkward, opportunity to push ballot reforms to eliminate the errors that helped Mr. Bush in Florida.
> 276

As it happened, Bush did enact his trademark tax cuts and signed a bill banning partial birth abortion, to the chagrin of the *New York Times*. But he also abided by their wish in signing the No Child Left Behind education bill, the McCain-Feingold campaign finance reform law and the Help America Vote Act.

The Help America Vote Act was actually a direct response to the disputed 2000 election. The bipartisan law set minimum state standards and provided federal money to states to improve and modernize voting machines, allow provisional ballots to be cast when there is a question, providing voting information and require a statewide voter registration database.

Bush was also very conciliatory upon entering office, nominating Clinton's Commerce Secretary Norm Mineta to be his Transportation secretary. He also kept Clinton CIA Director George Tenant.

Bush Wins Another Recount

Media recounts found that Bush would have won the election under the rules of a Gore recount, but ironically, that Gore could have possibly won in a statewide recount that also included overvotes. The Gore legal team didn't ask for a statewide recount or for overvotes.

The media consortium recount was paid for by several news organizations including the Associated Press, CNN, The New York Times, The Washington Post, The Wall Street Journal, The Palm Beach Post, The St. Petersburg Times and Tribune Media. If Gore's limited recount of undervotes in the four Democratic counties had proceeded, Bush would have won the election by between 225 and 493 votes, fewer than the 537, but still a victory.

However, the media consortium also found that if the overvotes had been counted statewide, Gore could have won by between 60 and 171 votes, depending on the standard used. That's under the most liberal interpretation of what would count as a Gore vote, but still enough to muddle even what was supposed to be the final word on the Florida tally—and enough to maintain the article of faith among Democrats that Florida was stolen.

As the *Washington Post* said, the recount only:

> *underscores what became apparent as soon as the polls closed in the nation's third most populous state Nov. 7, 2000: That no one can say with certainty who actually won Florida. Under every scenario used in the study, the winning margin remains less than 500 votes out of almost 6 million cast.*

The *Post* continued:

> Bush had less to fear from recounts than he thought. Under any standard used to judge the ballots in the four counties where Gore lawyers had sought a recount—Palm Beach, Broward, Miami-Dade and Volusia—Bush still ended up with more votes than Gore, according to the study. ... Had Bush not been a party to short-circuiting those recounts, he might have escaped criticism that his victory hinged on legal maneuvering rather than counting the votes. [277]

The *Palm Beach Post* took a bolder approach, saying:

> Al Gore was doomed. He couldn't have caught George W. Bush even if his two best chances for an official recount had played out.

A separate count by *USA Today/Miami Herald* analysis found:

> George W. Bush would have won a hand recount of all disputed ballots in Florida's presidential election if the most widely accepted standard for judging votes had been applied. [278]

There was room for Democrats to spin the results regarding the overvotes to their favor. Most Democrats, including Gore, did not raise a stink—perhaps spooked by Bush's post 9/11 popularity by the time the media recount was completed. But Gore's campaign manager Donna Brazile was certain that black votes were not counted in Florida:

> Something happened to some of those votes. Somebody tampered with them. [279]

The election revealed a clear divide in the United States, one in which Bush and Republicans seemed to have a clear advantage in the middle of the country—or "flyover country," while Gore won urban areas. Bush won 2,434 counties across the country while Gore won 644. Red states encompassed 2.8 million square miles of the United States, compared to 580,000 square miles for blue states. Republicans liked to point to a sea of red on the U.S. map, while Democrats were quick to point out there weren't as many people that lived in those states.

The divide was in place before the 2000 election—but the unusual outcome prompted intense study of the red-blue divide in the country. It's a divide that has mostly held in subsequent election, although President Barack Obama has captured traditionally Republican states such as Indiana, North Carolina (once) and Virginia (twice).

The honeymoon for the new president didn't last long. In another anomaly from the 2000 election that was overshadowed, the Senate was split 50-50. With Dick Cheney as Senate president, he was there to cast a tie-breaking vote and maintain a slim GOP majority, so it seemed. Then liberal Republican Sen. Jim Jeffords of Vermont announced he was becoming an independent, thus giving the Democrats a 50-49-1 edge. Jeffords caucused with the Democrats.

Then, America changed when terrorists flew planes into the World Trade Center and the Pentagon on Sept. 11, 2001. The politically divided nation rallied around Bush, as the president who was barely elected had stratospheric approval ratings in the 90s for a time.

That unity all fell with the Iraq war, and enough Democrats started to remember they thought the election was stolen. There were signs and bumper stickers that said "Re-Elect Gore 2004."

Given the choice of emulating Jackson's 1828 comeback or Tilden's 1880 passing the baton, Gore chose to follow the Tilden model. In 2004, Bush became the first winner of a disputed election since Thomas Jefferson to win re-election, defeating Massachusetts Sen. John Kerry.

But those four years would have clearly been much different with a President Gore.

CHAPTER FOURTEEN

President Gore

TO PARAPHRASE HILLARY Clinton, what difference does it make? That's what some limited government advocates would say about an Al Gore presidency.

Gene Healy, author of, *The Cult of the Presidency*, and vice president of the libertarian Cato Institute, said:

> *I often joke that if Rip Van Winkle fell asleep during the Florida hanging chads dispute, and woke up in 2006 to be told the president had signed the McCain-Feingold campaign finance reform bill, expanded federal involvement in education and signed the largest Medicare expansion since Lyndon B. Johnson was president, he would have assumed that Gore won the recount. The contours of the Bush or Gore policies would have been different, but the broad strokes are the same.* [280]

But that's not the only view of a Gore presidency.

"It would be a completely different world if Gore were elected by the Electoral College and not just the popular vote," said Jon-Christopher Bua, who worked in several media rolls in the Clinton administration, and was at the headquarters in Nashville on the confusing and emotional election night. [281]

Healy focused on domestic issues, while Bua referred to international matters. How different the world would be is always the question. But a different election result could have happened quite easily on a number of fronts.

Gore might have chosen a different legal strategy—one to at least attempt a statewide count before it was time for the Electoral College to certify votes. It would not have violated the Fourteenth Amendment, and had overvotes been counted, he might have won Florida's 25 electoral votes.

Or, other political factors might have occurred. If Gore had simply carried his home state of Tennessee, 11 electoral votes, it would have carried him to 276 to Bush's 260 electoral votes. Gore lost Tennessee for the same reason he lost other red states that he and Bill Clinton previously won together. Cultural issues played a big role and Clinton's impeachment scandal left just enough states ready to punish his successor.

To flip that argument around, one red state that might have forgiven Bill Clinton was Arkansas—a state that knew him well before the nation did. Clinton wanted to hit the trail for Gore. Gore wanted him to stay out of sight. But perhaps a Clinton solo appearance in Arkansas—it wouldn't even require the two to be seen together for national consumption—could have given Gore 272 electoral votes from Arkansas's six votes, leaving Bush at 265.

There are a number of scenarios that would have allowed Al Gore to be inaugurated president on Jan. 20, 2001, riding to the U.S. Capitol in a limousine with the president he shunned throughout the campaign.

Supporters and opponents of Bush recognize that he was—for better or worse—among America's most consequential presidents. Right or wrong, Bush made bold decisions—sometimes with popular support, such as the initial invasion of

Iraq, sometimes with the public firmly opposed, such as the surge that won what became an unpopular war.

The Iraq war was the defining decision of the Bush presidency that even many conservative one-time war supporters came to believe was a bad move in retrospection. Bush's presidency is also defined largely by how he responded in the aftermath of 9/11. But the Bush presidency was bigger—and very consequential on the domestic front as well. He was in office more than two years before the "shock-and-awe" campaign began in Iraq, and nearly nine months before terrorists flew planes into the World Trade Center and Pentagon.

It's not very likely Gore would have moved to establish an Office of Faith-Based and Community Initiatives, controversial at the time, though President Barack Obama kept the office and its initiatives intact. Gore clearly would have never signed the first Bush tax cut. He further, without hesitation, would have fully funded embryonic stem cell research. These were the top issues of Bush's pre-9/11 presidency and provides some contexts for what issues would or wouldn't come up in a Gore presidency.

Gore's Green Agenda

Gore, of course would have entered office with a different agenda focused heavily on the environment. By late March, the Bush administration announced it was abandoning any plans to get the Kyoto Protocol on climate change with 180 countries ratified by the Senate. This was of course a radical departure from what a President Gore would have done. However, Gore would have had very little chance of gaining ratification.

The environmental movement was in some disarray during the Bush years. This would have been profoundly different under Gore, said Robert Zelnick, author of the 1999 biography, *Gore: A Political Life*. Zelnick, a former Emmy-Award winning ABC News reporter and journalism professor at Boston University, said:

> *He had deep environmental concerns. I think the Gore environmental record would be very similar to that which is ascribed to our current president. There would have been less pain for the environmental community under President Gore. Gore is associated with things that have not been forgotten. He brought much needed attention to environmental advocacy and had a sensitivity to that issue.* [282]

There would have been a definite consequence to that focus on environmentalism, said Eric Patterson, dean of the Robertson School of Government at Regent University:

> *Gore's first nine months in office would have mostly been a continuation of the Clinton administration, but Gore would have staked out his own ground on the environment and technology. I'm not sure technology would be much different. But he would have had very pro-alternative energy policies and anti-oil policies for four to eight years. The oil boom that was allowed to happen under Bush would not have happened. Instead of costing $2 or less, we might be paying $4 or $5 now for gasoline today. The fracking revolution would not have occurred. All of the technology for fracking happened under George W. Bush.*

For a better understanding of this, it's worth looking at the Barack Obama administration's commitment to green energy through federal loan guarantees to gage how well Gore's programs could have survived. Solar and wind technology were even less developed in 2001. A 2015 analysis by the Institute for Energy Research found that the Obama spent $39 billion per year on average for solar energy projects, but solar was expected to generate just 0.6 percent of electricity for that year.[283]

A 2012 analysis by the Heritage Foundation, a conservative think tank, determined that of the 36 green energy companies the Obama administration had subsidized, more than half either declared bankruptcy or were facing extreme financial difficulty. Of the companies, two received more than $1 billion from the federal government and two received more than $500 million. The poster child for the failures was Solyndra, a politically-connected solar firm that got $535 million in loans from the Energy Department only to collapse and face an FBI investigation.[284]

Gore assuredly would not have sought expanding offshore drilling as Bush did, and would have stepped in the way of fracking. While he would have had a 50 plus one majority in the Senate, with Vice President Joe Lieberman casting tie breaking votes, it seems unlikely that he would ever get the Kyoto Protocol ratified, nor would he be able to push a cap and trade bill through Congress. His environmental agenda—which never had broad based public support—would have been pruned a bit but might have made some progress.

University of Dayton historian Larry Schweikart said:

> *Gore would have had still had a Republican Senate and Republican House. They wouldn't have funded many of his environmental plans or his domestic agenda. But, if Republicans in Congress were acting as an opposition party, they might not have run the deficit up as much as they did under Bush.*

As often happens when someone lionized by a movement is actually forced to govern, Gore's inability to achieve everything he wanted would have enraged some environmentalists who were certain that a Gore presidency would equal nirvana.

Ralph Nader would probably get some airtime denouncing

Gore as a corporate sellout, reasserting that it really was Bore and Gush. Nader would almost assuredly gain clout with the left, as would his third party building ambitions. That's because after the narrow Bush victory Nader became a pariah to the left, the man responsible for Bush. A President Gore could never be liberal enough for Nader, which would have been more than enough for the view on the far left that there's not a dime's worth of difference between the parties. Facing this pressure, Gore would by necessity be more liberal than Clinton and likely keep up "the people vs. the powerful" rhetoric. Whether that translated into policy is difficult to say.

Gore might have been limited in how far he would go. He would have no doubt faced pushback from House Republicans such as House Majority Leader Tom DeLay over his legitimacy in office, though probably far less from the media. With Vice President Lieberman, Gore would have a majority in the Senate for at least the first two years, which would allow South Dakota Sen. Tom Daschle—the headache for Bush—to be the majority leader and President Gore's valuable ally. It seems quite likely that with a Democrat in the White House, Vermont Senator Jim Jeffords would have remained a Republican who frequently voted with Democrats, particularly since there would be no reward for his switch. Since appropriations bills begin in the House, DeLay would have been a key roadblock to Gore and the Democratic Senate.

Gore the War President

After all of this, Gore's metal would be tested after Al Qaeda terrorists hijacked and flew jets into the World Trade Center and the Pentagon on Sept. 11, 2001.

Patterson of Regent University and author of *Ending Wars Well: Order, Justice and Conciliation in Contemporary Post-Conflict*, said:

> *Would Al Gore have been able to rally the nation after 9/11 the way Bush did? Would he have extended the war to Iraq? Any president would have had to do something after 9/11, but Gore might well have carried out targeted attacks in Afghanistan with cruise missiles. It might not have been with the goal of deposing the Taliban. His response after 9/11 would have been different. It would have been more European ... That's not the way a Texan does it. Gore would have taken a more European than Texan approach. He would have prioritized no women and children in harm's way. He would have sought international remedies. He would have viewed joining the International Criminal Court as a solution to terrorism. For better or worse, Guantanamo Bay would have never been established.*

One interesting factor to consider is whether the country would have *wrongly* presumed that the election of a Jewish vice president would have prompted more aggression from the anti-Semitic terrorists. That was a concern expressed by Florida State Sen. David Aronberg, who supported Lieberman's presidential campaign in 2004. Aronberg told the *Hartford Courant*:

> *There are people who say if Lieberman had been vice president on 9/11, the Jews would be blamed for that.*[285]

The Iraq Question

Zelnick chronicled Gore's hawkish streak in the Senate for his book, but thinks on balance a President Gore would not have taken the plunge into Iraq.

Zelnick said:

Tainted by Suspicion

> *Gore voted for the first Gulf War because he wanted to position himself as a liberal with a hawkish stance on Iraq. There is some inclination to believe a President Gore might have invaded Iraq, but I think unlike Bush, he would have faced a lot of push back from his own party over such a decision. So I think he would have backed away. If I had to bet, I would say he would not have taken the country into Gulf War II.*

The absence of the war in Iraq would have changed the Middle East and the world, said Jon-Christopher Bua, who for six years was an adjunct professor at the Georgetown University School of Foreign Service, and is now at Catholic University in Washington, D.C.

Bua said:

> *We would probably not have invaded Iraq. Saddam Hussein would still be a tyrant, but you would have two tyrants, Iran and Iraq, checking each other. Al Qaeda in Iraq would not have emerged and we wouldn't have ISIS, if there had been no war in Iraq. It started a power vacuum. Gore most likely would not have gone in that direction. He was not a neocon.*

Without an Iraq war, Bua said, there would have been no Arab Spring, which gave many people hope for a time at least, as it looked as if democracy might really spread in the Middle East. Old dictators—friends and foes to the United States—would still be in power such as Moammar Gadhafi of Libya and Hosni Mubarak of Egypt. The Middle East had dictators, but the argument goes, they were stable dictators.

This point is overstated, Patterson contends, and seems to imagine a good-old-days era for the Middle East. He said:

Tainted by Suspicion

> *The Middle East has always been unstable. Is the Middle East less stable today than before the invasion of Iraq? I think that's a hard case to make with evidence. What we're seeing is the crumbling of old regimes. Bush gave the region a shakeup, which was part of his freedom agenda.*

Beyond the domestic policy similarities, Gore might well have matched Bush on foreign policy, Healy, the vice president of the libertarian Cato Institute said:

> *Al Gore might have done many things different, including the Iraq war. But he was a hawk on Iraq during the 1990s. Had he been a Democratic president during post-9/11, there is a lot of reason to believe he would have set up a similar national security structure. Because he was a Democrat, he might have felt pressured to do something big to prove he wasn't a McGovernite in the wake of 9/11. Gore of course wouldn't have Cheney and Rumsfeld as his aides, who had an ideology of executive power for their own sake going back to the Ford administration, but 9/11 would have expanded the powers of the presidency regardless.*

Public opinion seems to be in line with Healy's skepticism about a different world under Gore.

A 60 Minutes/Vanity Fair poll in 2011—marking 10 years since 9/11—found 56 percent believed little would have changed had Gore been president. The public believes the Iraq war—and 4,000 American lives lost—would have occurred under President Gore. In fact, when broken down further, more independents, 62 percent, than Republicans, 57 percent, believed everything would have been the same. Meanwhile, almost half, 48 percent, of Democrats felt the same. [286]

Tainted by Suspicion

Others paint a different picture.

The 2006 book, *President Gore and Other Things That Never Happened: A Book of Political Counterfactuals*, asserts that after 9/11, Gore rallies the nation, and defeats an attempt by his vice president, Lieberman, to push a war in Iraq. By 2004, the Gore administration had killed Osama bin Laden, and the president was elected with a landslide victory. A fairly rosy scenario, but it gets rosier. Brent Budowsky, liberal columnist for The Hill newspaper, pictured a virtual paradise if Gore had ascended to the presidency in a column published Sept. 2, 2011—even asserting there would have been no 9/11 terror attack. Budowsky wrote:

> Had Gore been briefed by intelligence officers as Bush was in August 2001 about terrorist planes attacking buildings, Gore would have put our services on red alert and might well have prevented 9/11.

That seems quite unlikely, particularly since subsequent news reports as well as the 9/11 Commission determined in 2004 that the Clinton administration had as many as four missed opportunities to kill or capture Osama bin Laden in 1998 and 1999, but did not go forward. [287]

The first occasion came in December 1998, at a time when Clinton was engulfed in an impeachment scandal, when intelligences suggested that bin Laden was in Kandahar, Afghanistan. A strike was prepared to go, but Clinton's advisors opted against recommending it because no one saw bin Laden. The second opportunity came in February 1999, when it was believed bin Laden was at a hunting camp in Afghanistan. The Clinton administration worried the strike would kill princes from the United Arab Emirates who were also at the camp. In May 1999, another strike in Kandahar was aborted because of concerns for collateral damage. In July 1999, intelligence was imprecise so the plan for an attack did not proceed. Based on some reports, there were even more opportunities.

Bush took considerable bumps for failing to prevent 9/11, but Gore might have taken a worse thrashing from the public since he was part of the administration that failed to stop bin Laden over the course of several years before the worst terrorist attack ever on U.S. soil. With the commission report being released in May 2004, it would have considerably stung in a re-election year.

Gore, post-9/11, might have also set out to establish a new Department of Homeland Security, perhaps with a different name and slightly different structure, since a key intelligence problem at the time seemed to be that security agencies were too far flung.

Budowsky continued in the column:

> *Even if 9/11 had happened: Gore would never have made the blunder of invading Iraq. Those American lives of troops KIA would have been saved. He would have focused on Afghanistan, which would have been won for keeps most likely by 2003. Many American lives of troops KIA in Afghanistan would also have been saved and our Afghan mission would have ended successfully long ago.*[288]

We do know for absolute fact that Al Gore, the private citizen, strongly opposed the war in Iraq. Gore told the Commonwealth Club in San Francisco in 2002:

> *Great nations persevere and then prevail. They do not jump from one unfinished task to another. In just one year, the president has somehow squandered the international outpouring of sympathy, goodwill and solidarity that followed the 9/11 attack.*

Tainted by Suspicion

Gore continued:

> President Bush now asserts that we will take pre-emptive action even if we think the threat we perceive is not imminent. If other nations assert the same right, then the rule of law will quickly be replaced by the reign of fear—any nation that perceives circumstances that could eventually lead to an imminent threat would be justified under this approach in taking military action against another nation. [289]

Not much ambiguity. As a matter of fact, when most Democratic politicians such as Senators Daschle, Hillary Clinton and John Kerry, House Minority Leader Dick Gephardt and other leading Democratic lawmakers were climbing over each other to support the Iraq invasion, Gore was sort of a lone opposition voice.

Why would it be any different if Gore were president? It's because circumstances change when a politician isn't watching from the sidelines. Also, President Bill Clinton signed the Iraq Liberation Act of 1998, making it formal U.S. policy to support regime change in Iraq. Salon's Steve Kornacki wrote in 2011:

> But look a little closer and you'll realize that President Gore would have been hearing the same pleas. His own vice president would have been Joe Lieberman, perhaps the most hawkish Democrat in Washington on Middle East issues. Marty Peretz, his old friend and confidante, would have had Gore's ear and filled it with arguments for going into Iraq.
>
> Loud, influential, non-conservative media voices—like Tom Friedman and Peter Beinart—would have amplified these calls on the outside. Republicans would have been screaming for an invasion, and the public would have been on their side. Clinton could

285

> *barely hold them all back in the '90s; after 9/11, would Gore have stood a chance?*

Kornacki added:

> *Maybe Gore would have pushed through some new type of sanctions, or a few more rounds of weapons inspections. Hussein would have just thumbed his nose at all of this, and every time he did, the chorus in America would have grown louder.* [290]

Lieberman gets mentioned frequently, but it seems possible Gore might keep the hawkish William Cohen as his Defense secretary and longtime Democratic stalwart George Tenant—who was supremely assured Saddam had weapons of mass destruction—as the CIA director.

Gore may well have had Machiavellian reason to oppose the war in September 2002. He was months away from his December announcement that he would not jump back into the ring in 2004. So he might well have been thinking about running again—and saw a more crowded field shaping up than the previous time he ran. Though popular sentiment was behind the war, Gore might have had a hunch that when 2004 rolled around, it might be less popular. It would be the only way to set himself apart from the bandwagon brigade of Democrats backing the war. If this was his thinking, he ultimately did not have the stomach to go through another grueling contest. But, now we are dangerously approaching an entirely separate "what-if."

Gore, Patriot Act and Gitmo

Iraq isn't the only question on the national security front. The left loathed Bush for Guantanamo, enhanced interrogation, the NSA surveillance and other anti-terror tools—certain that only Bush and his supposedly sinister Vice President Dick Cheney would push this agenda. This presumption was of course before Obama.

Los Angeles Times editorial writer Michael McGough speculated that the President Gore might have taken many of these actions—as evidence by the record of the Clinton administration. McGough wrote:

> But what makes this 'what if' exercise so fascinating is that it is far from a slam dunk (as former CIA Director George Tenet, a Clinton appointee, might say) that a Gore administration wouldn't have done at least some of the things for which Bush has been pilloried. It was Clinton, not Bush, who defied the ACLU by signing the 1996 Anti-Terrorism and Effective Death Penalty Act, which Congress passed on the first anniversary of the Oklahoma City bombing.

The controversial Anti-Terrorism and Effective Death Penalty Act established new hurdles for a convict to challenge a state conviction in federal court and for criminalizing "material support" for terrorists. It also increased the likelihood of deportation of suspected terrorists and allowed prosecutors to use classified information not provided to the defense. Further, in 2006, Clinton's first CIA Director R. James Woolsey Jr., defended the NSA surveillance by the Bush administration, McGough noted:

> The point is that you don't have to be a 'loyal Bushie' or even a Republican to support some renegotiation of the relationship between liberty and security. Clinton did after the Oklahoma City bombing, and President Al Gore might well have followed suit after 9/11 with his own versions of the Patriot Act and the Terrorist Surveillance Program. [291]

Difference on the Home Front

It's noteworthy that during his most unpopular days, Bush maintained the support of most of the Republican base and conservative media in large part because the Left seemed to have such deep vitriol for the president. After he left office, more classic fiscal conservatism awakened against massive government debt and deficit spending. Bush began and Obama accelerated much of the fiscal irresponsibility. It wasn't entirely ignored during the Bush years. Conservative author Richard A. Viguerie wrote *Conservatives Betrayed: How George W. Bush and Other Big Government Republicans Hijacked the Conservative Movement*, while Bruce Bartlett wrote *Imposter: How George W. Bush Bankrupted America and Betrayed the Reagan Legacy*. Both books came out in 2006, the year Bush lost the Congress.

Bush indeed reversed much of what Reagan sought to do. Bush worked with Sen. Ted Kennedy on an education bill, widely received as a bipartisan achievement known as No Child Left Behind in January 2002, which was loathed for years by both parties after it was implemented. Bush pushed forward the largest entitlement expansion since the Great Society, signing a Medicare prescription drug plan in December 2003.

While it's certainly true Clinton sought a health care plan more expansive than what is today known as Obamacare, he didn't achieve it. Clinton was dragged by the Republican Congress to balance the federal budget and sign welfare reform. But the bottom line is, he did. He was a Democrat that declared "the era of big government is over." It seemed at the time as if Reagan had won the larger war of ideas. Then Bush came in and grew the government.

Craig Shirley, a presidential historian and head of Shirley and Banister Public Relations, said:

I don't think Gore would have been able to grow the

> *government in the way Bush did. He wouldn't have had a mandate. The long term consequences of the Bush administration was to fracture the Republican party between the big government Republicans and the conservatives. The conservatives controlled the party after Reagan before Bush.* [292]

A Republican Congress acquiesced to Bush's ambitious growth of government, but would have united against a Democratic president.

One sweeping piece of legislation Gore would have vetoed is the ban on partial birth abortion. Bush signed the ban in November 2003, the first federal ban of any kind on an abortion procedure since the Roe v. Wade decision in the Supreme Court in 1973. In 2007, the Supreme Court upheld the ban. Gore, formerly a pro-life moderate in the Senate, would have almost certainly had to veto for practical political concerns of keeping his base in line.

Speaking of the Supreme Court, John Roberts and Samuel Alito would not be serving on the court if Gore were elected. Gore would have named justices similar to Elena Kagan and Sonya Sotomayor. This would have changed major rulings on the Second Amendment, free speech, abortion and religious freedom that the court has handed down in recent years.

Four More for Gore?

Most certainly, the final test for Gore's legitimacy would arrive on Nov. 3, 2004—when Bush was re-elected over Sen. John Kerry. Would Gore have been so lucky?

Zelnick said:

> *I believe he would have won re-election in 2004. Gore was a pretty good politician, not a great one, not*

> *perfect. But he had political wisdom. He knew how institutions worked. He could accurately enough read the politics of the country. Gore benefited from having a father who was a U.S. senator and he benefited from experience, having run for the presidency before in 1988. Joe Lieberman as his vice president would have been a solid contributor to his presidency.*

Patterson, of Regent University, doesn't think so:

> *Gore probably would not have won re-election in 2004. It's unlikely for a single party to hold on to power for more than three terms. We saw the same thing in 1992 after 12 years of Republicans, people were ready for something different. Gore most likely would have been a one-termer. George W. Bush would have come roaring back in 2004, similar to how Andrew Jackson planned out his campaign for four years, or how Grover Cleveland planned his comeback. Or maybe Jeb would have run. It's very likely the Bush family would have had their long knives out.*

Given a Republican victory in 2004, Patterson thinks it's still plausible that Illinois Sen. Barack Obama might have emerged as a presidential contender:

> *Obama had no ties to the Clintons. He didn't owe the old party anything. He could have come on to the stage and won in 2008 or 2012.*

Bua, on the other hand, believes Gore might have been re-elected had he maintained the Clinton policies and the economy remained steady. But he asserted that the housing crisis in the United States was one part of a global economic crisis that hit in 2008 and 2009.

That would have been blamed on President Gore, fair or not. Further, Bua points to how deeply unpopular Bush was by the end of his second term, which almost ensured a Democratic victory in 2008. Thus, he thinks if Gore had been in office for four or eight years, there would not have been the political environment to propel Obama into the presidency:

> There would not have been a Barack Obama presidency. Barack Obama won the Nobel Peace Prize mostly because he wasn't George Bush. There was a demand for something new. Barack Obama was the right candidate for the right time.

***

But Gore did not become president. In some ways, it was almost a better deal. Instead of unsuccessfully pushing for unachievable climate legislation and being slammed by the environmental movement he cherished, Gore managed to make an Oscar-winning documentary, *An Inconvenient Truth*, and even better, he won a Nobel Peace Prize. He and Tipper divorced, which might have been less likely if they had ever been the first family. As a former first couple, they might have felt it would be impossible to part ways.

There were rumors that Gore would run for president in 2008, and rumors again he would challenge Hillary Clinton for the Democratic nomination in 2016. He did neither. Instead, Gore built up much sympathy for playing the role of the guy who should have won, a climate activist and a "recovering politician."

CONCLUSION

Did Anyone Really Steal Anything?

THE MOST SHOCKING assessment to make would be that of the four key elections examined in these pages, none were stolen.

That's right. There might well have been some skullduggery, but probably not enough to tilt the election. Despite the popular vote, all presidents were constitutionally elected.

In the nation's history, four candidates who lost the popular vote became president, but there was by no means anything illegal about it. The Electoral College decides the presidency, not the popular vote. Until the Constitution is amended, it will remain that way. There is an effort among some states to undermine the Electoral College by agreeing to have their electors vote for whoever won the national popular vote. While this might not honor the wishes of the voters in their own state, state legislatures have the right to apportion electors however they wish. Other states have debated proportional awarding of electoral votes—as Maine and Nebraska already have. But again, it's up to the states.

With regard to four disputed elections, Jefferson most certainly didn't steal anything since it was clearly understood that he was supposed to be the presidential candidate. That said, Burr did nothing wrong—at least not constitutionally. Under the pre-Twelfth Amendment Constitution, he was legally running for president not vice president. He didn't force the electors to give him an equal number of votes with Jefferson. Clearly, he handled things wrongly and paid a political price for his lack of loyalty while serving as Jefferson's vice president. But, he was within his rights with regard to the law.

In 1824, the system worked as it was supposed to work. That was certainly upsetting to Jackson and his supporters, but the will of the people was not the determining factor then—and isn't entirely now—in determining the presidents. With four candidates, no one received a majority, and the election went to the House where it was decided by the people's representatives. That's how it was supposed to work.

In 1876, it's quite complicated to discern who won and who lost the popular vote. There was absolutely voter suppression in southern states. That doesn't necessarily mean that Hayes would have won those states if more blacks and even more white Republicans were allowed to vote there. But knowing this, why wouldn't Republicans challenge the result?

Since there was no direct constitutional remedy—the House can only broker an election with no clear majority, this was an incomplete election as four states had multiple sets of returns—and Electoral Commission might have been the most sensible solution.

It's likely a better solution than limiting the matter exclusively to the courts, as happened in 2000. But, the 2000 dispute was of a different nature and concerned the legality of recounts standards and procedures. Justice David Souter's contention that it's best to handle this at the political level was almost a conservative argument. But, it was likely impractical.

The fact is, the case was litigated, and settled by the Supreme Court. On top of that, every credible recount showed that Bush won Florida, albeit by a thin margin.

Bush joined the club with the other son of a president (John Quincy Adams), a grandson of another president (Benjamin Harrison) and Hayes—all constitutionally elected presidents despite losing the popular vote.

As for the Kennedy-Nixon election that was never challenged, the fraud was almost certain, but if recent studies are correct, Kennedy would have likely at least carried the Electoral College even without the fraud. By no means is that condoning election fraud or other nefarious activities of the Daley machine—only saying that the machine might have carried less weight than once believed.

There is a moral case perhaps to be made for popular voting. It's an obvious cloud hanging over the elected president's head if he could not win more votes than his vanquished opponent. But, the Electoral College has a purpose of ensuring states have a say in the federal government.

Honest elections that have the public's confidence require safeguards against election fraud and voter suppression. Unfortunately, these protections are cast as being at odds. Even the most basic safeguards such as voter ID gets compared by demagogues to Jim Crow. One need only look at the Hayes-Tilden election to find that comparison insulting to America's intelligence and conscience.

Final point, the what-ifs are more than a thought-provoking exercise, but rather a demonstration of why elections matter. There is a dime's worth of difference—sometimes more—between presidential candidates. However, according to historians, that change was not always profound, but mattered.

END NOTES

[1] Gary Wills; *Negro President: Jefferson and Slave Power*; Mariner Books; 2005
[2] Kenneth Walsh; *The Most Consequential Elections in History: Thomas Jefferson and the Election of 1800*; U.S. News and World Report; Aug. 13, 2008
[3] History Central; 1800 Election Results; Jefferson vs. Adams
[4] John Furling; *Adams vs. Jefferson: The Tumultuous Election of 1800*; Oxford University Press; 2004 p. 15-16
[5] Presidential Biographies; www.WhiteHouse.gov
[6] Bernard A. Weisberger; *America Afire: Jefferson, Adams and the First Contested Election*; Perennial; 2000; Page 230
[7] Aaron Burr Biography; senate.gov
[8] Robert K. Wright Jr and Morris J. MacGregor; *Soldiers and Statesmen of the Constitution*; Center for Military History; 1987
[9] Paul F. Boller, Jr.; *Presidential Campaigns from George Washington to George W. Bush*; Oxford University Press; 2004; p. 10
[10] Paul F. Boller; *Presidential Campaigns*; Oxford University Press; 2004; Page 12
[11] Library of Congress;
[12] Phillip G. Henderson; *The Presidency: Then and Now*; Page 143; Rowan & Littlefield; 2000
[13] Joseph Cummings; *Anything for a Vote: Dirty Tricks, Cheap Shots*

and October Surprises in U.S. Presidential Campaigns; 2007; Page 26

[14] Paul F. Boller; *Presidential Campaigns from George Washington to George W. Bush*; Oxford University Press; 2004; Page 13

[15] C-SPAN Booknotes; http://www.booknotes.org/Watch/161310-1/Bernard+Weisberger.aspx

[16] C-SPAN Booknotes; http://www.booknotes.org/Watch/161310-1/Bernard+Weisberger.aspx

[17] C-SPAN Booknotes

[18] *The Case for Tammany Hall Being on the Right Side of History*; National Public Radio; March 6, 2014

[19] Bernard A. Weisberger; *America Afire: Jefferson, Adams and the First Contested Election*; Perennial; 2000; Page 238

[20] John Ferling; *Adams vs. Jefferson: The Tumultuous Election of 1800*; Oxford University Press; 2004 p. 128

[21] John Ferling; *Adams vs. Jefferson: The Tumultuous Election of 1800*; Oxford University Press; 2004 p. 127

[22] Paul F. Boiler; *Presidential Campaigns*; Oxford University Press; 2004; Page 13

[23] Joseph Cummings; *Anything for a Vote: Dirty Tricks, Cheap Shots and October Surprises in U.S. Elections*; Quirk Books; 2007; Page 27

[24] Paul F. Boller Jr.; *Presidential Campaign from George Washington to George W. Bush*; Oxford University Press; 2004; Page 10-11

[25] Ron Chernow; *Alexander Hamilton*; Penguin; 2004; Page 613

[26] Library of Congress; http://www.loc.gov/resource/mtj1.022_0628_0629/?sp=1&st=text

[27] Paul F. Boller; *Presidential Campaigns;* Oxford University Press; 2004; Page 14

[28] Aaron Burr Biography; senate.gov

[29] Bernard A. Weisberger; *America Afire: Jefferson, Adams and the*

First Contested Election; Perennial; 2000; Page 259

[30] Gary Wills; *Negro President: Jefferson and Slave Power*; Mariner Books; 2005; 77

[31] Gary Wills; *Negro President: Jefferson and Slave Power*; Mariner Books; 2005; Page 76

[32] Bernard A. Weisberger; *America Afire: Jefferson, Adams and the First Contested Election*; Perennial; 2000; Page 263

[33] The American Experience; The Dual; PBS; 2000

[34] Bernard A. Weisberger; *America Afire: Jefferson, Adams and the First Contested Election*; Perennial; 2000; Page 260

[35] Booknotes; C-SPAN

[36] Bernard A. Weisberger; *America Afire: Jefferson, Adams and the First Contested Election*; Perennial; 2000; Page 263

[37] Bernard A. Weisberger; *America Afire: Jefferson, Adams and the First Contested Election*; Perennial; 2000; Page 270

[38] Bernard A. Weisberger; *America Afire: Jefferson, Adams and the First Contested Election*; Perennial; 2000; Page 270

[39] Jefferson letter to Monroe; Feb. 15, 1801; Founders.Archives.gov

[40] Bernard A. Weisberger; *America Afire: Jefferson, Adams and the First Contested Election*; Perennial; 2000; Page 270

[41] Larry Schweikart and Michael Allen; *A Patriot's History of the United States*; Sentinel; 2004; Page 154-155

[42] John Ferling; *Adams vs. Jefferson: The Tumultuous Election of 1800*; Oxford University Press; 2004 p. 208

[43] Paul Johnson; *A History of the American People*; Harper Perennial; 1999; Page 165; 1997

[44] Gary Wills; *Negro President: Jefferson and the Slave Power*; A Mariner Book, Hougton Mifflin Company; 2003

[45] Susan Dunn; *Jefferson's Second Revolution: The Election Crisis of 1800 and the Triumph of Republicanism*; Houghton Mifflin Company; 2004; Page 215

[46] John Ferling; *Adams vs. Jefferson: The Tumultuous Election of 1800*; Oxford University Press; 2004 p. 201

[47] Wm. Sullivan; *The Public Men of the Revolution: Peace of 1783 to the Peace of 1815 in a Series of Letters*; Carey and Hart; 1847; Page 437

[48] John Ferling; *Adams vs. Jefferson: The Tumultuous Election of 1800*; Oxford University Press; 2004 p. 196

[49] Interview for this book.

[50] Interview for this book.

[51] Interview for this book.

[52] Interview for this book.

[53] Interview for this book.

[54] Interview for this book.

[55] Interview for this book.

[56] Interview for this book.

[57] Senate Floor Speech by Sen. Robert C. Byrd; West Virginia Democrat; *That Great Enigma*; U.S. Congressional Record; 100th Congress; Page 31914; Nov. 13, 1987

[58] William F. Weeks; *The Impeachment of Federal Officers*; Harper's Weekly, Jan. 28, 1905

[59] David O. Stewart; *American Emperor: Aaron Burr's Challenge to Jefferson's America*; Simon & Schuster; 2011; Page 257-258

[60] Donald Ratcliffe; *The One Party President Contest: Adams, Jackson, and 1824's Five-Horse Race*; University of Kansas Press; 2015; Page 2

[61] Paul Johnson; *A History of the American People*; Harper Perennial; 1999; Page 219

[62] Donald Ratcliffe; *The One Party President Contest: Adams, Jackson, and 1824's Five-Horse Race*; University of Kansas Press; 2015; Page 114

[63] Paul Johnson; *A History of the American People*; Harper Perennial; 1999; Page 219

[64] Paul F. Boller; *Presidential Campaigns*; Oxford University Press; 2000; Page 38

[65] Bruce Walker; *Countering the National Popular Voter Narrative*; American Thinker; October 20, 2012

[66] Donald Ratcliffe; *The One Party President Contest: Adams, Jackson, and 1824's Five-Horse Race*; University of Kansas Press; 2015; Page 2

[67] James Taranto and Leonard Leo; *Presidential Leadership After Disputed Elections*; Free Press, 2004

[68] Donald Ratcliffe; *The One Party President Contest: Adams, Jackson, and 1824's Five-Horse Race*; University of Kansas Press; 2015; Page 2

[69] University of Virginia; Miller Center; John Quincy Adams: Campaigns and Elections

[70] Donald Ratcliffe; *The One Party President Contest: Adams, Jackson, and 1824's Five-Horse Race*; University of Kansas Press; 2015; Page 199

[71] University of Virginia; Miller Center; John Quincy Adams: Campaigns and Elections

[72] H.W. Brands; *The Life and Times of Andrew Jackson*; First Anchor Books; 2005; Page 375

[73] Paul F. Boller; *Presidential Campaigns*; Oxford University Press; 2000; Page 34

[74] University of Virginia; Miller Center; John Quincy Adams: Campaigns and Elections

[75] Robert McNamara; *The Election of 1824 was Decided in the House of Representatives*; About.com

[76] Donald Ratcliffe; *The One Party President Contest: Adams, Jackson, and 1824's Five-Horse Race*; University of Kansas Press; 2015; Page 167

[77] Paul E. Teed; *John Quincy Adams: Yankee Nationalist*; Nova Science Publishers, Inc.; 2006; Page 166

[78] Larry Schweikart and Michael Allen; *A Patriot's History of the United States*; Sentinel; 2004; Page 201

[79] Donald Ratcliffe; *The One Party President Contest: Adams, Jackson, and 1824's Five-Horse Race*; University of Kansas Press; 2015; Page 94

[80] Larry Schweikart and Michael Allen; *A Patriot's History of the United States*; Sentinel; 2004; Page 202

[81] Donald Ratcliffe; *The One Party President Contest: Adams, Jackson, and 1824's Five-Horse Race*; University of Kansas Press; 2015; Page 71

[82] Thomas D. Clark; Biography of Henry Clay; Henry Clay Estate

[83] Jon Meacham; *American Lion: Andrew Jackson in the White House*; Random House; 2008; Page 44

[84] Larry Schweikart and Michael Allen; *A Patriot's History of the United States*; Sentinel; 2004; Page 202

[85] *Disputed Election of 1824*; History Central; http://www.historycentral.com/Ant/Disputed.html

[86] Joseph Cummins; *Anything for a Vote*; Quirk Books; 2007; Page 43

[87] NDDB; William H. Crawford profile

[88] University of Virginia; Miller Center; John Quincy Adams: Campaigns and Elections

[89] Donald Ratcliffe; *The One Party President Contest: Adams, Jackson, and 1824's Five-Horse Race*; University of Kansas Press; 2015; Page 229

[90] Robert McNamara; *The Election of 1824 was Decided in the House of Representatives*; About.com

[91] *Disputed Election of 1824*; History Central; http://www.historycentral.com/Ant/Disputed.html

[92] Paul Johnson; *A History of the American People*; Harper Perennial; 1999; Page 219

[93] Jon Meacham; *American Lion: Andrew Jackson in the White House*;

Random House; 2008; Page 44
[94] Paul F. Boller Jr.; *Presidential Campaigns*; Oxford University Press; 2004; Page
[95] *Disputed Election of 1824*; History Central; http://www.historycentral.com/Ant/Disputed.html
[96] Paul F. Boller; *Presidential Campaigns*; Oxford University Press; 2004; Page 39
[97] Roger Mutaz; *Presidents Fact Book*; Black Dog and Leventhal Publishers; 2009; Page 110
[98] *Disputed Election of 1824*; History Central; http://www.historycentral.com/Ant/Disputed.html
[99] University of Virginia; Miller Center; John Quincy Adams: Campaigns and Elections
[100] Paul F. Boller; *Presidential Campaigns*; Oxford University Press; 2004; Page 36-37
[101] Paul F. Boller; *Presidential Campaigns*; Oxford University Press; 2004; Page 40
[102] Paul F. Boller; *Presidential Campaigns*; Oxford University Press; 2004; Page 37
[103] Jeffrey Jenkins and Brian Sala; *The Spatial Theory of Voting and the Presidential Election of 1824*; American Journal of Political Science; 1998
[104] John Quincy Adams; *First Annual Message*; December 6, 1825; Online by Gerhard Peters and John T. Woolley, *The American Presidency Project*. http://www.presidency.ucsb.edu/ws/?pid=2946
[105] Roger Mutaz; *Presidents Fact Book*; Black Dog and Leventhal Publishers; 2009; Page 110
[106] Paul Johnson; *A History of the American People*; Harper Perennial; 1999; Page 219
[107] Donald Ratcliffe; *The One Party President Contest: Adams, Jackson, and 1824's Five-Horse Race*; University of Kansas Press; 2015; Page

228
[108] Joseph Cummins; *Anything for a Vote*; Quirk Books; 2007; Page 46
[109] Interview for this book.
[110] Interview for this book.
[111] Interview for this book.
[112] Interview for this book.
[113] Interview for this book.
[114] Interview for this book.
[115] Roger Matuz; *Presidential Fact Book: The Achievements, Campaigns, Events, Triumphs, Tragedies and Legacies of Every President from George Washington to Barack Obama*; Black Dogs and Leventhal Publishers; 2009; Page 127
[116] Larry Schweikart and Michael Allen; *A Patriot's History of the United States*; Sentinel; 2005; Page 207-208
[117] H.W. Brands essay on Andrew Jackson from the book, *Presidential Leadership: Ranking the Best and the Worst in the White House*; Edited by James Taranto and Leonard Leo; Free Press; 2004; Page 47
[118] Interview for this book.
[119] Larry Schweikart and Michael Allen; *A Patriot's History of the United States*; Sentinel; 2005; Page 214-215
[120] Randy Dotinga; *Election Season: Remembering the Strange Election of 1876*; The Christian Science Monitor; Nov. 5, 2012
[121] Jeffrey Lord; *The Democrats Missing History*; The Wall Street Journal; Aug. 13, 2008
[122] William H. Rehnquist; *Centennial Crisis: The Disputed Election of 1876*; Knopf; 2004; Page 18
[123] Interview for this book.
[124] Paul Johnson; *A History of the American People*; Harper Perennial; 1999; Page 363
[125] Michael Zak; *Back to Basics for the Republican Party*; 2003; Page

119

[126] Paul F. Boller; *Presidential Elections*; Oxford University Press; 2004; Page 139

[127] William H. Rehnquist; *Centennial Crisis: The Disputed Election of 1876*; Knopf; 2004; Page 52

[128] Michael Zak; *Back to Basics for the Republican Party*; 2003; Page 119

[129] Paul F. Boller; *Presidential Elections*; Oxford University Press; 2004; Page 133

[130] Paul F. Boller; *Presidential Elections*; Oxford University Press; 2004; Page 133

[131] Paul F. Boller; *Presidential Elections*; Oxford University Press; 2004; Page 134

[132] Paul F. Boller; "Presidential Elections;" Oxford University Press; 2004; Page 134

[133] Frank Freidel and Hugh Sidey; *The Presidents of the United States of America*; White House Historical Association; 2006; WhiteHouse.gov

[134] William H. Rehnquist; *Centennial Crisis: The Disputed Election of 1876*; Knopf; 2004; Page 48-50

[135] Paul Johnson; *A History of the American People*; Harper Perennial; 1999; Page 363

[136] William H. Rehnquist; *Centennial Crisis: The Disputed Election of 1876*; Knopf; 2004; Page 71

[137] Joseph Cummins; *Anything for a Vote*; Quirk Book; 2007; Page 118

[138] William H. Rehnquist; *Centennial Crisis: The Disputed Election of 1876*; Knopf; 2004; Page 77

[139] Samuel Tilden Biography; National Park Service; NPS.gov

[140] William H. Rehnquist; *Centennial Crisis: The Disputed Election of 1876*; Knopf; 2004; Page 71

[141] Joseph Cummins; *Anything for a Vote*; Quirk Book; 2007; Page

118
[142] Paul F. Boller; *Presidential Elections*; Oxford University Press; 2004; Page 136
[143] Michael Zak; *Back to Basics for the Republican Party*; 2003; Page 119
[144] Joseph Cummins; *Anything for a Vote*; Quirk Book; 2007; Page 118
[145] Roy Morris, Jr.; *Fraud of the Century: Rutherford B. Hayes, Samuel Tilden and the Stolen Election of 1876*; Simon and Schuster; 2003; Page 143
[146] Paul F. Boller; *Presidential Elections*; Oxford University Press; 2004; Page 136
[147] William H. Rehnquist; *Centennial Crisis: The Disputed Election of 1876*; Knopf; 2004; Page 89-90
[148] *Finding Precedent: Hayes vs. Tilden*; Harper's Weekly; http://elections.harpweek.com/09Ver2Controversy/Overview-1.htm#1
[149] Paul F. Boller; *Presidential Elections*; Oxford University Press; 2004; Page 136
[150] *Finding Precedent: Hayes vs. Tilden*; Harper's Weekly; http://elections.harpweek.com/09Ver2Controversy/Overview-1.htm#1
[151] Ari Hoogenboom; *Rutherford B. Hayes: Warrior & President*; University Press of Kansas; 1995; Accessed through Rutherford B. Hayes Presidential Center, http://www.rbhayes.org/hayes/president/display.asp?id=512&subj=president
[152] *Finding Precedent: Hayes vs. Tilden*; Harper's Weekly; http://elections.harpweek.com/09Ver2Controversy/Overview-1.htm#1
[153] Ari Hoogenboom; *Rutherford B. Hayes: Warrior & President*; University Press of Kansas; 1995; Accessed through Rutherford B.

Hayes Presidential Center, http://www.rbhayes.org/hayes/president/display.asp?id=512&subj=president

[154] William H. Rehnquist; *Centennial Crisis: The Disputed Election of 1876*; Knopf; 2004; Page 98

[155] *Finding Precedent: Hayes vs. Tilden*; Harper's Weekly; http://elections.harpweek.com/09Ver2Controversy/Overview-1.htm#1

[156] Ari Hoogenboom; *Rutherford B. Hayes: Warrior & President*; University Press of Kansas; 1995; Accessed through Rutherford B. Hayes Presidential Center, http://www.rbhayes.org/hayes/president/display.asp?id=512&subj=president

[157] *Finding Precedent: Hayes vs. Tilden*; Harper's Weekly; http://elections.harpweek.com/09Ver2Controversy/Overview-1.htm#1

[158] William H. Rehnquist; *Centennial Crisis: The Disputed Election of 1876*; Knopf; 2004; Page 111

[159] Paul F. Boller; *Presidential Elections*; Oxford University Press; 2004; Page 135

[160] William H. Rehnquist; *Centennial Crisis: The Disputed Election of 1876*; Knopf; 2004; Page 101

[161] Ari Hoogenboom; *Rutherford B. Hayes: Warrior & President*; University Press of Kansas; 1995; Accessed through Rutherford B. Hayes Presidential Center, http://www.rbhayes.org/hayes/president/display.asp?id=512&subj=president

[162] *Finding Precedent: Hayes vs. Tilden*; Harper's Weekly; http://elections.harpweek.com/09Ver2Controversy/Overview-1.htm#1

[163] N.R. Kleinfield; *Counting the Vote: President Tilden? No, but Almost, in Another Vote that Dragged On*; The New York Times;

Nov. 12, 2000

[164] Ari Hoogenboom; *Rutherford B. Hayes: Warrior & President*; University Press of Kansas; 1995; Accessed through Rutherford B. Hayes Presidential Center, http://www.rbhayes.org/hayes/president/display.asp?id=512&subj=president

[165] Danielle S. Margolies; *Henry Watterson and the New South*; University Press of Kentucky; 2006 Page 42

[166] Scott Farris; *Almost President: The Men Who Lost the Race But Changed the Nation*; Lyons Press; 2012; Page 296

[167] Ari Hoogenboom; *Rutherford B. Hayes: Warrior & President*; University Press of Kansas; 1995; Accessed through Rutherford B. Hayes Presidential Center, http://www.rbhayes.org/hayes/president/display.asp?id=512&subj=president

[168] *Report of the Committees of the Two Houses Upon Method of Counting the Presidential Vote*; Published in full in Harper's Weekly, Feb. 2, 1877, Page 82

[169] Ari Hoogenboom; *Rutherford B. Hayes: Warrior & President*; University Press of Kansas; 1995; Accessed through Rutherford B. Hayes Presidential Center, http://www.rbhayes.org/hayes/president/display.asp?id=512&subj=president

[170] William H. Rehnquist; *Centennial Crisis: The Disputed Election of 1876*; Knopf; 2004; Page 174

[171] Paul F. Boller; *Presidential Elections*; Oxford University Press; 2004; Page 140-141

[172] Ari Hoogenboom; *Rutherford B. Hayes: Warrior & President*; University Press of Kansas; 1995; Accessed through Rutherford B. Hayes Presidential Center, http://www.rbhayes.org/hayes/president/display.asp?id=512&subj=president

[173] Ari Hoogenboom; *Rutherford B. Hayes: Warrior & President*; University Press of Kansas; 1995; Accessed through Rutherford B. Hayes Presidential Center, http://www.rbhayes.org/hayes/president/display.asp?id=512&subj=president

[174] Ari Hoogenboom; *Rutherford B. Hayes: Warrior & President*; University Press of Kansas; 1995; Accessed through Rutherford B. Hayes Presidential Center, http://www.rbhayes.org/hayes/president/display.asp?id=512&subj=president

[175] William H. Rehnquist; *Centennial Crisis: The Disputed Election of 1876*; Knopf; 2004; Page 178

[176] *President-Elect Hayes: Hayes Arrival in Washington, His Trip From Columbus to the Nation's Capital, His Reception by the General of the Army and Senator Sherman*; The New York Times; March 3, 1877

[177] Paul F. Boller; *Presidential Elections*; Oxford University Press; 2004; Page 137

[178] David Goldfield; *America Aflame: How the Civil War Created a Nation*; Bloomsbury Press; 2011; Page 526

[179] Paul F. Boller; *Presidential Elections*; Oxford University Press; 2004; Page 137

[180] Michael Zak; *Back to Basics for the Republican Party*; 2003; Page 121

[181] Ray Morris, Jr.; *Fraud of the Century: Rutherford B. Hayes, Samuel Tilden and the Stolen Election*; Simon & Schuster; 2004; Page 253

[182] Interview for this book.

[183] Ari Hoogenboom essay on Rutherford B. Hayes in *Presidential Leadership: Rating the Best and Worst in the White House*; Edited by James Taranto and Leonard Leo; A Wall Street Journal Book Published by Free Press; 2004; Page 103

[184] *The Union! It's Dangers! And How They Can be Averted: Letters from Samuel J. Tilden to Hon. William Kent*; 1860; Page 14-15

[185] Edited by John Bigelow; *The Writings and Speeches of Samuel J. Tilden*; Harper and Brothers; 1885 Page 400-404
[186] Interview for this book.
[187] Steve Tally; *Almost America: From the Colonists to Clinton: A 'What If' History of the U.S.*; Harper Collins; 2000; 178
[188] Interview for this book.
[189] Ari Hoogenboom essay on Rutherford B. Hayes in *Presidential Leadership: Rating the Best and Worst in the White House*; Edited by James Taranto and Leonard Leo; A Wall Street Journal Book Published by Free Press; 2004; Page 102
[190] Ari Hoogenboom essay on Rutherford B. Hayes in *Presidential Leadership: Rating the Best and Worst in the White House*; Edited by James Taranto and Leonard Leo; A Wall Street Journal Book Published by Free Press; 2004; Page 101-102
[191] *On This Day-November 2, 1878*; New York Times; NYTimes.com
[192] Paul F. Boller, Jr.; *Presidential Campaigns*; Oxford University Press; 2004; Page 157
[193] Miller Center on the American President; University of Virginia; *Benjamin Harrison: Campaigns and Elections*
[194] Harper's Weekly; Explore History; 1888 Presidential Election; http://elections.harpweek.com/1888/Overview-1888-1.htm
[195] Miller Center on the American President; University of Virginia; *Benjamin Harrison: Campaigns and Elections*
[196] Paul F. Boller, Jr.; *Presidential Campaigns*; Oxford University Press; 2004; Page 157
[197] Interview for this book.
[198] Michael Zak; *Back to Basics for the Republican Party*; 2003; Page 129
[199] Harper's Weekly; Explore History; 1888 Presidential Election; http://elections.harpweek.com/1888/Overview-1888-1.htm
[200] Paul F. Boller, Jr.; *Presidential Campaigns*; Oxford University

Press; 2004; Page 158

[201] Paul F. Boller, Jr.; *Presidential Campaigns*; Oxford University Press; 2004; Page 159

[202] Paul F. Boller, Jr.; *Presidential Campaigns*; Oxford University Press; 2004; Page 160

[203] Frank Freidel and Hugh Sidey; *The Presidents of the United States of America*; White House Historical Association; 2006

[204] Paul F. Boller, Jr.; *Presidential Campaigns*; Oxford University Press; 2004; Page 161

[205] Interview for this book.

[206] Peter Carlson; *Another Race to the Finish*; The Washington Post; Nov. 17, 2000

[207] Bruce Bartlett; *Wrong on Race: The Democratic Party's Buried Past*; Palgrave Macmillan; 2008; Page 161

[208] Miller Center on American Presidents; *John F. Kennedy Campaigns and Elections*; http://millercenter.org/president/biography/kennedy-campaigns-and-elections

[209] Bruce Bartlett; *Wrong on Race: The Democratic Party's Buried Past*; Palgrave Macmillan; 2008; Page 161

[210] Bruce Bartlett; *Wrong on Race: The Democratic Party's Buried Past*; Palgrave Macmillan; 2008; Page 162

[211] Sean Trende; *Did JFK Lose the Popular Vote?*; Real Clear Politics; Oct. 19, 2012

[212] Steve Allen; *JFK's Popular Vote Victory: The Myth*; Capital Research Center; Nov. 12, 2013

[213] Steve Allen; *JFK's Popular Vote Victory: The Myth*; Capital Research Center; Nov. 12, 2013

[214] Sean Trende; *Did JFK Lose the Popular Vote?*; Real Clear Politics; Oct. 19, 2012

[215] Sean Trende; *Did JFK Lose the Popular Vote?*; Real Clear Politics; Oct. 19, 2012

[216] Letter from Gordon Tullock, Reply by Francis Russell; *Did Nixon Beat Kennedy?*; New York Review of Books; Nov. 10, 1988
[217] Sean Trende; *Did JFK Lose the Popular Vote?*; Real Clear Politics; Oct. 19, 2012
[218] Peter Carlson; *Another Race to the Finish*; The Washington Post; Nov. 17, 2000
[219] Peter Carlson; *Another Race to the Finish*; The Washington Post; Nov. 17, 2000
[220] Gerald Posner; *The Fallacy of Nixon's Graceful Exit*; Salon; Nov. 10, 2000
[221] David Greenberg; *It's a Myth that Nixon Acquiesced in 1960*; The Los Angeles Times; Nov. 10, 2000
[222] Peter Carlson; *Another Race to the Finish*; The Washington Post; Nov. 17, 2000
[223] David Greenberg; *Was Nixon Robbed?*; Slate; Oct. 16, 2000
[224] Peter Carlson; *Another Race to the Finish*; The Washington Post; Nov. 17, 2000
[225] David Greenberg; *Was Nixon Robbed?*; Slate; Oct. 16, 2000
[226] David Greenberg; *Was Nixon Robbed?*; Slate; Oct. 16, 2000
[227] Adam Cohen and Elizabeth Taylor; *American Pharaoh: Mayor Richard J. Daley: His Battle for Chicago and the Nation*; Back Bay Books; 2001; Page 264
[228] Peter Carlson; *Another Race to the Finish*; The Washington Post; Nov. 17, 2000
[229] *The Drama Behind President Kennedy's 1960 Election Win*; National Constitution Center, Nov. 7, 2014
[230] Peter Carlson; *Another Race to the Finish*; The Washington Post; Nov. 17, 2000
[231] David Greenberg; *Was Nixon Robbed?*; Slate; Oct. 16, 2000
[232] Peter Carlson; *Another Race to the Finish*; The Washington Post; Nov. 17, 2000
[233] David Greenberg; *Was Nixon Robbed?*; Slate; Oct. 16, 2000

[234] David Greenberg; *Was Nixon Robbed?*; Slate; Oct. 16, 2000
[235] Judy Keen; *Chicago Ties Cast Shadow on 1960 Presidential Win*; USA Today; Sept. 26, 2010
[236] Edward Foley; *Ballot Battles: The History of Disputed Elections in the United States*; Oxford University Press; 2015; Page 224
[237] Interview for this book.
[238] Interview for this book.
[239] Interview for this book.
[240] Interview for this book.
[241] Interview for this book.
[242] Eric Poole; *The Grudge Match: At the GOP Convention, 2000 Seems Like 1992, That's Because Bush is Asking Voters, did you Get It Right Back Then?*; Time; Aug. 6, 2000
[243] Frank Freidel and Hugh Sidey; *The President of the United States of America*; White House Historical Association; 2006; WhiteHouse.gov
[244] *The 2000 Campaign: Excerpts from the Democratic Candidates Debate at the Apollo Theater*; The New York Times; Feb. 22, 2000
[245] Eric Pooley; *The Grudge Match: At the GOP Convention, 2000 Seems Like 1992, That's Because Bush is Asking Voters, Did you Get it Right Back Then?*; Time; Aug. 6, 2000
[246] Editorial Board; *Gore's Clinton Fatigue*; Wall Street Journal; Aug. 8, 2000
[247] Paul F. Boller, Jr.; *Presidential Campaigns*; Oxford University Press; 2004; Page 407
[248] NAACP National Voter Fund October 2000 TV commercial; Transcript access through The George Washington University; http://www.gwu.edu/~action/ads2/adnaacp.html
[249] Richard Berke; *Democrats See, and Smell, Rats in GOP Ad*; The New York Times; Sept. 12, 2000
[250] Ronald Brownstein; *Polls Show Victory Could Come Without Winning Popular Vote*; Los Angeles Times; Nov. 3, 2000

[251] Paul F. Boller, Jr.; *Presidential Campaigns*; Oxford University Press; 2004; Page 412

[252] Larry Schweikart; *48 Liberal Lies About American History*; Sentinel; 2008; Page 156

[253] Washington Post Political Staff; *Deadlock: The Inside Story of America's Closest Election*; Public Affairs; 2001; Page 47

[254] Bill Sammon; *At Any Cost: How Al Gore Tried to Steal the Election*; Regnery; 2001; Page 92

[255] Bill Sammon; *At Any Cost: How Al Gore Tried to Steal the Election*; Regnery; 2001; Page 84

[256] Joseph Cummins; *Anything for a Vote*; Quirk Books; 2007; Page 280

[257] Bill Sammon; *At Any Cost: How Al Gore Tried to Steal the Election*; Regnery; 2001; Page 78

[258] John Fund; *The People Have Spoken. Will Al Gore Listen?*; The Wall Street Journal; Nov. 10, 2000

[259] Bill Sammon; *At Any Cost: How Al Gore Tried to Steal the Election*; Regnery; 2001; Page 80

[260] Bill Sammon; *At Any Cost: How Al Gore Tried to Steal the Election*; Regnery; 2001; Page 151

[261] J.K. Dineed; *It's War Over Military Votes*; The New York Daily News; Nov. 21, 2000

[262] Paul F. Boller, Jr.; *Presidential Campaigns*; Oxford University Press; 2004; Page 411

[263] Bill Sammon; *At Any Cost: How Al Gore Tried to Steal the Election*; Regnery; 2001; Page 209

[264] Washington Post Political Staff; *Deadlock: The Inside Story of America's Closest Election*; Public Affairs; 2001; Page 163

[265] Washington Post Political Staff; *Deadlock: The Inside Story of America's Closest Election*; Public Affairs; 2001; Page 164

[266] Washington Post Political Staff; *Deadlock: The Inside Story of America's Closest Election*; Public Affairs; 2001; Page 165

[267] Washington Post Political Staff; *Deadlock: The Inside Story of America's Closest Election*; Public Affairs; 2001; Page 211-212

[268] Washington Post Political Staff; *Deadlock: The Inside Story of America's Closest Election*; Public Affairs; 2001; Page 207

[269] Washington Post Political Staff; *Deadlock: The Inside Story of America's Closest Election*; Public Affairs; 2001; Page 207

[270] Washington Post Political Staff; *Deadlock: The Inside Story of America's Closest Election*; Public Affairs; 2001; Page 210

[271] David Kaplan; Excerpt of *The Accidental President: How 413 Lawyers, 9 Supreme Court Justices; and 5,963,110 Floridians (Give or Take a Few) Landed George W. Bush in the White House*; Newsweek; Sept. 16, 2001

[272] Bill Sammon; *At Any Cost: How Al Gore Tried to Steal the Election*; Regnery; 2001; Page 251-255

[273] Interview for this book.

[274] Charles Krauthammer; *Defenders of the Law*; Washington Post; Dec. 15, 2000

[275] Editorial Board; *Supreme Court Fault Lines*; The New York Times; Dec. 14, 2000

[276] Editorial Board; *Mr. Gore's Farewell, Mr. Bush's Task*; The New York Times; December 14, 2000

[277] Dan Keating and Dan Balz; *The Final Word? Florida Recounts Would Have Favored Bush—But Study Finds Gore Might Have Won Statewide Tally of All Uncounted Ballots*; The Washington Post; Nov. 12, 2001

[278] Brooks Jackson; *The Florida Recount of 2000*; Factcheck.org; Jan. 22, 2008

[279] Jake Tapper; *What if They Hijacked an Election and No One Cared?*; Salon; Nov. 14, 2001

[280] Interview for this book.

[281] Interview for this book.

[282] Interview for this book.

[283] Institute for Energy Research; *Obama Subsidizes U.S. Solar Energy and Promises to do the Same in India*; Feb. 20, 2015

[284] Ashe Schow; *President Obama's Taxpayer Backed Green Energy Failures*; Daily Signal; Oct. 18, 2012

[285] David Lightman; *Religion, Israel Hobble Lieberman*; Hartford Courant; Oct. 26, 2003

[286] *The 60 Minutes/Vanity Fair Poll*; Vanity Fair; Aug. 29, 2011

[287] Dan Eggen and John Mintz; *9/11 Panel Critical of Clinton, Bush*; Washington Post; May 24, 2004

[288] Brent Budowsky; *If Al Gore Had Won*; The Hill; Sept. 2, 2011

[289] John Mercurio; *Gore Challenges Bush Iraqi Policy*; CNN; Sept. 23, 2002

[290] Steve Kornacki; *Why President Gore Might Have Gone Into Iraq After 9/11 Too*; Salon; Aug. 30, 2011

[291] Michael McGough; *If Gore had Won*; The Los Angeles Times; Aug. 23, 2007

[292] Interview for this book.

CPSIA information can be obtained at www.ICGtesting.com
Printed in the USA
BVOW03s1313020816

457645BV00002B/4/P